HONE
MY AUTOBIOGRAPHY

Pino Iacaruso

Published by:
AS YOU LIKE IT
HARBURY   WARWICKSHIRE

British Library Cataloguing-in-Publication Data.
A catalogue record for this book is available
from the British Library.

Copies of this book can be obtained
at a cost of £12.00 plus £2.50 p&p
from Pino Iacaruso, Rosello, Harbury, Leamington Spa, CV33 9JD.
Tel: 01926 612417

Photographs – the author's collection
Food colour photos – Mike Inch
Croquembouche – Lionel

ISBN 978-0-9556320-0-6
Printed in Great Britain by
Arthur H. Stockwell Ltd.
Torrs Park   Ilfracombe
Devon

To my Father Edilio and to my brothers and sisters,
Savina, Giovanna, Lucio and Mario

Il Papá: Il mio lavoro si svolgeva sempre sulle navi della Marina Militare e tornavo a casa una o due volte l'anno, ma sapevo che mi aspettavano Lina, una moglie stupenda, purtroppo venuta a mancare quattordici anni fa e cinque figli di cui Pino era il maggiore. In quegli anni, in un certo senso, mi sostituiva come capo famiglia. Pino è sempre stato altruista e lavoratore instancabile prima in Svizzera e Inghilterra.

Oggi mi commuove l'idea che abbia scritto un altro libro anche se ciò non mi sorprende; chissà cos'altro dovrò aspettarmi!!
Edilio Iacaruso, Rosello 2006

Papa: My work took me away from home as I was employed by the Military Navy as a civilian chef and I used to come back home once or twice a year, but I knew that my wonderful wife, Lina, was waiting for me, sadly she died fourteen years ago, we had five children of which Pino was the eldest.

Often in those early years, Pino acted as head of the family. Pino has always been an unselfish man, a tireless worker first in Italy then Switzerland and England.

Today I am moved at the idea that he has written another book but I am not surprised; whatever will be next!!

[On March 4th 2007 Papá died in Rosello. He was aware that the second book would be published sometime this year]

Edilio junior: My father is my best friend and the best dad in the world. He has always looked after me. Even through his terrible illness he was very strong and positive as though nothing was wrong, for which I admired him immensely.

As a child my holidays were spent in Italy, which, I loved and still do. Being with all my family and friends is always fantastic and of course my love for the Italian food continues but never a tiramisu to match my Fathers.

My Father is a very special man to me and he has always encouraged me to work hard and respect people. I have learnt a lot from him and I love him very much.
Edilio Iacaruso. London 2006

Edilio: Mio padre, il migliore papà del mondo, è il mio piú caro amico; anche durante la sua malattia si è preso sempre cura di me. L'ho sempre ammirato poiché dimostrava la sua forza e la sua positività come se nulla fosse accaduto.

Fin da bambino mi è sempre piaciuto trascorrere le mie vacanze con lui e la sua famiglia in Italia. Mi ha inculcato l'amore per l'arte e la cucina italiana.

Mio padre è un uomo speciale, mi ha sempre incoraggiato allo studio, al lavoro e mi ha trasmesso il rispetto per il prossimo. Ho imparato molto da lui e gli voglio molto bene.

I Fratelli: Non ricordiamo molto di nostro fratello Pino poiché all'età di quattordici anni, lasció il nucleo famigliare per andare a Roma. Ciò nonostante ha lasciato l'impronta di sé per le sue capacità umane e artistiche; è una persona solare, dinamica ed intraprendente ed oggi ne da conferma con quadri, libri e una squisita cucina.

Possiede una forza interiore immensa capace di risollevarlo dalla malattia che lo ha colpito nove anni fa.

Savina, Lucio, Giovanna e Mario

My Siblings: We do not remember much about our brother Pino since at the age of fourteen he left the family home for Rome. But in spite of that he has left an impression of himself of his human capacity and artistic talents; he is a solar person, dynamic and energetic. And today he gives us the confirmation with his paintings, books and his exquisite cucina.

He possesses an immense interior strength and his capability to overcome the illness which struck him down nine years ago.

I nipoti: Cosa possiamo dire di nostro zio Pino; avessimo noi Le sue capacità... ci aiutrebbero molto! Parlare di nostro zio ad amici o parenti acquisiti è per noi un grande orgoglio. Non c'è bisogno di raccontare molto di lui, ma quel poco basta a mostrarlo come esempio per i nostri figli e la loro generazione.

Mario, Giuliana, Milena, Mariano, Anna, Umberto, Andrea, Paola e Jacopo

My Nephews and Nieces: what can we say of our Uncle Pino; We wish we had his ability, his skills, his talents.............. it would help us a lot!

To talk of our Uncle to friends and our relations it gives us great pride. There is so much to talk about him but the main thing is to demonstrate that he sets an example for our children and future generations.

Contents

FOREWORD
by Elisabeth, Lady Hamilton

I was delighted when Pino and Caroline asked me if I would write the foreword to Pino's autobiography. I had much enjoyed his earlier book of recipes and reminiscences, *Flavours of Rosello*, and looked forward to hearing more about his extended family in Italy and his career as a chef. Pino brought the manuscript over and I started to read it as soon as he had gone. Before long I became totally absorbed in the narrative. *Honey* is a love story, not only about Pino's love for Caroline and his family, but also about his love of food, of cooking, of people and of life itself.

Pino is a third-generation cook. Cooking is in his blood; he tells us that almost every man in the Abruzzo region where he comes from would wish to become a chef. To read the book is to feel the warmth of Pino's personality, the camaraderie, the bustle and the heat of the kitchens where he has worked (although sometimes this was too much – 'it wasn't warm, it was *boiling*' is how he describes one of the kitchens). We sense his love of food, of fresh ingredients of the finest quality – newly picked strawberries brought into the kitchen in baskets, free-range chicken, succulent and mouth-watering when cooked, aubergines with lovely shiny purple skins, the beautiful colours of Mediterranean ingredients kissed by the sun. Pino is no mean artist and he writes with an artist's eye for colour, bringing vividly to life the different environments where he has lived and worked – the hotels in Italy, the Swiss patisserie, embassies, Kensington Palace, and his own home in rural Warwickshire – all peopled with a rich kaleidoscope of the human beings he met and worked with, including all the members of his family. 'Never a day goes by when I don't think about them,' he writes. There were the porters in the Rome hotel who covered up for him when he left the baked apples in the oven and forgot all about them; the male dishwasher who had once been a monk; Eduardo, the master chef who expressed himself in cooking and presentation and his refined style and art; Princess Margaret popping into the kitchen and smelling and stirring the contents of the saucepans (and sometimes tasting them too); and his perfectionist employer in the Chelsea house who became infuriated when Pino forgot to buy the black-cherry conserve to go with the rice pudding. Then there was the virtuoso pianist Richard, who worked for Pino in his gap year and who became almost as interested in the *art culinaire* as he was in music, so much so that Pino would not have been surprised to see him glazing an apple flan with one hand and playing Beethoven's Fifth with the other.

There were the great occasions like the banquet for the King and Queen of Spain at the Spanish Embassy, the Thyssen wedding party, and the working holiday at the country home of Prince and Princess Michael of Kent. Pino paints a picture of a world of beautifully laid tables, perfectly presented food and immaculate service. These were the high points – but we also learn about the hard work, the times when Pino was learning his craft and when a typical day could be spent dipping tomatoes into boiling water and peeling them ready for the pasta sauce in the evening. Caroline and Pino, in setting up their own business, Take Two Cooks, have made a great success of the venture, combining as a team in a partnership that also worked well when Pino was the chef and Caroline, with her flair for administration, was the major-domo for the delightful Finnish Ambassador and his wife. But none of this was achieved without hard work and dedication.

Every life has its ups and downs, and the most moving part of the book lies in Pino's simple and undramatised description of the illness from which he has emerged more than ever ready to bless the sunrise each day and full of gratitude for those who helped him through this trauma. As he puts it himself, 'I never wanted to be a recluse,' but one can only admire his courage and determination for getting back into the world with such a different face from the one that everyone had known before.

Pino has explored so many aspects of the culinary art, from the most skilled patisserie to the simplest home-made fare. He has praise for the fashionable nouvelle cuisine with its artistry and its delicate flavours. But, he writes, 'it is still hard to beat a lovely home-cooked meal, when all the family and friends sit around a big dining-room table . . . and the favourite family dish is brought to the table to be served.'

'The crispiest roast potatoes, and steaming vegetables are also placed on the table. Long arms are stretched out from all directions to serve. The gravy boat and the sauces are passed around. Glasses are filled up with wine to make a toast and to celebrate before the meal. This is followed by a delicious bread-and-butter pudding.' And, he adds, fine wines alone do not make a happy occasion. In his opinion a table needs food lovers and an empty stomach with a jolly crowd.

For good measure Pino has included recipes from the most sophisticated to the most simple. 'I would never turn down a good shepherd's pie,' Pino writes, and his recipe is here for you to try, with that extra touch of some grated carrot, which I am sure will make it all the more delicious. So when you have tried out a recipe or two, settle down with this story that Pino tells, of himself and the lovely Welsh girl he married, of their much loved son Edilio, of the sights and sounds of his life in town and country with baked croissants and beautifully cooked meat and fish. Read – and enjoy!

Walton, Warwickshire, 2006

GREETINGS FROM FINLAND
by Camilla Tötterman, Ambassadress of Finland, London, 1976–84

What a pleasure and what a relief it was to have Pino as chef during our eight happy and busy years in London!

In the first few months before the Iacarusos changed our lives, we never knew what next to expect from the kitchen. I have vivid recollections of various calamities. Once a beautiful large salmon was served raw. The chef at that time claimed that his recipe said a few minutes in a warm oven. So he had done the right thing. His recipe, though, was for steaks of salmon. Another day, another chef prepared a supposedly Mediterranean speciality, a dish of raw, mashed shellfish, a black and slimy mess. Then again burnt meat, and so on. . . .

However, these worrying and difficult times soon became just a bad memory. We were fortunate in acquiring Pino to take charge as chef in the embassy residence. A long period of highly professional activity and smooth teamwork began. We could relax and enjoy Pino's excellent cuisine. Not only skilfully and deliciously prepared courses but they were elegantly and artistically arranged without fuss and frill. His ability to create culinary sensations was unsurpassable and covered the entire range of the gastronomical scale. Even simple dishes became small wonders in his experienced hands.

Pino soon became well known and esteemed amongst our guests, friends and colleagues in the diplomatic corps. I always found it rewarding to exchange views with Pino. His professionalism and his amiable personality alike continued over the years to be a source of satisfaction and delight.

We remain grateful for the happy years with our dear friend maître chef Pino and his admirable Caroline, who worked with him in such perfect harmony.

It is gratifying to note how Pino's artistic talent and urge have not only carried him over times of diminished health but have grown even stronger in later years. This has been manifested in *Flavours of Rosello* and in his fine watercolours when expressing himself so well in both words and colours.

My family and I wish him every success with his new book and in his professional and artistic activities as well as personal happiness in the coming years.

Helsinki, Finland, 2006

By John Watkinson
Consultant ENT/Head & Neck and Thyroid Surgeon,
The Cancer Centre, Queen Elizabeth Hospital,
University of Birmingham, NHS Trust,
Edgbaston, Birmingham.

Pino Iacaruso – the champion chef – is larger than life and his reputation goes before him. I was first asked to put pen to paper by Pino and his wife Caroline, when they asked me to contribute to the foreword of his previous book, *Flavours of Rosello*. This turned out to be a tremendous success and was a tribute to his artistic and culinary skills. To experience his cooking ability, with raucous laughter in the kitchen surrounded by beautiful pictures is a real treat. Well done, Pino!

Nearly ten years ago, Pino suffered from head and neck cancer. He fought this disease with great dignity and came through a stronger person. He subsequently donated some of the proceeds of his book to a charity called Get A-Head, which is dedicated to helping patients with head and neck diseases, especially those with cancer.

Times move on and Pino decided to go ahead with his second book. Sadly, this was coupled with a development of a further head and neck cancer for which he had to undergo more surgery. He has come through this yet again fighting fit, and this new book is a testament to his courage and strength.

I wrote a few years ago that doctors should not make friends with their patients. Again, I say, rules are there to be broken and I value Pino as a true friend. We're always there to be proved wrong and remember – of all the things which wisdom provides to make life entirely happy, much the greatest is the possession of friendship [Epicurus].

John and Esmé Watkinson, Birmingham, 2006

Again, some of the proceeds from *Honey* will be donated to the Get-A-Head charity. www.getahead.org.uk

MY DREAM

As a child, I remember
I had a beautiful dream
Of this great creative art
Of being a chef.

At the age of fourteen
I had left school
And waiting for the departure
To seek new beginnings.

With a suitcase packed
Full of clothes and enthusiasm,
For the long journey
To Rome I began.

At first a little apprehensive
To a new city,
Then the discovery of
The fine culinary delights.

The future, and my life
Looked happy and
Full of interesting things
New Places to go.

Finally to England
To my new life.

Then my world was
Shattered at the feel
of a lump and my little
Face was scarred for life.

Now I have learned
To smile again.
My passion for
Food, painting and music
As never deter.

My dream now, as a wise
And tolerant man,
Is as strong and deeper into me,
As when I was a child.

Pino Iacaruso

IL MIO SOGNO

Da ragazzo, mi ricordo
di aver avuto un bel sogno
di questa grand' arte
di fare il cuoco.

All'eta di quattordici anni
ho lasciato scuola
e aspettavo la partenza
di cominciare un nuovo inizio.

Con una valigia giá piena
di panni ed entusiasmo,
per il lungo viaggio
a Roma cominciai.

Al principio un pó apprensivo
della nuova cittá,
poi la scoperta delle
delizie culinarie.

Il futuro, e la mia vita
sembrava felice e
piena di cose interessanti
nuovi posti da visitare.

Finalmente in Enghilterra
per una nuova vita.

Poi il mio mondo s'era
rotto al toccar una ciste
e la mia piccola faccia
era sfregiata per la vita.

Adesso ho imparato
a sorridere di nuovo.
La mia passione per
cibo, pittura e musica
non mi ha mai deluso.

Il mio sogno adesso, come
un uomo saggio e tollerante,
é piú profondo dentro di me,
come quando ero ragazzo.

July16th 2003, Old Hunstanton,Norfolk.

PRESENTATION OF DISHES

Nil posse creari de nilo
LUCRETIUS c.94–55 BC
Nothing can be created out of nothing.

In former years, the presentation of dishes was somewhat elaborate, and laborious. Head chefs used to spend whole days and large quantities of ingredients to create new dishes to display for buffet and banqueting. The presentation had to be beautiful and impressive for the eye and tasty to the palate.

When I started working at the Belgian Embassy in Rome in my early days in the kitchen with the chef, Eduardo, he was decorating a whole baked sea bass. After he had removed the skin he sat at the table with black truffles, patiently slicing them, cutting out different shapes with a tiny pastry cutter, and then he meticulously placed them in aspic over the salmon to transform this beautiful fish into a masterpiece as if it were a piece of jewellery.

For the galantine of chicken, the meat had to be pounded in a mortar then sieved, before pistachio nuts and truffles were added to it. It was then rolled back into the chicken skin, sewn and boiled, and displayed in a fan shape, before finally being glazed and surrounded with a border of aspic flavoured with fresh tarragon. At the end, after I had been sieving meat for hours, I had the most horrendous headache!

For pastillage, a mixture of icing sugar, egg whites and Arabic gum was made into a mass, rolled out, and then cut into fancy shapes or put into moulds to dry out before being assembled to present desserts and puddings. These were known as masterpieces of culinary architecture.

A chef who is a colleague of mine, and also a great friend, Benito Franchescelli, worked at an embassy in London. His passion was making sugar-work. He used to serve his desserts with sugar roses and petals at dinner parties to impress the guests. He was called by his ambassador one day and asked not to make them any more, because when he was invited out, his host felt embarrassed that his chef could not decorate the dessert in the same way.

The presentation of dishes is now as simple as possible, but one can still make a beautiful display of gastronomic delights. Cold terrine, pâté or mousses can be presented in soufflé dishes, cut-glass bowls with beautiful design, or simply placed on serving dishes with a white serviette underneath to set them off and keep them in place. Eggs in tartelettes with hollandaise sauce, with the deep-yellow colour from the hollandaise and the green from the watercress, can be simply served on a round dish, and the contrast is simply beautiful. There is an interesting way of presenting fillets of soles in white wine sauce that I can suggest. A fish shape can be drawn on a piece of cardboard and then cut around. When the fillets of soles are ready, hold the fish-shaped card over the dish and sprinkle finely chopped parsley.

This will decorate the dish instantly, with the contrast of the green parsley and the white sauce as a background. This beautifully presented dish can be achieved with little effort. Serve with a crescent of puff pastry.

For roast quails on a bed of potato straw nests, the potato nests can be arranged on a serving dish, the birds placed on the straw nests with a hard-boiled quail's egg under the bird. This dish was served at the fifth wedding of Baron Heini Thyssen when he married Carmen 'Tita' Cervera at Daylesford House. It was a splendid three days that I stayed helping to prepare the wedding breakfast. More about that later, but Caroline has introduced this wonderful recipe to our general repertoire.

I spend a lot of time preparing the vegetables, maybe two or three different kinds. Stuffed courgettes, tomatoes or some beautiful aubergines with their lovely shiny purple skin can be prepared in so many ways. Vegetables offer us an endless variety of colour and versatility in the kitchen that is unique. Here is the way I serve French beans, mangetout, swede, cauliflower and leeks: Firstly I cook them, cool under running water and drain them. Then I arrange all the vegetables in a beautiful manner in an ovenproof dish, add a little seasoning, a few knobs of butter and finally warm them up in a hot oven for about 20–25 minutes. The effect is stunning and the vegetables are ready to serve.

The desserts, such as fresh fruit flans, gateaux, bavaroise, soufflé and other puddings are generally best presented whole. They can all be served with sauces or with a jug of cream. I personally think that, unlike restaurants where the desserts are portioned for a reason, in our own homes there is nothing nicer at the end of a meal when the hostess brings to the table a lovely home-made pudding and everyone gasps in anticipation of a slice!

When we have a dinner party at home, Caroline and I will always discuss the menu first. What would be appropriate, what is available, and what would please our friends most to eat? We go through this process every time together, and we work very much as a team to enjoy the evening with our guests.

I also sketch the dish in my mind and I 'paint' it the way it should look. The experience in one's years of cooking plays an important part too. The serving dishes and china are without doubt the making of an attractive meal, and the ability to visualise all this in time without panicking before serving your guests is most important.

One formal dinner party that I cooked for the Prince and Princess Michael of Kent that stays in my mind would have been totally wrong in a household who studied their menus, and yet it was most successful at the time, and was praised by everyone.

**Eggs in Tartelettes
with Sweetcorn
Hollandaise Sauce**

***

**Coulibiac of Salmon
Dill Sauce**

***

Wild Rice
Carrots Vichy
Mangetout

***

Soufflé Grand Marnier
with Orange Segments

Can you see what is wrong with this menu? Maybe it sounds delightful to you, but for me it should not contain eggs in every course.

THIS IS WHAT THE WORLD ... THINKS OF ME

For over 26 years, Pino has been an inspiration through both his work and personal life. First, he has taught me an incredible amount about cooking both through watching him AT work and by working WITH him. He is one of a rare breed of chefs who, with an amazing generosity of spirit, will freely share his ideas, skills and personal recipes.

On a personal level, Pino has been a sincere and valued friend who has taught me the true meaning of courage. Through serious illness, he has remained positive, cheerful and looking forward to his next venture.

Pino's books have been a labour of love, a reflection of a truly remarkable man.

Teresa Barclay, London

After Pino's recent spell in hospital I feared lack of time and the essential energy to complete might well have delayed publication of this book. I should have known better! Pino is after all a professional. Isn't it basic to a chef's training that come hell or high water he meets his deadlines, never keeps his audience waiting, never lets his standards waiver (unless of course like Pino's they are constantly improving)

Naturally, I, and all your northern fan club are expecting great things from this second course of memoirs and recipes, pictures too, what a fistful of talents!

By the by it always raises a smile when I tell your admirers Pino's most used term of endearment for Car is that delectable culinary ingredient "honey".

It takes "Two Cooks" to please every palate and that you two most certainly do, so remember team no meal is complete without a touch of the dolce. So while welcoming your new book we will still be eagerly awaiting dessert – stick with it Pino, this has to be a trilogy!

Julia Cheetham, Kirkennan, Scotland

PLANNING MENUS AND CHOOSING WINES

The grand parties of yesteryear, with ten or more courses, now belong to the past. These days, a dinner party with more than four courses is already exceptional. However, the traditions, procedures and service at the table remain, as do the rules of good taste and the logic of planning a meal. Good planning is required when deciding on the food and drink to be served. While always considering tasty and healthy dishes, something must be chosen that will be enjoyed by both hosts and guests. You must also take into consideration personal limitations of time and experience. If you are planning a hot lunch or dinner, bear in mind that it will be impossible to serve a hot starter, hot main course and a hot pudding without help. You could have one, or maybe two, hot courses, or possibly a hot course and a hot pudding, or it is even quite acceptable to only serve a hot main course. Even when I was working at the embassies and private houses with plenty of help, a big kitchen with a large kitchen battery, and time to discuss and organise things, the rules remained the same.

Begin by offering your guests an aperitif to prepare the stomach and the palate, such as a glass of white wine or a glass of old-fashioned sherry; or follow my preference, which is a glass of champagne.

One of Princess Michael of Kent's favourite aperitifs is champagne mixed with peach nectar, served with cheese straws, cheddar cakes or canapés. That really is a lovely way to welcome guests.

Choose your wine carefully and remember those that you have enjoyed most before. The wrong wine can ruin a meal and that would be a great shame after all the preparation and hard work.

OEUFS POCHES AUX MAIS
EN TARTELETS
SAUCE HOLLANDAISE

CANARD A L'ORANGE
RIZ SAUVAGE
MANGE-TOUT
CAROTTES VICHY
TOMATES GRILLES

SOUFFLE AU CHOCOLAT
EN CHARTREUSE

JEUDI
LE 11 FEVRIER
1988

BAR À L'ANGLAISE

———

PINTADES TRUFFÉES
POMMES DUCHESSE

———

ASPERGES D'ARGENTEUIL
SAUCE MOUSSELINE

———

SURPRISE NORVÉGIENNE

———

FRUITS

ROME, 23 FÉVRIER 1984

M

Saumon Mousse

- - -

Selle d'Agneau Rôti
Pommes Parisiennes
Chouxfleur au Beurre
Épinard à la Crème
Carottes aux Peiselées

- - -

Meringue Noisette
Sauce Framboise

- - -

Fromage

Café

- - -

Jeudi, le 16 Avril

Crème de Céleri

Bouchées aux Crevettes

Bœuf à la Cuiller
Pommes Rissolées

Fonds d'Artichauts
à la Hollandaise

Dame Blanche

Fruits

Rome, le 13 février 196..

INTRODUCTION

Gratus erga Deum beatitudine vitae
Grateful to God for the blessing of life

I have been inspired by my mother's endless meals cooked from the safety of our homely, small kitchen. And I always remember talking to her and my friends for this passion and love for this great art of cooking which not only satisfies my own appetite and stomach, but also brings satisfaction to others. It has been with me for as long as I can remember, from a very young age, as if I were born with a wooden spoon in my hands.

The reason for my love of cooking is more than the fact that it is in my blood, it goes back much further. My paternal grandfather, Giuseppe (I was named after him), was a chef and went to Naples with his family. Sadly I never knew him, as he died at the age of forty of pneumonia, when my father was four years old, my father's elder sister seven and his younger brother two years of age. They all came back to the village.

My grandfather left 7,000 lire to the three of them, which his daughter, Concettina, had invested for her dowry and got married; my father, Edilio, also used the money to get married; and his other son, Luigi, got married too and bought a pig with those few lire that he had left.

My grandfather's origin was not from Rosello, but from Borello, a village six kilometres away. He came to our village, met and married my grandmother Felicetta; and his sister Antonina married in another village, called Pescopennataro, where as a young boy I would go to spend my few weeks of summer holiday.

My father and his brother, Uncle Luigi, became chefs, following in my grandfather's footsteps. Then came the turns of me and my brothers, Lucio and Mario, who also after finishing school went straight into the kitchen.

My father, Edilio, went to work in Naples as a kitchen boy and lodged with an old family friend whilst he was working in restaurants and learning his skills, before moving later on to work in private houses. Eventually after he married he joined the Italian Navy as a civilian chef shortly after the war. He gave nearly all his working life to the navy, staying with them for forty years until his retirement. He has worked on many huge ships, has crossed every ocean and sea and has been all over the world in calm and rough water. During his working life he was awarded the silver and bronze medals for his service by the Ministry of Defence.

As a young man he was tall, slim and good-looking, always clean-shaven and well dressed. He had red shiny hair and was nicknamed 'The Red' by everyone in the village. He has always been a provider for his family. We never wanted for anything. We have a lovely home in the village, and I still go home every year for a two weeks' holiday to a warm welcome and a plate of pasta. We have a nice time together with good meals and a siesta in the afternoon. I know that the morning I have to leave to return to England, you can see the sadness on his face.

One year with my son, Edilio, we walked down the piazza towards the bus stop to take the coach for Rome. We kissed goodbye. Edilio and I got on the coach, and I thought he was still standing near the door to wave to us, and by the time I bought the tickets from the coach driver, I turned around thinking that he was still standing on the road. I looked up and from the coach back window I saw my father walking straight back home with his head down and without looking back. I never saw him doing that before. We both felt very sad. To this day, I am still known as the son of Edilio the Red.

My maternal great-grandmother was born in Rosello. Her name was Antonina Candolfo, nicknamed and known as 'La Storna', meaning the bay horse. She married Domenico Valerio. Her hair went white at an early age; she was a strong healthy girl, full of vitality and a dynamic woman, and the saying that went in those days stands true today – she was as strong as a horse! Maybe that is where I get my strength from.

They had five children and the youngest, Nicolino, married my grandmother, Concettina Margiotta, who was also nicknamed 'La Storna'. She was a woman with a slim figure and fit, quick on her feet with an equine nose and a lovely soft smile. Her silver hair was pulled back into a bun. She was left-handed, a trait which I, my brother Lucio, and my sister Giovanna have inherited. It was to her that my mother Lina and her brother Domenico Valerio were born. My mother Lina was also nicknamed 'La Storna' married my father Edilio Iacaruso and they had five children.

I was born on 9 June 1948. I am the first of five children, followed by my sister Savina born two years later, in 1950, then my brother Lucio was born in 1951 and my other sister, Giovanna, was born in 1955. My other brother, Mario, is the youngest and was born in 1962.

The old village of Rosello was built upon a steep and stony hill named *Il Colle,* facing north-east. Hundreds of uneven cobblestone steps, brilliant and worn out by the constant treading, divided the village down the middle. Small stone houses were built stacked up, one next to the other, with their tiny windows and red tile roofs, lining the village streets. At the top of the village there stood the old church, which scholars estimate dates back to the end of the 12th century. The inside was cool and painted white. There were several small altars around the sides, decorated with saints and flanked by columns; and on the ceiling a white cast dove representing the Holy Spirit welcomed a large congregation. Next came the high campanile with an arched doorway.

To the north-west there is a ring of hills, behind which rises La Maiella, the highest mountain in the whole of the Apennines. The hill is capped with a massive rock, rising into the sky, which dominates the village. The very first houses were built during the 12th century below the foot of this rock. We Rosellani looked upon this rock as a friend and protector, and it was given the name *La Torre* (meaning the tower). As a little boy, I clambered over it to play amongst the cracks and the loose ivy with my friends. I remember there was a circle of bricks around the very top. They have now worn away, but in the olden days this was a lookout tower, and it would have been manned for protection.

From here you could admire the most magnificent view of valleys and woods, with many scattered villages amongst multicoloured cultivated fields that looked like duvet covers. And there was open countryside as far as the eye could see.

During the Second World War, Rosello was destroyed by German troops. The order was given that everybody should evacuate the village immediately. Young men went into hiding in the countryside, including my Uncle Mimi. Some of the young men were captured and taken to a camp, and later all of them escaped except one who was killed by a landmine. So the elderly, women and children went to a little church called The Madonna of the Grace. This was about a mile away from Rosello on a beautiful green hilltop.

Included were my mother and grandmother, who sought refuge from German occupation forces. My mother, who had been very young at the time, told me stories of the horror and shock she went through during the days they spent crammed together on the church floor, and of the other families who stayed in their own chapels in the cemetery.

One November day, a heavy fog was hanging in the air and they could not see the village at all. Miraculously all the houses were screened by this blanket of fog so they could not see their village being destroyed. The muffled sound of the mines exploding echoed around them accompanied by flashes of red flames while the houses were burning.

The day after, the German troops moved further on to another town called Sulmona (still in the Abruzzo region); and they returned to the village to find it buried in rubble and dust. Only four houses were left standing. I believe the officers had used them for their own accommodation.

Many people emigrated after the war, some never to return; others have rebuilt their ruined homes; and some others have built new homes on their land.

Many years later my father had a large four-storey house built, which is the family home today. My Aunt Concettina told me the story of how they had their home destroyed but the land still belonged to the Iacaruso family. We have a large piazza with a three-tiered carved stone fountain with a large octagonal base, with a large bowl also octagonal in the middle and a smaller bowl on top with a spray of water gushing down. Men spend time there. They sit on wrought-iron benches, under the shade of elm trees. They chat about everyday life and reminisce about the past, with an 'if' (sé) and a 'but' (peró) while they look around and let the time pass.

One warm Sunday morning after Mass, the usual gathering before dispersing for the Sunday lunch saw a pigeon land in the fountain's small bowl to drink some water and to rest. Suddenly the group of men interrupted their conversation and theirs eyes focused on the fountain to admire the pigeon and to make a few comments.

"Oh, what a beautiful pigeon! I wonder from where he comes from," said Nicola.

"He must have been so thirsty . . . with this heat," replied Corrado.

"Perhaps he is a wild one or he has got lost," intervened Carlo.

"Or he could be a carrier pigeon," added Domenico.

"Oh yes, perhaps he is taking a message to your wife," answered Nicola.

The pigeon moved his head and looked around. I imagine that he couldn't believe the attention that he was given. He splashed his wings in the water, made a little fuss and flew away. We have no pigeons in Rosello and that little event gave the men the opportunity to talk about something different.

The fountain and the piazza are the life and soul of every village; there is also the town hall, the church, the school, the shops, the post office, and stalls where outsiders come and sell their goods. You greet friends and meet people going on their way and exchange news with them. The Mayor, Domenico Cimino, and the priest, old Don Peppe, were seen as two big authorities, in charge of their posts, and they commanded respect and adherence to the law. The town hall took care of its citizens and all the necessities that the village required, and the church took care of its congregation. Young and old were proud of their mayor and their priest. They were well respected by the people and one would go to them to ask for help and to seek advice.

The village has expanded, and looks prosperous. And still people have had to leave Rosello to seek work and they have set up home all over the world. Many of the children of those who left Rosello went on to university, and not so many work as chefs these days. They have studied to become doctors, lawyers, and other chosen professions. The poor village, Rosello, is dying out and during the winter with the snow it is very quiet; but still many of the people return to Rosello in the summer months.

Our first house was amongst a cluster of houses that is typical of an Italian village. From the cobbled street, we had to walk down half a dozen steps and under an old stone archway (portico), turning right where it would lead to a small square courtyard surrounded by four walls and windows. Facing us there was a green painted door where we kept our Rosina (more about her later), and on the left wall of the courtyard was our arched front door.

Inside the house we had the kitchen, and a sitting area with a fireplace at the far end of the room. There were two fairly large windows opposite the front door. In this room we would do everything. We sat, we ate our meals, we played, we did our homework and we drank the water from a copper ladle of the copper basin collected from the fountain. We had an upstairs bedroom and it was a little crowded with us all, but we had the most fabulous view from the balcony overlooking the village houses.

This was my maternal grandmother's house, where I was born, along with my sisters, Savina and Giovanna, and my brother, Lucio. This is where I spent my earlier and happy years of my childhood together with my siblings, and with my mother and grandmother. My father used to come back home perhaps two or three times a year as he was at sea.

At the age of eight or nine we left this house and went to live at another house at the other side of the village, which was more spacious and more comfortable; and my youngest brother, Mario, arrived.

My grandmother was in seventh heaven. She had a small flowerbed and a nice-sized garden with an apple tree in the middle, and she loved to grow all sorts of vegetables.

The old house was left empty for many, many years until my Uncle Mimi came back from Argentina and renovated it. Now, after his death, and the death of his only son, Nicolino, my uncle's wife, Anita, with her daughter-in-law, Maria Rosa, and her adopted daughter, Giovanna, lives in it.

In April of 1952 my Uncle Mimi went to that faraway land. I was four years old. I vaguely remember his face, like a hazy imprint in my mind, but I don't remember his departure. He also left behind his wife and their son, his sister and his mother.

He went to join his four brothers-in-law, who had already been well established in Argentina for several years, running their own businesses. Years later his wife, Anita, and their only son, Nicolino, went to join him in Argentina. I think that for him the motive was to seek a better life and also a pinch of fortune. His profession was a builder, and he could turn his hand to almost anything in the building trade. He had a very hard time in Argentina, and life had not been very kind to him.

Once he sent a photograph of himself standing in a garden in Buenos Aires. His face was as I had remembered, with gentle features and a soft smile. We were filled with emotion at this black-and-white picture – especially his mother, who placed it in a frame on the mantelpiece. In 1968 his beloved mother died whilst he was away from home.

In 1982 he came back for the first time to Rosello after thirty years away and stayed for several months. He did some masonry work in the village. I will never forget the look on his face when entering our home. My father had fetched him from Rome Airport and the first disaster occurred when he picked out the wrong suitcase from the carousel, opened it up to discover ladies' clothes – they had to return to the airport once more, at great expense, by taxi.

When he arrived in Rosello he made his way into our home and entered the corridor, his eyes looking in every direction to see where his sister was, whilst she was coming down the marble staircase very carefully, one step at a time due to her bad diabetes, which had damaged her feet. They hugged and held each other in their arms and cried like small children. He was a good man with a touch of melancholy and a sad look in his eyes. I was very fond of my Uncle Mimi.

He went back to Argentina with the idea of returning to Italy for good. The departure date was set and they sold everything they possessed. Then at the last minute horrendous bad luck struck. Their son was taken into hospital with a massive brain haemorrhage but somehow he pulled through it. This sucked away their strength, energy and finances. Eventually they came back home to a bad start.

Nicolino couldn't work as planned because of his ill health and my uncle started to suffer with bad arthritis. In later years he needed a wheelchair to get around. All of the family had to take care of them both. What should have been a new beginning, and happy days ahead for them, was a disastrous and a sad setback. It was like something you might see in films, and yet it happened to this innocent family. I would go and visit my uncle when I was in Rosello.

I can always remember in the summer, when we lived in the old house all four of us children sitting round the table, having breakfast in the mornings. The windows

22

were wide open and the morning sun overlooked the terracotta red roofs below our house. The warm milk from the pan spilled onto the old wooden table, and slices of our own home-made bread were piled on a plate. There were grains of granulated sugar scattered on the table; they had missed our big white bowls, which we ate our breakfasts from. The table would be covered in flies attracted by the spilled milk and the granulated sugar, and we were forever brushing them away. In my mind, it seems that there were hundreds of them flying around. Then we would set off to school.

I was very close to my mother, Lina Valerio. She was very kind, with a gentle manner, very organised and always busy looking after us. Our grandmother (maternal), who lived with us, helped to bring us up as if we were her own children and we called her Mum too. There was a never-ending pile of clothes to be washed, and in those days the clothes had to be boiled outside in a big caldron over a tripod in front of the house. My mother had to act not only as a mother but also as the head of the family in making decisions, as our father was away at sea working. He would come back home every three or four months just for a few weeks on leave. I always remember my mother being there for us, and reassuring us with her presence. At times she was pensive and looked worried as if something was wrong, but we were too young to understand. Sadly my mother died in 1991 and not only her spirit lives on but also her nickname, Lina della Storna.

I am a third-generation chef. My father wanted me to study so that I would have a diploma like everyone else. He used to tell me that he wanted me to become a stationmaster – a clean and respectable profession. He thought that going to work in a kitchen was dirty with long hours and hard work, and that I would never be free from duty. He only wanted the best for me. Alas! though, I had made my mind up and there was nothing he could do. This passion grew deeper and I became even more curious to find out about food.

I had been invited to a christening at a neighbour's and, when the starter was brought to the table, I was staring at the small-diced multicoloured vegetables. They looked interesting and pretty, and tasted delicious. I was too shy to ask its name, but later, when I went to Rome, I discovered that it was a Russian salad.

As schoolboys are today, I was always eager to see the school front door shut at the end of another school year. I started school at the age of six. The classroom was on the ground floor, with large windows overlooking some old kitchen gardens and rows of tiled roofs on old houses. My first teacher, Signor Ercolino Maranzano, a tall and strict young man from Giulipoli, a nearby village, used to arrive in the morning in all kinds of weather on his Vespa to teach us.

I had to wait fifty years to meet someone from his own family. And in August 2004, during my watercolour exhibition at Rosello Town Hall, I had the pleasure of being introduced to his daughter, Renata. She is a charming and intelligent lady and she lives in Rome. We talked a lot, and she wanted to know what I was doing and where I was living. I got very excited on recounting my early school days with her father and how much I remembered him. She was delighted that one of her father's pupils had such a talent. She admired my work and was amazed by the mixed varieties and subjects of the many paintings.

The first year he let all the class draw lines, circles and little squares, but I never paid enough attention when I should have been doing sums and short division. I never did get the hang of these things that didn't make sense to me, and I failed that first year.

My first school companion was called Nicolino Percario. He too left our little village at a very young age to go into the kitchen, and we are still friends to this day.

I remember that one day I was very naughty and I didn't want to go to school. I hid myself in the street below our house behind a stack of wood and my godmother, Commara Antonina, saw me crouched down. Then she looked up and shouted to call my mother, leaning out of the window, and told her what she had seen. My grandmother pulled me all the way down to the school and I was crying my eyes out. We crossed a deserted piazza – all the children were already in the classrooms. Ercolino was very angry with me and I didn't do it ever again. I never forgot that day in my life. I spent two years with him.

My second teacher, Mimi Cimino, was the village mayor for nearly twenty-five years. He was severe and we were frightened of him. He could freeze the entire class with his look alone on entering the room. We were all well disciplined and we were taught all sorts of subjects: grammar, history, mathematics and others, but I excelled at drawing. There was always lots of homework and we had to learn poetry by heart and recite it the next morning. There was a saying in our village that if Mimi taught you, you couldn't fail to receive a good education.

I used to share my desk with another companion and friend, Ludovico Marchesani. We were two inseparable friends. We used to dress up as cowboy and Indian, and we lived near to each other. We grew up together and shared our dreams and our village streets.

Then at the beginning of the sixties we parted. He went to work in Milan, and I went to Rome. In forty years we have seen each other only once. He has married a girl in the north of Italy and I know from his family that he is the owner of his own restaurant. We never kept in touch and I don't even remember the town where Ludovico lives!

The classroom was on the first floor and overlooked the piazza, the fountain and the town-hall clock tower, which wasn't much help as we couldn't help but look at the time and count how long we had to go before we were let out. I spent two years with Mimi.

My third and last teacher was Don Marino, the father of our local doctor, Mario Zanna. He was an elderly and very nice gentleman who was always smartly dressed and had enormous patience and understanding. He had huge lungs, but even Don Marino would run out of breath and become very exasperated on the occasions when we did not listen to what he was saying. We all liked him, though – for his patience and gentleness with us. We had a great respect and high regard for him, so much that when the old class get together we still talk about Don Marino. At the age of thirteen, I finished school with my school certificate.

I became friendly with Dr Zanna, and in the meantime he took up dentistry and opened a dental surgery in another village nearby, at Villa Santa Maria. I would go with him to keep him company and to help prepare the studio before the patients started to arrive. We would leave our village at around nine in the morning, and he would see and treat his patients all through the morning and return home after two o'clock in the afternoon. His family were very charming and kind to me and they would make sure that I always had lunch with the Doctor before going back home.

One of his friends and colleagues was looking for a young person to train as an dental assistant in his laboratory, in a big town of our region in Pescara. His parents and wife wanted very much for me to take the job and go to work with him. They kept repeating what a nice person he was, and that I would be working in a better environment, earning more money. I could be near home, rather than in Rome starting my career as a chef in a hot kitchen.

But I had already planned my future and there was no going back. They meant well and they liked me very much. I think they were a little disappointed with me. But I couldn't see myself as an deontologist with a long white coat and handling dentures! I never told anyone about this offer so here I have to borrow the famous quotation from one of the most distinguished English actors, Sir Michael Caine, who said " . . . and not a lot of people know that!"

In the winter months, school began at nine o'clock in the morning and would finish at 1.30 in the afternoon. This was due to bad weather. With deep snow, blizzards and very cold winds we would push our way through with heavy boots and coats covered in snow up to the school door. At the far end of the classroom a log fire was burning in a terracotta stove to warm up the classroom before the class would begin.

The municipal and school caretaker, Peppe Colaizzo, was responsible for this job. I remember this elderly man very well. He was a gentle and kind person with thinning hair and soft brown eyes. He would sweat and run out of breath, while carrying pieces of wood in his arms from one classroom to another. We liked him, though, and we used to tease him like a bunch of very naughty children. We would rush forwards and put our hands on the stove to feel the heat.

In the spring days the lessons were earlier and we had the piazza all to ourselves in the mornings before school. Two hundred or more pupils gathered and ran around playing all sorts of games before a teacher would wave his hand into the air to show that it was time for class. In May and in June, for a treat, when the weather was getting warmer, and the teachers were in good spirits, the entire school would close for the day. It was time for a *passeggiata* (a walk in the countryside for a bit of fresh air) and for singing folk songs. We would look at the farmers working in the fields, a shepherd looking after his flock and we would admire the beauty in the nature that surrounded our village. The girls would pick up the little daisies while we boys would be looking to see if we could find a bird's nest in the shrubs. They were the exciting moments of our school days.

On returning home later in my life, I have noticed changes to the village life. The school building is still there but the old wooden front door has been replaced with a ghastly metal one. My first classroom has been transformed into a post office and a life-insurance company which used to occupy my classroom on the first floor has closed down too. A few years back, there were a dozen children in the building at one time, then there were six children, and then it soon came to an end. This was an end of what was once a pillar of our village life where even the desks are part of my memories.

I also started to go out after dinner to the village bar and joined old school friends for a drink or two and a get-together. Not always, but some evenings when there was a good crowd and it was not too cold with a clear sky full of shining stars, we would go around the village serenading the girls with a dear friend, Peppino, who could play the accordion. We would walk around the streets, stopping under the houses where we knew that girls lived. It was great fun and so romantic to serenade. These were moments that I will never forget, as long as I live. There is something magic about this time – something that I know does not last for ever. Two to three songs were played to each girl with us singing along – perhaps out of tune but we tried our best! They would switch the light on just for a few seconds to let us know that they had heard us. Then we would move on quietly to the next one. (If you are ever serenaded, don't get up and look out of the window, otherwise you would ruin the mystique.)

I was growing up and I had to find a job, otherwise the villagers would start gossiping: "What is he doing all day? He is too lazy. He does not like work."

A relation of the family, Antonio Margiotta, who lived in Rome, promised to help me find work as an apprentice in an embassy or a private house. But it was very difficult and there were lots of fruitless promises. The chefs were a closely knit circle in those days – some kind of mafia, although I don't like to use this word! They guarded and protected their own places. When they needed someone to help, they would give the job to a relative or to a family friend. They did not know me, and a job never materialised.

Finally, another friend, named Quinto Terreri, found a job for me in Rome. I will never forget the morning of 9 March 1963, as I waited for the coach in Rosello, together with my mother, grandmother, brothers and sisters.

We were standing at the side of the road as the seven-o'clock coach for Rome arrived, and I can remember my mother and grandmother sad and tearful, knowing that the time had come for me to leave home.

I was only fourteen years old and life would never be the same again. I boarded the coach, bought a ticket, sat quietly in one of the empty back seats, and the coach moved on. I turned my head around, looking at the village and thinking at the same time of my childhood spent there. I knew the bends and the bumps in the road and could sense where I was. As we rounded the last bend, called *La Cerashe* (the cherries), the red terracotta roofs disappeared behind me, and I whispered goodbye to myself.

THIS IS WHAT THE WORLD ... THINKS OF ME

A Pino lo conozco desde 1982. Era el propietario de la casa que alquilé en Londres. Desde el primer momento, se comportó como un amigo. Es amable, cariñoso y siempre está a ayudarte. Como "chef" siempre me ha sorprendido por su indiscutible talento, con munús extraordinarios-no puedo olvidar tantos y tan deliciosos platos con los que me ha hecho disfrutar y descubrir que la comida es mas que alimentarse.

Como persona tan solo puedo añadir que lo considero como uno de mis mejores amigos.

I met Pino in 1982. He was the owner of the house in London that I rented. Since that first time, he behaved like a friend. He is kind, lovely and always ready to help.

As a chef, I have been always surprised by his exceptional talent, with extraordinary food that is more, much more, than simply eating.

Finally there is nothing more to add, just to say that I consider him one of my best friends.

Manuela Ferrer-Ibanez, Sevilla

I have known Pino for many years as a loving husband to Caroline and devoted father to Edilio, with many great qualities, not least conquering adversity and added to this a zest for life and living, not many of us, alas, possess.

He is a passionate creative person always willing to share his ideas and creations with others, much loved and admired and an inspiration to us all.

Ann Boughton-Leigh, Santon, Isle of Man

Pino Iacaruso is an extraordinary chef who has led an extraordinary life. And perhaps even more extraordinary, he writes about it with warmth, eloquence and charm while his wonderful recipes simply ooze Italian sunshine.

Alison Davison, Editor of foodie magazine

I feel privileged to count Pino as a personal friend. His skills, knowledge and courage have been an inspiration to me. He has a tremendous passion for food, sourcing and using the best ingredients to prepare food of such great quality, and all this with dedication and modesty.

John Heller, A.C.F. Maitrisse Escoffier, Palmes Culinaire Cordon Culinaire

SPAGHETTI ALLA CARBONARA
SPAGHETTI WITH BACON

To find the origin of this dish, we must not look back to the time of the Carboneria in Rome, a patriotic mercenary plot that was similar to the Guy Fawkes' plot, but simply, this name was given by adding freshly milled black pepper to the spaghetti just before serving. This was to make it darker.

250g/8oz pancetta or streaky bacon unsmoked
6 tbsp olive oil
1 clove of garlic crushed
4 eggs size 4
200ml/6fl oz double cream
60g/2oz freshly grated pecorino or Parmesan cheese
600g/1lb 5oz spaghetti
Salt
Freshly ground black pepper

Cut the bacon into small strips; crush the garlic and fry in olive oil making sure not to let the pancetta get too crispy as it could become too hard. Remove and discard the garlic and keep the bacon in the frying pan with the oil to one side. Beat the eggs, double cream, Parmesan cheese and a few rounds of black pepper together. Keep also on one side.

Cook the spaghetti until it is al dente in plenty of salted water according to instructions. Before draining, add one glass of cold water and stir, this will shock the pasta and will stop it cooking. Return the drained spaghetti to the pan, add the bacon and the egg mixture, stir well and taste for seasoning. Serve with plenty of black pepper on top.

The heat from the pan and hot drained spaghetti should be sufficient to heat the egg and bacon sauce. If it is too runny for your liking, return the pan to the heat and stir for a few seconds.

This dish is very quick and easy to make, and is tasty too. I recommend not overdoing the seasoning, and the quantity is plenty for six people.

Serves: 6
Preparation: 15 minutes
Cooking: 12–15 minutes

INSALATA DI ASPARAGI CON PROSCIUTTO DI PARMA
ASPARAGUS SALAD WITH PARMA HAM

This is a light and delicious antipasto for the warm summer days.

2 fresh bunches of asparagus
2 fresh bunches of watercress, washed
3 eating apples (coxes)
12 very thin slices of Parma ham

Sauce Vinaigrette:
4 tbsp olive oil
1 tbsp wine vinegar
1 tbsp lemon juice
2 tbsp natural yoghurt
1 good pinch mixed herbs
Salt
Freshly ground black pepper

Trim and tie the asparagus. Boil in plenty of water with a little salt and 2 slices of lemon. Cook until tender to the touch but not overcooked. Lift out the asparagus bunches and plunge in cold water to stop further cooking and then drain them. Cut the asparagus stems if they are too long. Keep to one side.

To make the vinaigrette: Whisk all the ingredients together in a bowl until well combined.

Place the watercress on 6 plates or in a large serving dish, cut the apples into thin wedges and arrange them around the plate. Then beautifully and artistically arrange the Parma ham and the asparagus. Spoon the vinaigrette over the salad and serve with warm ciabatta bread.

Serves: 6
Preparation: 30 minutes

Chef's note: As an alternative to asparagus you could use also fresh green figs, or melon like the charentais.

CARCIOFI ALLA ROMANA
BRAISED GLOBE ARTICHOKES

One of the most attractive and appetising ways of preparing these artichokes is alla romana

6 large globe artichokes
1 lemon
3 tbsp finely chopped parsley
30g/1oz fresh white breadcrumbs
2 cloves garlic, peeled and finely chopped
1 tsp crumbled mint leaves
Salt
Freshly ground black pepper
8 tbsp olive oil

Begin preparing the artichokes by bending back and snapping off the outer green part of the leaves.

With a pair of kitchen scissors cut off the top halves of the next two or three rounds of leaves while you are holding the artichokes stem. With a sharp knife, slice at least 25mm/1in off the top of the entire central cone, eliminating all the green part. You can now look into the centre, where you will find at the bottom some small, pale leaves with prickly tips curving inwards. Cut off all the little leaves and scrape away the fuzzy choke beneath them with a small knife or a melon baller being carefully not to cut away any of the heart.

Trim away all the green up to the base of the artichoke, keeping only the white part. Rub with the lemon, squeezing juice over the cut portions so that they will not discolour.

In a bowl, mix the chopped parsley, the breadcrumbs, the garlic, mint leaves and salt. Set aside one-third of the mixture and press the rest into the cavity of each artichoke, rubbing it well into the sides of the cavity.

Choose a heavy-bottomed casserole just large enough to contain the artichokes. Place the artichoke tops pointing upwards and stems facing down – fit with a tight-fitting lid

Sprinkle the rest of the parsley mixture, add the olive oil and enough water to cover one third of the artichokes leaves. Soak a piece of greaseproof paper in water, wide enough to cover the casserole. Place the lid and cook over a low/medium heat. Check if tender and easily pierced with a fork. Lightly brown under a grill.

Serves: 6
Preparation: 20 minutes
Cooking: 35–40 minutes

Chef's note: Cooking times vary according to freshness and tenderness of the artichokes. If they are tough and take a long time to cook, you may add 2–3 tablespoons water from to time to time. They should be served either lukewarm or at room temperature.

BRUSCHETTA
ROMAN GARLIC BREAD

The name bruschetta comes from bruscare, which means 'to roast over coals', the original and still the best way of toasting the bread. As a child I used to eat the bruschetta sitting next to our fireplace during the winter months.

12 slices Italian white bread cut into 37mm/1½in thick
4 cloves garlic, lightly crushed and peeled
8 tbsp olive oil, as green as you can find
Salt
Freshly ground pepper to taste

Preheat the grill. Put the sliced bread over an oven tray. Toast the bread on both sides to a golden brown under the hot grill.

Rub one side of the toast while still hot with garlic. Discard the garlic as it dries up and take a fresh clove. Put the toast on a dish garlic-rubbed side facing up, and pour a thin stream of olive oil over it. Not a few drops, but enough to soak each slice very lightly. Add a sprinkling of salt and a twist or two of freshly ground pepper per slice. The toast is best served while still warm.

Serves: 6
Preparation: 20 minutes

Chef's note: Top the bruschetta with slices of beef tomatoes and oregano or with Mediterranean vegetables.

MY VILLAGE

I smell the odour of the woods and the perfume
of your air, and the fields in flower,
and the morning rise, slowly, I can see the smoke,
and the beautiful colour of the countryside.

I see you, my village on the steep hill:
your houses stacked up like a mast on the top
and the smoothly scattered, vibrant turf.
Now the life is not the same again.

You don't see me between the poplar trees and streams,
as I happily leap and run down again,
but your singing in me doesn't fade.

I feel the beautiful day in my being
That I will take in my heart with quiet spirit;
land of my dear Fathers, in the flower of my youth.

PAESE MIO

Sento l'odor del bosco ed il profumo
dell'aria tua, dei prati in fiore
e del mattin levarsi, lento, il fumo
vedo, e della campagna il bel colore.

Te vedo, paese mio, erto sul colle:
le tue case arroccate in su la cima,
sparse al pian sulle vivide zolle.
Ora la vita non è quella di prima.

Né mi vedi fra i pioppi e nei ruscelli,
giù per balze ancor correndo lieto,
ma il tuo canto in me più non si perde.

Sento nel petto vivi i giorni belli
che porterò nel cuor con spirto quieto;
terra dei padri cari, età mia verde.

Enisio A. Di Tullio (1963)

PENSIONE ALFA – ROME

Canis ingens, catena vinctus in pariete erat pictus
superque quadrata littera scriptum 'Cave canem'
PETRONIUS AD 1st century
A huge dog, tied by a chain, was painted on the wall
and over it was written in capital letters 'Beware of the dog'

The work that Quinto Terreri had found for me was as an apprentice chef at a small hotel not very far from Rome's main railway station. It was called the Pensione Alfa. The days before the departure were full of excitement and preparation.

What was I going to take with me? What was needed once I had left the comfort of my home? I remember my mother made me try on some of my father's white kitchen jackets to see if they fitted me. Fortunately, they were the right size. I looked good in them and took three or four with me. My mother went through the other clothes and packed a suitcase for me. My grandmother put in the case a few buttons, cotton and needle and an old pair of scissors, which I've still got to this day on the mantelpiece, and they are very much treasured.

The coach stopped halfway at Cassino in the main piazza for fifteen minutes. Looking up high, towards a blue sky, for the first time in my life I saw the *Abbazia* of Montecassino, which I had heard so much about. It is an enormous high building with thick stone walls as if it were a fortress, dominating the valley down below. A narrow road winding up like a snake leads to this religious retreat. There are coaches that can take you up to visit the abbey and, after so many years, sadly I have never been to visit it.

The cashier, and the barmen in the Bar Italia were invaded by a coachful of hungry and thirsty people. As soon as we walked in we were hit by the wonderful aroma of freshly roasting coffee, while a large selection of fresh home-made mouth-watering pastries and gateaux were irresistibly displayed behind the thick glass counter. There was a rush to eat. With one hand holding a pastry, and the other a cappuccino, we had to get back on the coach; and we had travelled no less then three hours before we went on the new motorway just opened to Rome. My face pressed against the glass window, and my eyes were glancing at every corner of the landscape as the coach moved on. One of my most vivid recollections of the journey to Rome was of groups of humble local people, dressed in bright clothes. Men and mostly women on the verge of the motorway were planting shrubs and small plants in the soil to stop the earth and stones rolling down. Years later, this provided us with the most beautiful view of plants dotted with yellow broom flowers and oleanders in full bloom.

We arrived in Rome in the middle of the afternoon. Quinto and another dear friend, Michele Margiotta, travelled on the same journey. Michele also became a chef at a young age. He followed in the footsteps of his older brother, Donato, as an apprentice many years before me in the restaurants of Naples, which he so much loved for the good food.

Naples is famous for pasta dishes, sweet pastries and coffee espresso – they like it 'hot as a fire, black as a woman's hair, and sweet as a kiss'. It is a fascinating city with such a diversity of travellers throughout the centuries. The natural beauty of the bay has attracted many artists to this magnificent and chaotic place.

However, Michele had had a change of heart and he was starting a new job at a big hotel, Massimo D'Azeglio, and Quinto was starting at the Nova Roma, in the capital next morning.

We got out of the coach under a cloudy grey sky. The noise of the cars was unbearable, and the bustling of people everywhere – a total confusion – frightened me. There I was in the Eternal City, Rome, the city that I couldn't wait to set foot in to start my new life, and I was horrified! I was frightened like a little bird, which leaves his nest for the first time and tries to fly. If I had had a mirror and looked into it I probably would have fainted. We set off – or rather, they set off with me following behind.

My mother had made me wear my best heavy woollen suit with chequered red and black squares that later I discovered was similar to the chef trousers. She wanted me to look smart – *fare bella figura,* as we say in Italy. Even though it was still March I felt boiling hot. We reached a crossroads, and in front of us I saw two giant Roman pine trees. I froze, staring at the height of them and thinking about what would happen if they came crashing down! Those pine trees are still imprinted on my mind and when I go back to Rome and happen to be in that area I go to look at them and it reminds me of my first day in Rome.

Quinto took me to meet the owner and the chef at Pensione Alfa, where he had worked as a young chef before me. On first impressions, it was not at all what I had expected. I couldn't turn back now, though. This was the pensione, on the fifth floor, where I was going to start my career and change my life. The kitchen was small and old-fashioned painted all in white with a high ceiling. At the far end there was a large, heavy stove; a big fridge occupied the right-hand side; and on the left there was the kitchen sink for general use. There was a table-island in the middle of the kitchen for preparation and other uses, and a large window on the left-hand side, looking down at a courtyard where there was a fire station (*pompieri*). Every time they were called out we were the first to hear the sound of the blaring siren. "Oh, not again!" the chef would complain.

The whole place was strange to my eyes. Having been taken into the kitchen, I was asked if I wanted something to eat. The chef gave me a plate of spaghetti. He just picked it up with his bare hands, put it into a colander, and heated it in boiling water before draining it and giving it to me. I had never seen anyone do that before at home, and I couldn't have said I didn't like it. It put me off straight away, until I realised that this was how a commercial kitchen worked.

The following morning, I was called early with a big shout by the lady owner to start my first day at work: "*E ragazzo* [boy], get up!"

And what a shock it was! After so many years the memory of it can still send cold shivers down my spine. And oh, the bedroom! It was so small that it was either the suitcase or me in there.

In the kitchen I started with washing up the breakfast dishes, then preparing and cleaning vegetables and finally waiting for the chef to arrive before cooking for lunch would start. Everything was so different, and I felt homesick for the village and my family I had left behind. I began to wonder what I had done.

The pensione was in Via Nazionale, leading to Piazza Esedra, one of the most beautiful piazzas in Rome. It was busy with people going about their business in all directions, and beautiful boutiques with chic shops, bars and restaurants on both sides. In the centre of the piazza is a huge, impressive, round fountain, which dominates the whole piazza. The fountain is carved in stone and has four statues of young ladies, each one holding a different animal in a contorted pose. Water gushes up from under them. There is a bronze statue on top of the fountain of a man holding a huge fish with its mouth open, from which water spouts high in the air. I could feel the light breeze and the coolness of the running water all around the fountain. I would sit at the edge, take a letter from home out of my pocket and read it all the way through perhaps once, twice or more and watch all those people moving and walking in every direction in this busy city. I would reflect on my life and the future ahead of me.

One night I had the most amazing dream. I dreamed that I was back at the village, and going back home, then I saw my mother's face and she was walking towards me and we met. I looked at her and said in a sort of lament as if I was tired, "Where have you been, Mum? I have not seen you for a long time. I have to make my own bed every day now, and wash all my clothes. I have missed you so much." This dream will never leave me. It is still vivid in my mind and I will never forget it.

The chef, Francesco, was a very good teacher. He was a nice man and he was patient and understanding. He explained things such as the ingredients and the methods many times over, as you have to with someone like me who was without any kitchen experience. He taught me a lot and, for me, the time spent with maestro Francesco Mangoli, was the basis of all my learning.

Francesco had been born and bred in Rome. He was elderly, totally professional, dedicated to his work and well known amongst other chefs in the Roman circle. The first thing he taught me was how to make béchamel sauce (a white sauce) for macaroni cheese (*maccheroni gratinati*), and I have always remembered to add fresh grated nutmeg to give a nice flavour. *Spaghetti alla carbonara*, a truly Roman dish with unsmoked bacon and hard sheep's cheese, fresh pancetta and *pecorino romano* was another dish I was shown. Another time he made a sweet pastry with apricots and almonds, called *crostata di albicocche* in Italian. It was the very first *crostata* that I had ever seen – quite delicious. When I was in the kitchen waiting for the chef to arrive, I kept opening the fridge, cutting out a small piece and then eating it, until there was not much left for the others!

After my fifteenth birthday I asked the chef for a short break to go home. I needed the working permit from Rosello Employment Agency if I wanted to find another job. I was working at the pensione without a permit and under age and that made it impossible for me to move on.

For the first time in my life, I returned home by train. I caught the midnight train from Rome's main station, and I wouldn't be home before nine o'clock the next morning. The train left the bright lights of the Rome platform, and set out towards a dark sky. The dim light of the compartment and the sound of the squeaking wheels made me soon go to sleep. I woke up at four in the morning, feeling cold as a new day was breaking, and for the first time in my life I saw the dawn. It was getting light. The mist was rising gently amongst the hills, the trees and the houses as the train was going through the countryside. The glass window panel was wet with condensation, and I wrote my name on it. The sun was appearing slowly from behind the mountains with its bright sunrays. As a young boy I was fascinated and mystified to watch the transformation of the aurora.

A few months later, I decided to look for another job at a big hotel near Rome's main station. I liked this hotel so much for it was huge and impressive. Along the way I had become friendly with some of the young chefs who worked there, and they encouraged me to go for an interview. I went along full of enthusiasm and hope that I might have a stroke of luck. I turned up at the back of the hotel, at the staff entrance, and asked a security man if I could see the head chef. A nice, friendly person appeared in one of the side doors in his complete uniform to see this important young man.

I asked the chef, "Do you have a job for an apprentice in your kitchen?"

"Not at the moment," he replied; "the chef's brigade is complete. How long have you been working in the kitchen?" he asked.

"About four months," I replied.

"With whom are you working?"

"I am working with Francesco at the Pensione Alfa."

"I know Francesco very well," the chef replied. "No, I am sorry, I can't help you."

Being so young at the time, I felt hurt and upset by his reply. I suppose I expected a better job with very little experience too soon.

I went back to work for the evening shift. Francesco came into the kitchen and was already changed into his whites to start cooking for dinner. He looked at me straight into my eyes and said, "Do you think that I don't know where you have been this afternoon? You went to see the chef Pavia Saccone, at the Mediterranio Hotel for work. I just saw him outside in the street and he has told me. You have barely arrived in Rome, and you are already looking for another job? I could have found you another job with my colleagues when the time was right the same way I did with my other apprentices."

I stood like a post and I remember not saying a word. I felt ashamed of myself for what I had done and it was very foolish of me even to think about it. Francesco and my employees were very nice and understanding towards me. They had met my father once on his way home and I must say they were very charming to him. I do not comprehend why I was so restless and eager to move on at such a young age when I had all my life in front of me.

Not satisfied enough by what I had already done, I thought that I should go to a catering school hotel and learn how to cook. On the way back to work I met a dear friend of mine, older than me, Eugenio Cimino, also from Rosello. I told him of my idea.

He turned around and not looking pleasant at all towards me he said, "What did you put in your mind this time, Pino? You have to study and work hard in these places and if that was your intention, why did you not study when your father told you so? They were true and saintly words. I did not dare to say anything.

I must confess that at times, in my early days, weeks and months in Rome before I did settle down, I regretted it. And I never told that to my father. I suppose I was too proud to admit it, and I knew deep down inside me what would have been his answer . . .

I was dreaming already of higher places – to work with other younger chefs and to learn my skill fast. The moral from this part of my life is that the mentality of changing work and being restless in a young mind has never changed from day zero and it will never change. I had learnt my lesson, though, and after that when I went to look for new work I never revealed where I was working.

In the afternoon, before returning to work for the evening shift, I used to walk around so that I would get to know Rome, and particularly the many interesting places throughout this corner of the magnificent city.

Via Vittorio Veneto, the street most renowned in the sixties, was where the film *La Dolce Vita* had been filmed. It was a street to be visited, and it was the street where the word paparazzo was invented. Photographers would stand around here with cameras for a chance to shoot the celebrities. There were lots of well-known bars and restaurants with smartly dressed waiters sporting long white aprons, serving a clientele of elegant, rich and famous people. Beautiful people would sit at tables outside, enjoying *la dolce vita*, sipping Martini and eating their gourmet food, slowly but with gusto under a decorated marquee in a world of their own. I would look at their faces, searching for somebody to recognise – maybe someone I had seen in a magazine? – perhaps a famous diva, an actor, an actress or maybe a millionaire?

From Piazza Venezia to Via del Corso, a well-renowned street flanked on both sides by shops, boutiques and luxurious restaurants and bars with bright lights, and counters with tasty gateaux and patisserie. I could only savour them with my eyes and I never set foot inside this haven of elegance. Leading to Piazza del Popolo (The People's Square) at the end of del Corso there are twin domed churches. This theatrical set of a large piazza has a tall obelisk in the centre with four Egyptian lions, each lying on four fountains, and the piazza is encircled by statues and monuments.

Four palazzi dominate the four corners of the piazza. On one corner is an old restaurant and bar called the Canova, with outside chairs, open umbrellas for shade and waiters with impeccable service, serving tourists with a traditional Roman cuisine on the pavement. I would stand there thinking what it might be like to sit there, looking in as if it was a pretty toy-shop window.

Four decades later on my way home I often return to Rome and we stay at a beautiful hotel called Giulio Cesare with all the comforts. We are always welcomed by the head concierge, Pierluigi, with the words, "Welcome to your home in Rome." This hotel is within walking distance from this beautiful piazza and together with my family we sit and enjoy the meals and the view from the tables that once I used to look at from outside. I smile and think how life has changed so much and how happy it makes me feel.

Years later my brother Lucio was working at Harry's Bar in the Via Veneto. On one occasion, on our way back to England, I took my wife, Caroline, to visit him. We were very impressed. It was a very smart restaurant; two barmen were ready to serve the famous Bellini cocktail and a selection of beautiful canapés on the bar counter. My brother was very pleased to see us and we were introduced to his colleagues amongst the restaurant staff. To please Lucio we had lunch there as well. Caroline wanted to eat outside, alfresco. The maître d'hôtel handed out the menu, and after a few minutes came back to the table, a notebook and a pen in his hand.

"Shall we start with an aperitif?" the maître d' suggested.

"*Si, si,*" we nodded in agreement.

"May I recommend a seafood antipasto? just a small starter."

"*Si, si.*"

"Would you like anything to drink with your meal? Can I suggest a nice bottle of Frascati wine?"

"*Si, si, va bene,*" came the answer again.

"Can I suggest a pasta dish, a small plate of fresh *tagliatelle alla Bolognese?*"

Being an Italian, one couldn't turn it down. "*Si, si,* bring also the tagliatelle." But the portion was quite large.

"The chef has cooked roast veal for lunch. I recommend it. It's very good and tender. Two slices each with tiny roasted potatoes and vegetables."

He wanted to look after us well and to make sure we were having a good time. With a brother working in the kitchen it was very hard to say no!

"Have you chosen the dessert yet? We have vanilla ice cream with glacé chestnuts (*marrons glacés*). It's Sophia Loren's favourite ice cream!"

Well, if it's Sophia Loren's favourite *gelato*, it must be ours as well!

Looking back to that day I remembered when I joined the Hotel Michelangelo years before. Nello Marinari, a kitchen porter, said, "A good maître d'hôtel makes you eat what he likes." Indeed, thinking about that lunch, Nello's wise words still echo inside my ears.

We got up from the table, lighter in our pocket, full and dizzy. The heat was unbearable. Caroline wanted me to look for a chemist to buy an Alka-Seltzer to help us to digest the meal and we both took a dose each and hastened to our hotel for a siesta.

THIS IS WHAT THE WORLD . . . THINKS OF ME

When I first met Pino several years ago I was struck by the immense courage of this man and his many gifts especially his painting and his garden creativity not to forget the joy of his cooking and also his Italian sense of humour almost as humorous as the Irish! With deepest respect and love for Pino.

Netta Burt, St. Leonards, Hertfordshire

Pino tu sei il mio orgoglio, ti voglio bene e ti auguro che il tuo futuro sia colorato e limpido come le tue pitture.

Pino you are my pride, and I am deeply fond of you. I wish you that your future will be coloured, and clear like your paintings.

Rita Candolfo, Ferrara

Pino ama la vita. Dio ti da la forza di continuare nel cammino per il tuo futuro.
Il tuo coraggio e la forza nell'afrontare a sconfiggere la malattia sia da esempio per tutti noi. Grazie per il dono della tua dell'amicizia nonostante la distanza che ci separa.

Pino loves life to the full. God gave you strength and continuity in the walk of life. Your courage and the spirit to overcome your illness you are an example to us all.

Thank you for the gift of your friendship that you give to us freely however many miles we are apart.

Franca e Amelia Caracino, Milano

PASTA AL FORMAGGIO
MACARONI WITH THREE CHEESES

For this dish I prefer penne or rigatoni. I find the small macaroni absorbs too much sauce and are fussy to eat. The cooking time of pasta varies according to quality. Good pasta always takes longer as the semolina is harder; inferior quality pasta cooks more quickly with bad results such as sticky pasta.

500g/1lb 2oz pasta
1½ litre/3 pints milk
1 Mozzarella cheese, cut into cubes
90g/3oz Parmesan cheese
90g/3oz Dolce latte cheese
60g/2oz butter
60g/2oz flour
Nutmeg
Salt
Freshly ground black pepper

One ovenproof dish measuring: 36cm/14in long by 25cm/10in wide. Buttered.

Fill a large saucepan with salted water and bring to the boil. Cook the pasta according to instructions, stirring occasionally so it does not stick at the bottom of the pan. Pour the pasta into a colander, cool under running water and leave to drain.

Melt the butter, add the flour and cook for 1–2 minutes by stirring with a wooden spoon.

Bring the milk to the boil and add the roux and stir with a whisk so no lumps form. Add salt, pepper and nutmeg and leave the sauce to thicken. Cook for 2–3 minutes. Add two tablespoons of Parmesan cheese. Adjust seasoning.

Put the pasta into a clean bowl, and then add the mozzarella (reserve some mozzarella cheese to sprinkle on top), the Dolce latte cheese and the Parmesan cheese, a little salt and a few rounds of black pepper, and mix. Pour one third of the white sauce over the pasta and mix well, taste for seasoning. Put the pasta into an ovenproof dish, smooth the top and add the remaining sauce and cheese. Dot the pasta with a few flakes of butter and bake to a light brown top.

Serves: 6
Preparation: 20 minutes
Cooking: 35–40 minutes
Oven: 180°C/350°F/Gas 4

Chef's note: To avoid disappointments of a dry macaroni cheese, bake the pasta in the oven in a bain-marie.

POLLO ALLA CACCIATORE
CHICKEN FRICASSÉE WITH PEPPERS AND TOMATOES

This is a classic Italian dish, and it is delicious. It can be prepared ahead of time and let the chicken cool in its sauce. When reheating, simmer very slowly, covered, until the chicken is hot.

1 roasting chicken weighing 1.35kg/3lb cut into 12 pieces
4 tbsp olive oil
110g/4oz plain flour
Salt
Freshly ground pepper, a few twists of the mill
150ml/5fl oz dry, white wine
½ medium onion, finely chopped
3 peppers one green, red and yellow, with seeds removed, cut into strips
2 cloves of garlic
1 tin Italian tomatoes, coarsely chopped with their juice

Wash the chicken pieces in cold water and pat dry very thoroughly with kitchen paper. Choose a frying pan or saucepan large enough to contain all the chicken pieces comfortably, without crowding.

Heat the olive oil in the frying pan over moderately high heat. Coat the chicken pieces in the flour on both sides, shake off the excess, and put in the frying pan, skin side down. When one side has turned golden brown, turn the pieces over and brown the other side, lift them out onto a dish, add salt and pepper and keep warm.

Tip the frying pan and draw off most of the fat with a spoon. Turn the heat high, add the wine and boil rapidly to reduce by half. Lower the heat and add the chopped onion and garlic, and cook for 5 minutes, stirring a few times. Add the browned chicken pieces, all but the breasts. (Breasts cook faster, so they can be added later.) Add the sliced pepper and chopped tomatoes and the juice. Adjust to slow simmer, and cover. After 10 minutes add the breasts and continue cooking until tender, about 30 minutes.

Turn and baste the chicken a few times while cooking. Adjust seasoning.

Transfer the chicken to a warm dish. If the sauce in the pan is too thin, raise the heat and boil to reduce until thickens, stirring as it boils. Pour over the dish and serve.

Serves: 6
Preparation: 30 minutes
Cooking: 30–35 minutes

CROSTATA DI ALBICOCCHE
APRICOT PIE

This is a well-known dessert in Italy and can be found at almost every sweet counter where it is eaten, with expresso or cappuccino coffee, at tables set outside. It is sold in many good Italian delicatessens and you can order crostata freshly baked at your local patisserie.

Pasta Frolla (see recipe opposite)
400g/14oz good quality apricot jam
1 egg, beaten size 4, mixed with
2 tbsp double cream
30g/1oz whole almond, skinned
Icing sugar, to dust

Make the pastry in advance and leave to rest and preheat the oven.

With a pastry brush, grease the inside of the flan tin and dust with a little flour. Roll out three quarters of the pastry to about ½cm/¼ in thick and line the 24cm/9in loose-based flan tin, ensuring that the pastry is even. Trim off any surplus and press the edges of the flan dish with your fingers to raise the pastry a little higher than the edge. Pinch the edges of the flan with your fingers to form a decorative edge. Spread the apricot jam over the pastry and scatter over the skinned almonds.

Roll out the remaining pastry. Beat the egg and brush the sides of the flan. Cut the pastry into strips and use to form a lattice decoration over the pie. Brush with the remaining egg/cream and bake. When cold, unmould, dust with icing sugar and serve.

Serves: 6
Preparation: 15 minutes
Cooking: 30–35 minutes
Oven: 170°C/325°F/Gas 3

PASTA FROLLA

250g/8oz plain flour
110g/4oz icing sugar
150g/5oz butter
4 egg yolks size 4
A little orange or lemon rind

Place in a large bowl the flour, sugar, butter and rind, and rub together with fingertips. Make a well in the middle and add the egg yolks. Gradually blend all the ingredients, place on a worktop and knead for a few minutes. Shape into a ball, wrap in a cloth or cling film and place in the fridge for at least 4 hours. Roll out the pastry as you would any other.

Do not overwork this pastry, as it is extremely delicate. It is even better made the day before required, and placed in the fridge overnight. This pastry is well known and used in many varieties of patisserie in Italy, such as for fruit flan bases, tartlets or crostata. Here it is also known as pasta detta Napoletana.

Makes: 600g/1lb 5oz
Preparation: 15 minutes

HOTEL PARIOLI

Mele al forno con la crema inglese é un matrimonio fatto in paradiso
Baked apples and custard a marriage made in heaven

Ambition and a free spirit drove me to look for a new job, which I found through a colleague. He knew of a hotel where they were looking for a young apprentice in the most residential area of Rome – at the Hotel Parioli. I was very enthusiastic at that age about this new job. I felt full of inspiration and strong, seeing myself with a proper chef's uniform, and looking forward to working with a team of chefs and sharing working experiences. The kitchen was very big and fully equipped compared to the one I had just left behind; and chefs at the hotel were of mixed ages.

My new colleague, Sergio, led me through a service once. From the service area you could see the preparation room, with its white-tiled walls, large fridges and long white marble tables, which ran the length of the entire room. Kitchen workers were singing in their bright overalls whilst they were cleaning vegetables or cutting large joints of fresh meat. There was the familiar sound of knives being sharpened against the steel and the constant running of cold water.

It was here that I went on the day of my interview. The head chef came out from his office. He was a very short man with a small nose and a very small fine moustache. He wore a white uniform, and a tall white hat which made him look taller. It hid his bald head. I noticed he had tufts of thick grey shiny hair showing on his neck, and a thin, well-sharpened pencil tucked behind his right ear ready to take any notes. "You must be Pino," he said, and we shook hands. "I am Gigino Mariotta and I welcome you to our kitchen. I hope you are going to be happy here with us." Chefs were seen as father figures in those days; they ran their kitchens and they commanded respect and kept good discipline. Although this one would lose his marbles sometimes!

As we were introduced, I thought to myself, 'Dare I ask any questions?'

"I see Sergio has given you the chef's tour!" he said.

"Indeed," I replied.

"Yes, it's one of our house jokes," he told me, smiling. "But you must be thirsty from your journey and the heat! I hope Sergio will give you a cold drink. I'm in a hurry to prepare a special dessert for tomorrow for an engagement party which is being held in the banqueting room."

What he was about to concoct was a beautiful dessert called *la bombe surprise*, which required a long process of preparation. On top of a flat circular serving plate, a ring of ice would be placed, from a mould. In the centre of this hollow ring would be placed a small battery light. Resting on the ice would then be a layer of sponge, on top of which *la bombe* itself was placed. The bombe was three layers of ice cream – raspberry, chocolate and a special cream mousse. Over this, whipped cream was piped to cover it, and the peak was garnished with a strawberry or some pineapple leaves. At the engagement party, *la bombe* would be brought in after the guests had finished their main courses. The lights would be switched off, then the battery light in the middle of the dessert would be turned on, and voila! a beautiful glow from inside the ice would shine through the room.

During the service time he couldn't control his nerves and would jump up and down next to the hotplate like a little boy! As soon as the restaurant was full of diners he would shout for the food to go out, no matter if the dishes were ready or not. I remember one day when we were extremely busy, and he was shouting to another chef, Nicola, to send out a pasta dish. The poor devil was hurrying, sautéing and tossing the penne in the air and they were falling back like a cascade in the pan and still they were cold.

"Via, via, let go, let go," he kept shouting.

"But, chef," said Nicola, "the pasta is still cold!"

"Never mind, never mind."

Nicola in disbelief shrugged his shoulders and in desperation sent the dish out.

Sometimes the food was kept in the hotplate ready to be sent out. Once, he called out for one of our main dishes prepared by my chef, Stefano. He handed it out to me and I took it to the hotplate. I placed the meat dish straight inside and closed the doors, and, because of the shouting and the confusion in the kitchen, the head chef wasn't aware of what I had done. I was so frightened by him that I didn't say anything. I assumed that he saw me placing the meat dish in the hotplate.

The head chef kept calling for the main-course dish.

Stefano said, "I have given it to you, chef."

The head chef said, "I don't have it."

They started exchanging words in loud voices and I was thinking, 'What have I started now?'

They became so angry that they nearly started a big row between the two of them until Stefano remembered that I had put it into the hotplate – problem solved!

I was placed to work with the senior sous-chef, Stefano Tafano, who was in his forties. He was a tall man with broad shoulders, very energetic and quick on his feet. He wore a foot-tall well-starched hat at all times, which gave him an even greater presence. He had great patience with me, and understanding too as I did not have a lot of experience in the kitchen. I did not find Tafano intimidating; he was jolly and very helpful – an interesting person. During our meals at the kitchen table he would reminisce about the past while the brigade listened.

I recall once he said that his father was blowing up rocks with dynamite sticks to make roads in his village and every time there was a loud bang the villagers would say, "Those bloody Tafanis – when are they going to stop making such a nuisance?"

Stefano worked very hard in his position, as a sous-chef, running from one end of the kitchen to another. I listened and tried very hard to understand the way things were made, and made myself useful in a new job and in a new environment. It was very hard work, and tiring. One had to react quickly and promptly, especially when the head chef called for an order to be sent straight away to the dining room.

The mornings were not as exciting as I thought they might have been. My first job was to place a large cauldron of water on the stove and bring it to the boil. Then I had to throw in handfuls of ripened tomatoes at a time and, after a few seconds, lift them out with a colander and plunge them into cold water. Then I would squeeze the skin out with my hands, getting splashed with tomato juice all over my white jacket, and then chop up the flesh. This was the first stage to make-litres of tomato sauce; and then there were other various and endless things to prepare and to sort out.

Outside was another glorious summer day. The sun was beating down. I wanted to be outside! It was hardly ten o'clock and the stove was already overheated. Phew! I felt exhausted.

On the left side of the stove, a few feet away, a tiled half wall concealed a very large kitchen sink where two kitchen porters washed up an array of saucepans and the kitchen utensils. It was like a sort of a window, and they couldn't help but overlook the section in which I was working, and seeing me so young and lost in the heat and the melee of the kitchen. They kept telling me, "Change job, Pino. You are far too young to be here. Why don't you start a new career? Look for something less hectic and stressful."

They were hard-working men with families at home and they had spent all their life washing saucepans, and cleaning big kitchens. They knew all about the long hours that you need to work when you are in catering. I remember how kind and humble these people were. They wanted to help and to advise me to look for a different future away from the kitchen.

The Parioli borough of Rome was a very smart and residential area, with luxury apartments, and concierges in dark uniforms at the doors, but there was not a place where you could go to sit and relax on an afternoon in the shade of a Roman pine tree.

I would catch the number 39 bus and travel all the way near to the main railway station where there are public gardens and meet some friends and colleagues for a chat and a little company.

One day, the head chef asked me to make some baked apples, and with his supervision I completed the task, put the apples in the oven and went off on my usual bus ride, without a care in the world.

I returned to the kitchen and one of the porters asked me, "What did you put in the oven?"

"Nothing," I replied.

"Didn't you put some apples in to bake?"

I suddenly remembered. I shrieked with fear of what I had done, and what the head chef was going to say of my being so forgetful.

There was a strong smell of burning sugar and smoke coming out from the oven door, and when they opened it they found the apples and the copper saucepan so badly burned that it had to be thrown away. They hid my mistake from the head chef and the others and not a word was ever said about it. Those nice porters had saved my skin!

The kitchen was always short of chefs, and at times an agency would send replacements to fill the vacancies for short periods of time. A chef arrived as a part-timer. He was a very tall man with a very big nose and a very small moustache. "I am Mario Pellegrino," he said while he was strapping the apron on. He seemed sure that he was good at his work and he was perhaps a bit full of himself. Strangely enough, he was from near my village, Rosello – a village called Villa Santa Maria. He told me, after being there a while, that I would never make it as a chef and if I did, it would take a very long time. I was too young to say anything. I felt wounded inside by his words, but I kept quiet. After so many years, I still remember what he told me. Perhaps his words were wise and prophetic. That drove me harder to become who I am today, and to prove not only to him but also to myself that he was wrong.

A new director arrived from Milan. He was slim, sharp-eyed and smartly dressed with new ideas to improve the hotel's performance. His look alone was enough to frighten the hell out of us. The kitchen suffered the first casualties and some of us lost our jobs, and that included me.

On the day that I was leaving the hotel, I was standing in the tradesman's entrance with my suitcases ready to go. Standing with me was one of the dining-room managers called Carlo Pisano. He looked very smart in a light-grey suit and tie; and behind the desk there was another man who supervised the deliveries and personnel coming in and going out from the hotel. His name was Romano Di Rienzo. He once recounted to me how much he would have liked to have been a chef; and he had worked in the hotel kitchen as an apprentice for a while, but he couldn't cope with the hard work and heat and he always felt exhausted. When he went to bed at night, the hours were never long enough. And when the alarm clock went off in the morning to wake him up, it was like a shock, he said.

Romano must have given a mighty shock to the midwife and to his mother when he came into this world. He was born with two penises, which he proudly showed to newcomers. One was large and one small and they were on top of each other as if they were a sort of an upright double-barrelled shotgun, if you see what I mean. Such a gift!

I stretched my hand to say goodbye to them both and suddenly I burst into tears. Then the manager said, "Hey, where do you think you are going to – America?"

Romano looked at the manager and replied, "He has got *affezzionato* here and he is sad to leave his friends."

They both kept repeating these words looking at each other. It sounded like it was a funny comedy. I think they must have both felt embarrassed by me. At the age of sixteen, I was crying like a child, and I was only going a few hundred yards away to the Belgian Embassy.

THIS IS WHAT THE WORLD . . . THINKS OF ME

Pino! From the moment we met I felt his warm heart, loving spirit and gentle soul, the deep pride for his family and heritage...and whatever delicious dish was in the making!

Pino! Who reaches out to others with his massive generosity. The Renaissance man: artist, author and world-class chef. The adoring and adored father and husband to Edilio and my dear friend, Car.

Pino! The man who smiles through adversity and pain overcomes with determination and grit.

"Hello Honey" he says, across the miles of telephone line between us. And the caress of his words brightens my day. Pino-thank you for being in my life. I love you.

Pamela Harvey-Blinn, Petaluma, California

A mon fidèle ami Pino que je connaîs de nomhreuses années je lui souhaite tout le success qu'il mèrite pour ce livre.

Je sais que son rêve s'est realisé grâce â son courage, la persèverance et â son talent qui son ses qualités essensielles.

J'attend avec beaucoup d'impatience ce livre, qui j'en suis sûre sera un enchantement et me permettra de m'echapper dans un autre monde.

To my constant friend Pino that I have known for many years. I wish him every success that he deserves for this book.

I know that his dream has been realized thanks to his courage, perseverance and with his talent and many qualities.

I wait with very much impatience for this book. And I am sure it will be an enchantment that will allow me to escape into another world.

Catherine Fresnel, Bruxelles

I am often asked whether I grow my own herbs or vegetables. I do grow herbs and wild strawberries. I have created a footpath where I grow three different kinds of thyme and sage, and marjoram, sorrel and rosemary grows in a flower bed.

I would rather leave the task to my greengrocer, Paul Mugleston of Country Fayre in Harbury. He is a remarkable man with a great deal of knowledge of his job and he is a well-known man at the markets around Warwickshire and neighbouring counties. He is a jolly man and he is well thought of.

Whenever I ask Paul for a certain fruit or vegetable that may be in season or not, he replies, "When do you want it for? I will do whatever I can," and more often than not, he gets it.

I never see Paul as just another seller of fruit and vegetables but as a true professional with experience and love for his job.

LEGUMI ALLA MEDITERRANEA
ROASTED VEGETABLES MEDITERRANEAN STYLE

A dish of summer vegetables, flavoured with thyme and garlic. It is delicious served as an accompaniment. Also mixed with penne or rigatoni pasta and couscous for a tasty starter.

2 fresh large aubergines
1 bunch of baby carrots on the hoof
2 fresh courgettes, medium size
2 fresh peppers, mixed: red, green or yellow
18 ripe vine tomatoes or cherry tomatoes
2 spring onions, cut into fine rings
2 cloves of garlic, crushed
Olive oil
4 sprigs of fresh thyme or marjoram
Salt
Freshly ground black pepper

Preheat the oven.

Remove the green part of the aubergines. Cut the unpeeled aubergines in half widthways, and then slice again lengthways and make slices of about 1cm/¾in thick. Peel and trim the green foliage from the carrots by leaving 1cm/½in on the end and boil for a few minutes until al dente. Meanwhile, cut the courgettes widthways at an angle, slice each piece ½cm/⅛in and keep to one side. Cut the peppers in half. Remove the green stalks, the seeds and cut into four. Remove the hard white veins with a knife, rinse under cold water and drain. Fry the tomatoes with a very little olive oil with 1–2 sprigs of thyme till light brown, lightly season and keep to one side. Chop two spring onions into fine rings and also keep to one side.

In a large oven tray pour some olive oil and place the aubergines, one next to each other. Drizzle with olive oil and add salt and pepper and bake for 15 minutes. Turn the aubergines over, making sure that they are just soft enough to the touch but not too mushy. Remove from the tray and put in a dish. Repeat the same way with the courgettes, but they require less cooking time. Roast the peppers with some thyme and the clove of garlic, adding more olive oil if necessary whilst cooking. Do not let the vegetables overcook or become too brown. Keep each vegetable separately for the colours.

To serve: In a large dish place the carrots in the middle. Arrange the vegetables by starting with the red peppers, then follow with the other vegetables to form a beautiful display. Sprinkle over the chopped onions, drizzle with some olive oil and a dash of balsamic vinegar, and serve.

Serves: 6 or more
Preparation: 30 minutes
Cooking: 20–25 minutes
Oven: 200°C/400°F/Gas 6

Chef's note: The vegetables can be cooked the day before. I would recommend to warm them up slightly – they taste better by taking the chill off.

SALTIN BOCCA ALLA ROMANA
VEAL ESCALOPES WITH PARMA HAM

The dish is Roman in origin and the word saltimbocca means 'jump in the mouth'.

12 slices veal escalopes,
sliced no more than ½ cm/¼ in thick – about 250g/8oz in all per portion
6 slices Parma ham
12 large fresh sage leaves
A little olive oil
Freshly ground black pepper
150ml/5fl oz dry white wine
A knob of butter

First beat the meat out to make it a little thinner. It just needs to be stretched a bit. Cut the Parma ham in half and lay on top of the veal. Because the ham slices won't be precisely the same size as the veal, overlap the pieces to make a rough fit.

Now place a sage leaf in the centre of each piece and secure it with a cocktail stick (using it as you would a dressmaking pin). Heat the oil in the frying pan until fairly hot. (You may need to fry the escalopes twice.) Fry the slices of veal with the sage leaf side up for 2 minutes, then flip the pieces over and fry them for another 2 minutes. Season with a few twists of pepper but no salt as there is enough in Parma ham. Now transfer the veal to a warm serving dish.

Pour the wine into the frying pan and let it bubble and reduce for a minute, then add a knob of butter and let it become a syrupy sauce. Spoon the sauce over the veal and serve.

Serves: 6
Preparation: 20 minutes
Cooking: 4 minutes

Chef's note: This recipe also works extremely well with slices of pork fillet.

MELE AL FORNO
BAKED APPLES

6 large cooking apples
A handful of sultanas
6 tbsp caster sugar
A little melted butter

Sugar Syrup:
1 glass white wine
4 tbsp caster sugar

Custard Sauce:
550ml/20fl oz single cream
6 egg yolks
2 level tsp cornflour
4 level tbsp caster sugar
1 vanilla pod

Wipe the apples and remove the cores using a melon baller, but not all the way through. Make a light cut in the skin around the middle of each apple. Place the apples in an ovenproof dish. Fill the cavity of each apple with sultanas. Brush the butter all over the apples and sprinkle 1 tablespoon of caster sugar over each apple. Pour the wine in the dish, add the sugar and scatter a few sultanas. Bake in the centre of a preheated oven, turn the dish around occasionally.

Put the cream in a saucepan with the vanilla pod and heat over a very gentle heat without boiling. Remove the pan from the heat, cover and leave to infuse for 10 minutes. Remove the vanilla pod.

Whisk the egg yolks, cornflour and sugar in a bowl. Gradually stir in the hot cream. Strain the custard back into the pan or into a double saucepan with hot, not boiling, water in the base. Stir the custard continuously over very low heat until it is creamy and thick enough to coat the back of a wooden spoon. Serve with the baked apples.

Serves: 6
Preparation: 10 minutes
Cooking: 30–35 minutes
Oven: 180°C/350°F/Gas 4

Chef's note: If the custard does overheat and start to look granular, don't worry. Remove it from the heat and continue to stir, it will become smooth again as it cools because the small addition of cornflour does a very efficient stabilising job.

THE BELGIAN EMBASSY

Se nulla metti in pentola, niente prendi fuori
If you don't put anything into the pot, you don't get anything out

I eventually found my next job through a fellow chef, as a kitchen assistant at the Belgian Embassy in Parioli. This is one of the best residential areas of Rome, where there are many embassies and large private houses. The Belgian Embassy was one of the most beautiful houses with impressive wrought-iron gates at the entrance, and a huge garden at the back with lily ponds, orange trees and exotic plants. This was the perfect venue where the Ambassador would give cocktail parties for the Roman aristocracy, drinking fine champagne with glazed canapés in the warm summer evenings.

The Ambassador was the career diplomat, Baron Poswick, from an old Belgian aristocratic family. He was an elderly man and reserved, with many years in the diplomatic corps. We addressed his wife as "Madame la Baroness". The Ambassador rarely came into the kitchen and when he wanted to speak to the chef he would knock at the kitchen door and very politely ask for something or thank the chef for the wonderful meal he had cooked. Madame la Baroness, however, would come to see the chef more often, to discuss the menus and the kitchen budget.

The embassy was well renowned for entertaining and good food. I started working with the head chef, Eduardo Coletta, a stocky man with thinning hair, who loved his work. Like me he had come from a small village – Roio del Sangro, not very far from Rosello. Almost every male from our region, the Abruzzo region became a chef. The Abruzzo region is known the world over for the chefs it produces and many of them started their careers in Rome at embassies and in private houses, all those years ago. Eduardo was a true professional, with a small thin moustache. He was a very serious man and a strict disciplinarian and my mentor. My friend and colleague, Egidio Gentile, and I were not even allowed to speak in the kitchen, or make any comment whatsoever. We had to obey his orders and rules, and do things exactly as he wanted. My colleague and I once took some apples from the kitchen cupboard without a second thought, but were severely reprimanded by him.

We felt this was unfair, but did not realise at the time he had to work within a very strict budget. When I later started to run my own kitchen, I did not like it when staff used to take food without asking and this always reminded me of Eduardo. Egidio and I lived in the embassy where we shared a room on the third floor. We would go down first thing in the morning to prepare various vegetables or make fresh crisps to be served with roasted chicken for the staff lunch. (And what a chicken! I would have given anything to eat a quarter of that chicken. We had to make a mixture of sea salt, pepper and sprigs of rosemary, brush the chicken with butter and sprinkle the ingredients inside and out to coat the bird. It would then be roasted and the end result was mouth-watering free-range chicken, succulent and brown all over with a crispy skin.) We would then see the chef coming through the kitchen door with heavy shopping bags. He would leave them on the table for us to sort out, while he was changing into his whites.

The kitchen was spacious and in the shape of a square. It was well lit with natural light coming through the front door and through a large window on the left-hand side, which looked out over a small patio with trees and shrubs. It gave a good sense of solitude and privacy, because you would never know what was going on in the outside world. Opposite the front door, two new gas cookers were installed before I started working there, and on the right-hand side, the most wonderful display of copper saucepans hung from the wall on brass hooks. Under the window, an old wooden table was scrubbed daily and constantly used for preparing vegetables to make soup (*zuppa di legumi*), different types of meat and various other culinary uses. The kitchen sink was opposite the saucepan wall and in the middle an old coal stove with a wooden and Formica top was used as a table to eat our meals at, although this was removed when necessary. The coal stove was ancient and was still used occasionally when there were large functions. A small amount of coal was kept in the coalbunker outside. The stove had to be lit first thing in the morning to build up a powerful heat, so we could cook on its rings and roast large joints of meat.

A lovely dish I learnt here was sole fillets in white wine sauce (*filetti di sogliola al vino bianco*), one of my favourites for taste and presentation, or a large prawn salad with citrus dressing (*insalata di granchi con salsa di cedri*).

In my opinion, Eduardo's pièce de résistance was his roast pheasant. He would dissect the cock pheasant into four parts by removing the head and neck, the wings, and the tail. The main body of the pheasant was plucked and roasted and then the head, the wings and the tail were reconstructed using a large, raw potato and wooden skewers. The finished effect had the appearance of a beautiful whole pheasant, which was put on the dish with the carved meat and roasted chestnuts around it. The base of the potato had to be slightly flattened in order to make the newly recreated pheasant stand up. I remember once when Eduardo was braising a beautiful silver sea bass wrapped up in greaseproof paper and gently basting the fish at the mouth of the oven. Silver foil was not even thought of at that time.

Next to the cookers, there was a door leading into the larder, which was a long and narrow room with a small window at the end to let the cool air in. On top of the fridge, two rectangular wooden trays had to be kept filled with freshly baked biscuits for when the Ambassadress had guests for tea. In a white cabinet alongside the wall were mixing bowls, and fresh fruit was also kept there. On the right side of the larder was a lower table with a marble top, which the chef used as a desk to write menus and to make pastries.

I can remember once when the chef spent most of the morning in the larder.

We were wondering what new creation was going to appear. He eventually came out with a couple of baking trays and on each one was a large, thick round of puff pastry, egg-glazed, and marked with lozenges to decorate the lid. It was placed in the oven and when baked they looked spectacular – deep and wide with a beautiful gold crust all around. They were called giant vol-au-vents. Quite impressive! That kitchen was a fount of never-ending seeing and learning. Making the sugar icing (the fondant ice) for patisserie uses was the only time I have ever seen it made.

As we worked, he would give me and Egidio orders to chop, slice or peel various things while he would stand at the stove making sure that all the food he cooked was just right, and every dish that left the kitchen for the dining room looked impeccable to the last sprig of parsley. He, as a young man, had worked in Belgium and had a good command of the French language and great knowledge of haute cuisine.

Alfonso, the butler (*il maggiordomo*), was the calmest and most placid person I have ever met. I never heard him shout, and a swear word would never leave his lips. Never mind how busy he was, he would answer the telephone with the utmost polite manner and impeccable courtesy. He organised and worked on his own, and would ask his colleagues for help only when there were functions at the embassy. He couldn't have had a more appropriate name for a butler: Alfonso il Maggiordomo. Fluent in French, before laying the table he would come into the kitchen and ask the chef, "*Combien des fourchettes?*" (How many forks?) At times they would converse in French so we couldn't understand the little gossip amongst themselves.

Alfonso had a good sense of humour too. At times he would appear at the kitchen door and ask the chef if he could tell us a joke that most probably had been made up by himself to raise a laugh in the kitchen.

There was a great working and amicable rapport between Eduardo and Alfonso, and this is the secret for a successful dining room.

The Ambassador held at least one lunch or dinner party every week. If the party, for example, was at Friday lunchtime, we had to work all day on the Thursday to prepare for the lunch the following day. That wasn't too bad as we could have a break in the afternoon before the evening meal. If instead it was an official dinner party, we had two days of hard work and preparation for the party, but it was worth it every time. It was fascinating to see such a master chef at work – the way he expressed himself in cooking and presentation and his refined style and art to show his skill to the world of gourmets. I used to watch every move in case I missed a trick. I was very lucky to be in the right place at the right time working with Eduardo.

The dishes that the chef used to cook were mostly from the classic French and Italian cuisine. There were lamb kidneys that were thinly sliced, dusted with flour and sautéed in hot butter for 2–3 minutes, seasoned with salt and pepper, and flambéed with a good dash of brandy. These were served on bread croutons (*crostini*) and sprinkled with chopped parsley. There were vol-au-vents with prawns and mushrooms. And another favourite was cardoons with marrow. The cardoons are from the artichoke family and they are cooked in court bouillon, then put on a tray with beef marrow and then sprinkled with fresh parsley and served. Fresh button mushrooms were sautéed in butter, seasoned with salt, pepper and a squeeze of lemon juice. Double cream was then added; it was reduced a little and then spooned onto croutons and sprinkled with chopped parsley.

A legumier, with fresh boiled leeks would never be served without a sauce boat filled with a gleaming hollandaise sauce. *Asperges d'Argenteuil* are the finest and most renowned French asparagus and are known for their violet-tipped end. Bundles of this delicate plant were never served as a starter, but as a vegetable with a main course that was accompanied with sauce mousseline.

Another dish, which was more unusual and required some skill, was *gnocchi à la Parisienne*. These tiny dumplings are made of choux pastry with Gruyère cheese. The mixture is spooned into a piping bag fitted with a plain nozzle. Portions of the mixture, the size of chestnuts, are squeezed out over a saucepan filled with salted, boiling water. The gnocchi float to the top, and they are then lifted out with a perforated spoon. They are then transferred into a gratin dish covered with *sauce béchamel* (white sauce), placed in the oven and cooked until light brown.

Cannelloni had to be different from an ordinary pasta dish. Crêpes were used instead of sheets of pasta. The filling was made from ricotta cheese and spinach, and then the crêpes were rolled up with the filling, placed in a gratin dish, coated with a white cheese sauce and baked. Spaghetti, which was served as a treat, also had to be served in a refined manner. The pasta was cooked with a more anaemic look than usual (not al dente) and served in a silver dish with a knob of butter placed on top. The fresh tomato sauce was sieved (no pips were allowed) and fresh Parmesan cheese was served in a sauce boat. When it came to preparing the fresh spinach, our job was to remove the tiny stalks. As Eduardo would say, "These people do not eat the spinach stalks!"

At lunchtime fruit completed the meal. At dinner time there was always a dessert. Vanilla millefeuilles and rich chocolate mousse with brandy, are just two of the delicacies that were produced. What dominated most for the dessert at dinner was the beautiful soufflés: savoury cheese soufflé, vanilla soufflé, or passion fruit, and many other flavours.

Those years belong to another era from now, and so do the gentry, who had a finer and more delicate palate than today. The food, which was served on silver dishes, had to reflect their way of life. This was why everything was different to look at and in its taste to our usual home cooking.

Somehow I feel that we do not have time to really sit back and enjoy our food as we used to then, and when we do take the time it is so much more memorable. Why do we have not so much time to 'stand and stare'? We all live rushed lives, eating on the hoof, as they say.

Egidio and I were clearing the table. The three of us had just finished eating our lunch. The chef was in the back room writing the menu, and the kitchen door suddenly sprang open and Alfonso brought the most terrible news of the assassination of President Kennedy.

"President John Kennedy has been shot dead," said Alfonso; "the Ambassador has just told me. Suddenly, we were all in shock, as the rest of the world was too. As young as I was I felt very sad, as if I had known him personally, and I remember that I couldn't stop thinking about him.

That day, 22 November 1963, I had my afternoon off. I had an appointment to see a relative of mine, called Antonio, and he took me to see an epic film at the cinema called *How the West Was Won*. During the interval I asked him what he thought about the assassination of President Kennedy. I thought that he would sympathise with me and share the same sorrow at the President's death but instead he replied, "I belong to a different party!"

I felt a bit cold at his reply.

I went home for Christmas that year and paid a visit to my paternal grandmother, Felicetta. On my way out, I noticed a newspaper photo cutting of the late president on the desk. My grandmother said people had told her that he was a very good man, a man of peace.

I owe much to Eduardo – above all, the chance to learn the French gastronomy. He was an inspiration to one so young. While I was at the Belgian Embassy (part of the Holy See of the Vatican) many church dignitaries came to dine. This made the embassy well renowned for giving the most beautiful luncheons and dinner parties with superb food, and the guests spoke of the chef with great respect and admiration.

One does not usually hear of chefs owning their own saucepans, but Eduardo Coletta did. He had a magnificent set of hand-made copper saucepans, which my colleague and I had to keep immaculately clean for him. The everyday meals for the Ambassador and his family were quite simple, light, tasty and well planned. I know that many people from all over the world for whom I have catered prefer simple and tasty meals. Even in those days, an evening meal could be comprised of a soup followed by *oeuf à la coque* (boiled egg) and soldiers of toast, spinach purée and a green mixed salad tossed in olive oil with a dash of wine vinegar and a little seasoning, followed by fruit compote or cheese to finish.

Of course each lunch or dinner was different, but the basis of each menu was quite simple and imaginative: the freshest of ingredients and the finest quality possible, always superbly presented.

Many years later my brother, Mario, went to work with Eduardo, and when I used to go to Rome on my journey home to Rosello I would visit the chef and recount the past.

Eventually Eduardo retired and Mario went to work at the Italian Embassy to the Holy See at the Vatican, in Viale delle Belle Arti, with Eduardo's brother-in-law Umberto Marcotullio. He was a man, with a passion for cooking and a great presence. He was also from our own village, a well-known and respected chef in the Roman circle at the time.

When I first started my job at the Pensione Alfa, at the same time a school friend of mine, Nicolino Percario, was working with Umberto as a kitchen assistant for Prince and Princess Aldobrandini, who lived at the Villa Belvedere, which was famous for the most beautiful gardens in the picturesque town of Frascati, near Rome. This beautiful and small town is famous the world over for its famous Frascati wines. The vines grow on the sloped hills known for their legendary castles, which surround this region called Il Lazio. In Roman dialect the wines are called *er vino de lì castelli*. Umberto had been a resident head chef for many years working for the Prince and Princess, and his family lived nearby on the estate.

On one occasion I went to pay a visit to Nicolino. I waited in the old kitchen, which was furnished with old utensils and a vast battery of various-sized copper saucepans, until he finished to have his half day off and then we met with another companion, Lucio Iarusso, in the town piazza.

We had a long discussion about how we were going to spend that precious and single afternoon. Lucio was very much against the idea of shutting ourselves in the local cinema instead of enjoying that sunny afternoon. He suggested going for a walk and visiting the town. How sad Lucio was when he could not convince us and we all three went to the cinema!

THIS IS WHAT THE WORLD . . . THINKS OF ME

Pino comes from a village Rosello in Italy famed for producing world class chefs and I consider Pino to be one of the very best.

He has a true passion for cooking which is quite rare today and not only that is a dear and sincere friend.

Ann Franceshelli, Roio del Sangro and London

We are lifelong friends to Car and Pino and always eagerly await invitations to sample Pino's incredible feasts – the dishes always exquisitely presented – the preparation it seems at a speed of lighting. Pino is very generous with practical hints on the preparation of food – just try the recipes and reap the rewards yourself. Italy is here!

Hilly and Karim Hakim, London

I can claim to have known Car longer than anyone else in the world as I was acting nurse at her birth. She is my baby sister and I am delighted to have Pino as my brother in law.

He is loved by all who meet him, very talented in many ways and a perfect Roman gentleman.

Marie Elliott, Dunchurch

Pino Iacaruso...Renaissance man – Loving husband, father and dear friend. Artist, writer, gardener, superb Chef...and **hero** to all who know him. We love you Pino.

Kate Harvey-Brown, San Francisco, California

FILETTI DI SOGLIOLA AL VINO BIANCO
SOLE FILLETS IN WHITE WINE SAUCE

For the presentation of this beautiful dish see the photo on page 193.

12 fillets of Dover sole each weighing about 90g/3oz, skin removed
60g/2oz butter
2 shallots, finely chopped
250g/8oz button mushrooms, sliced
200ml/6fl oz dry white wine
300ml/½ pint fish stock
100ml/3fl oz double cream
Lemon juice to taste (2–3 tbsp)
Salt
Freshly ground black pepper

Beurre Manié:
30g/1oz butter softened and mixed with 30g/1oz flour

To garnish:
2tbsp chopped parsley
Crescents of puff pastry (see opposite)

Melt the butter in a frying pan, add the shallots and fry them slowly over a
moderate heat until soft. Add the mushrooms and allow them to sweat for a
little longer to let the mushroom liquid evaporate. Put these aside into an
ovenproof dish, measuring approx 34cm/13in long by 21cm/8in wide to
accommodate the fish.

Beat the fillets of sole to flatten slightly. Season lightly and fold them in two,
skin side inwards. Place them in the ovenproof dish and add the wine and the
stock. Cover with buttered greaseproof paper or silver foil and cook in a
preheated oven for about 10 minutes.

For the sauce: When the fish is cooked, carefully remove the fish onto a
plate with a slotted fish slice and pour the liquid into a saucepan through a
sieve, to collect the mushrooms and onions. Add the double cream to the liquid
and bring to the boil for a few minutes. This will reduce the liquid a little.
Thicken the sauce by whisking in the beurre manié. Whisk well to a smooth
sauce and add the lemon juice. Adjust seasoning.

Wash the ovenproof dish and put the mushrooms and onions back in the
bottom. Place the fish over the mushrooms and onions, and pour the sauce
over to cover the fillets completely. Keep warm in a fairly warm oven.

To serve: Sprinkle the chopped parsley over the sauce and garnish with warm crescents of puff pastry.

Serves: 6
Preparation: 30 minutes
Cooking: 10 minutes
Oven: 180°C/350°F/Gas 4

Chef's note: Other fish such as lemon sole, or a combination of cod, halibut, salmon, cut into cubes, and prawns can be easily substituted. This fillet dish has a good robust flavour and makes a splendid meal for a dinner party.

CRESCENTINE DI PASTA SFOGLIA
CRESCENTS OF PUFF PASTRY

250g/8oz puff pastry
1 egg yolk, size 4, mixed with a little double cream
1 pastry cutter

Roll out the pastry to a rectangle of 40cm/16in by 30cm/12in and 2mm/⅛in thick. Cut out with a pastry cutter, 8cm/3in round, ¼ moon pastry shapes (see photos on page 195). Brush with egg yolk, and with the back of a fork draw lines across the shapes to give a nice look when baked. Place on a lightly buttered and floured baking tray and bake to a golden colour. Remove from the tray and leave to cool. Reheat in the oven for four minutes before serving.

Makes: over 30
Preparation: 30 minutes
Cooking: 10–12 minutes
Oven: 200°C/400°F/Gas 6

Chef's note: These crescents can be made well in advance, kept in an airtight container for several days, and could be served with fish in white wine sauces, casserole dishes or soups.

SPUMA AL CIOCCOLATO BIANCO E NERO
RICH WHITE AND DARK CHOCOLATE MOUSSE

This is a lovely rich chocolate mousse to serve for a dinner party. The sponge could be omitted and the chocolate creams served individually or in a glass bowl.

Sponge layer:
3 eggs, separated
75g/3oz icing sugar, sifted
60g/2oz cocoa powder, sifted
Cocoa powder for dusting

Chocolate cream dark:
200g/7oz good quality dark chocolate
60ml/2fl oz of hot water
1 tsp instant coffee (optional)
4 tbsp brandy
4 egg yolks
200ml/7fl oz double cream, lightly whipped

Chocolate cream white:
200g/7oz good quality white chocolate
A little orange rind (optional)
50ml/1½fl oz warm water
200ml/7fl oz double cream lightly whipped

To make the sponge: Preheat the oven. Lightly butter a shallow 33 x 23 x 2cm/ 13 x 9 x 1in baking tin, line it with a sheet of greaseproof paper, and lightly butter and flour the paper, shaking off the excess flour.

Whisk the egg yolks with 60g/2oz icing sugar until thick and ribbon-like. Whisk the egg whites until frothy adding the remaining icing sugar gradually and whisking until stiff. Mix the whites into the yolk mixture, and fold in the cocoa powder. Spread the mixture on the baking tray and bake.

Turn out the cake onto a clean tea towel; remove the paper and fold the ends of the tea towel over the sponge. Leave to cool.

Using a 20cm/8in round spring loose-base cake tin, cut out a circle from the sponge. Lightly grease the side of the cake tin. Line the cake tin with greaseproof paper, place on a serving dish, then put in the sponge.

Serves: 6 or more
Preparation: 15 minutes

Cooking: 10 minutes
Oven: 180°C/350°F/Gas 4

To make the chocolate creams: Melt the dark chocolate with the water/coffee and brandy over a double boiler. Cool slightly, then mix in the egg yolks and one third of the lightly whipped cream, then add the remaining cream, very gently. Pour into the cake tin over the chocolate sponge and refrigerate.

Melt the white chocolate with the water. Add the orange rind, stir and leave to cool slightly. Fold in one third of the double cream, then add the remaining cream, very gently. Pour this white chocolate cream over the dark chocolate cream and refrigerate until set.

Before serving, release the cake tin, peel off the greaseproof paper, dust with cocoa powder and serve.

Preparation: 30 minutes
Setting time: 4 hours

L'ARTE DEL SOUFFLÉ
THE ART OF SOUFFLÉ

I have never had any problems with making soufflés, sweet or savoury, and I was lucky enough to work under a great maestro at the Belgian Embassy, who taught me the art in my youth. The chef enjoyed making them for the family he worked for, and I really learnt as I went along rather than going by a rule book. Throughout my career, I too have enjoyed making soufflés and have often been complimented on their flavour and presentation.

Always grease the soufflé dish with soft butter, and sprinkle with sugar (for a sweet soufflé) or breadcrumbs (for a savoury soufflé) and tip out the excess.

You should prepare the soufflé in a good heavy saucepan, using a wooden spoon to stir the mixture and a whisk to smooth it, and then gently mix in the rest of the ingredients with a wooden spoon.

Cool the soufflé base for a few minutes, and then add whatever liqueurs, juices or purées you are using, together with the beaten egg yolks.

Always use a china or stainless-steel mixing bowl that has been cleaned meticulously.

Make sure that there is no trace of fat or egg yolk in your mixture, which will reduce the bulk and lightness of the whites when you beat them. Use the wooden spoon to fold in the whites to the yolk mixture.

Always preheat the oven and check the temperature carefully. Cook soufflés on the middle shelf of the oven so the heat circulates evenly around. If the dish is too near the top of the oven, the crust will burn and the rising is impaired.

Serve immediately, dusting sweet soufflés with icing sugar as soon as they are removed from the oven.

When I was asked to cook at Kensington Palace for a dinner party, I would often serve a splendid soufflé for dessert, as it was a particular favourite of Prince and Princess Michael. I was familiar with the kitchen and every soufflé I cooked there would be cooked to perfection, with a top like a cupola drenched with icing sugar. As the butler took it through to the dining room it would waft behind it the most divine aroma.

SOUFFLÉ AL FRUTTO DELLA PASSIONE
PASSION FRUIT SOUFFLÉ

If you plan to serve this soufflé, buy the passion fruit hard and unbruised and let them ripen in their own time, as it is not always easy to find them ready to eat. They can take up to a week to ripen

6 ripe passion fruit
4 eggs, size 4, separated
90g/3oz caster sugar
Icing sugar, to dust
30g/1oz softened butter
60g/2oz castor sugar, to coat

You will need: 6 soufflé dishes (ramekins), of about 8cm/3in diameter and 4cm/2½in deep.

Brush the inside of the dishes with butter, tip the castor sugar into one dish and rotate it so that the entire surface is covered with sugar. Tip the sugar into the next dish and repeat the operation until all the dishes are coated with sugar. Remove any excess from the last dish.

Beat the egg yolks with 60g/2oz of caster sugar in a bowl until light and white (reserving 30g/1oz of caster sugar). Cut the passion fruit in half and with a teaspoon scoop out the flesh and the pips. Place a fine sieve over the egg mixture and press the fruit through the sieve until all the flesh has gone through.

This stage can be prepared well in advance and kept at room temperature. If you are serving this soufflé for a dinner party, I am afraid you must leave your guests at the end of the main course and go in the kitchen.

Beat the egg whites with a pinch of salt until the mixture forms a peak. Now add the remaining sugar and beat for 30–40 seconds until the meringue is shiny and glossy. Add one third of the passion fruit mixture and stir well with a wooden spoon, then add the remainder and fold gently, making sure that you mix the fruit at the bottom of the bowl. Place the ramekins on an oven tray, fill them evenly with the mixture and smooth the surface with a palette knife. Bake in a well-preheated oven. Dust with icing sugar and serve immediately.

Serves: 6
Preparation: 30 minutes
Cooking: 10 minutes
Oven: 200°C/400°F/Gas 6

HOTEL MICHELANGELO

Se avete fame mangiate, ma per favore non buttare via il mangiare
Gino's motto
If you are hungry, eat, but please don't throw the food away

Time moves on and so did I. I joined the chef's brigade at the Hotel Michelangelo, not very far from the Vatican Walls. It was one of the newest hotels, but it was nice for me to start work with other chefs, and they do say that it is good to gain more experience in life. The kitchen at the Hotel Michelangelo was extremely busy, especially for someone like me who had arrived from the quiet kitchen of the Belgian Embassy. Being a new arrival, I was fascinated and excited at the prospect of this new job. I was called *Signor Commis* by the senior sous-chef, Giorgio Della Franca, meaning that I did my job extremely well and meticulously, my skills having been refined by Eduardo.

The chefs would run about in all directions, everyone responsible for their own section. There was a lot of calling and shouting to get things moving more quickly. No one had time to explain anything if you asked at a busy time. The only way to learn about food and to become a good chef was to keep my eyes wide open and watch every move made by the other chefs, while I tried to cope with my work and make myself useful. There were more varieties of fish than I had ever seen before, and many different meats and vegetables. Here I discovered a different and more varied way of cooking and presenting dishes, although in larger quantities and at a faster pace.

The head chef, Gino Innocenti, was born and bred in the magnificent city of Florence, where he learnt his skill. Tuscany, where Florence is situated, is one of the most beautiful regions of Italy, renowned for its beautiful sun-drenched landscapes and its silvery olive groves and vineyards. Good food, wine, the purest olive oil, fine art and architecture, is found in abundance. Gino was a very pleasant man, well mannered and well spoken with a soft Florentine accent. He was a good chef, full of energy and life, with a strong presence and he was well respected. His motto for his chefs was: 'If you are hungry, eat, but please don't throw the food away'!

He introduced and showed us some dishes from his beloved Firenze: Tuscan bean soup, egg Florentine, stuffed trout with fine herbs, the famous thick T-bone steak and the chocolate-and-cream dessert *Zuccotto*.

The Michelangelo was the very first hotel where I worked with many other colleagues and it taught me a lot about a working life and companionship. I was the youngest chef in the kitchen at the time with a great future ahead in the *art culinaire*. I was a *commis entremettiers*, named after the cooks who prepared the entremets (literally, between dishes). In old French the term covered all the dishes which followed the roast, and included not only sweets but also vegetables.

My *chef de partie*, Giacomo Capodimonte, who came from the Isle of Ischia, was in his thirties, strict and a good teacher, and he explained to me a new way of cooking. Once I was pouring olive oil into a saucepan, and because I was being careful not to use too much of it, I placed my thumb in front of the bottleneck. He reprimanded me for not being generous with the oil by saying, "You do that in your home, not here." We got on well together and we were responsible for stocks, soups, all the vegetables and roast potatoes that were arranged around the main courses, and egg dishes, including omelettes. The senior sous-chef nicknamed me 'the King of the Omelettes', because they were that perfect!

Giacomo told me that while working at the Hotel Excelsior in Ischia in the sixties he and other chefs had to get up early in the morning to prepare refreshment for the film crew while filming *Cleopatra* with Elizabeth Taylor, Richard Burton and Rex Harrison. Imagine preparing for several hundred every day.

The staff quarters were literally across the street, where I shared one bedroom with three other kitchen staff, and many others colleagues shared rooms in the apartment provided by the hotel. The room was shared by me, Angelo, Fausto and Michele, who came from the Neapolitan region.

Michele came over to me and showed me a letter he had received from home. I thought he wanted me to see the good news, and share it with me. Instead he said, "Pino, can you read it for me? I can't read." The letter was from his mother. I read the letter without showing any disbelief or surprise that a young man barely one year younger than me was illiterate. I thought at the time that only people of an older generation and less fortunate than us could not read. I would reply to his mother's letters, as I would have done with my own mother. I sent to her all his news and kept her informed of his life.

Michele was a very handsome young man, tall, with thick blond hair and a good and generous heart. With no qualifications, he was one day working in the kitchen as a washer-up and another day somewhere else in the hotel.

This anecdote brings me back to my childhood, and to my friends at the time when we lived in the small village where I was born. It is one of the most mountainous regions of Italy – the Abruzzo region. High in altitude were the slumbering and beautiful mountains, away from the noises of chaotic cities. We enjoyed the light fresh air, the beautiful seasons and the tranquillity of our village life. We all had caring parents. We all went to the kindergarten and to school. We had the piazza, the fountain, the football pitch, and many other such pleasures all to ourselves. The Mayor made sure that the citizens wanted for nothing, and we were supported by the province of Chieti and by our unique and beautiful region with its motto: 'forte e gentile' (strong and gentle). This makes us very proud of our heredity and our place of birth, and we as a whole must have been the luckiest children in the world!

One Sunday morning there was no sign of Giacomo. The kitchen was already in full swing, the time was ticking away. I kept turning my head towards the kitchen door, hoping to see him walking in. The head chef, anxious, sent me to fetch him at the staff quarters. We thought that he might have overslept, or something might have happened to him. I walked out of the hotel door, and I was shocked to see my chef, my 'hero', with his head bowed pensively. He was holding a rosary and a prayer book in his right hand and he was walking back to the staff quarters. I hadn't realised that he was such a devout Catholic. 'He is not going to be the next pope!' I thought.

"Where have you been?" I said. "It's past eight o'clock and I was coming to call you."

"I have been to church, to morning Mass," he replied, and then added, "It's such a lovely day that I felt I should get up earlier and go to Mass. I had not realised the time. My watch reads a quarter to eight! It must have stopped."

I sighed with relief that all was well: and when I told him the correct time and that we were very busy, he hurried away to change.

Eventually Giacomo left the Michelangelo. He was missing the sea and returned to his beloved Isle of Ischia. I missed him very much.

I was left on my own for quite a while until a new section head chef was found to join my section. In the meantime by working on my own I discovered that I was born to be a chef. I felt that I coped well. I felt very confident.

At times there were fraught days. For example, when one or two trays of roasting potatoes gave off a funny smell, the head chef would shout at the top of his voice, "I can smell burning!" My other colleagues would have a good laugh at our expense!

I became very friendly with another colleague, the *commis sauciers*, Angelo Bilello. His *chef de partie* was the senior sous-chef, Giorgio. We worked opposite each other, and shared the big gas stove. We would compete against one another about who kept the top of the stove cleanest and most shiny. He was responsible for making the sauces – Bolognese, tomato, and others – and for roasting joints of meat, frying steaks, veal chops and fish.

Angelo was from the city of Enna, Sicily. We got on well together, in the kitchen and socially.

After a hot and busy day in the kitchen we would go out for a walk around the Vatican area, for sightseeing or for a drink at a bar. Sometimes we would go to the local cinema, St Pietro, which was another of our favourite pastimes.

Angelo told me once how he came to be in Rome. His father was a man with old traditions and a different way of thinking. His son was not allowed to leave home until after the military service, which is completed at twenty-one years of age.

Angelo didn't want to wait that long to start his life so he bought a ticket and jumped on a train bound for the capital. Once in Rome, he took a bus to St Peter's Square and asked a traffic warden for the Hotel Saint Angelo. He was told that there wasn't such a hotel, but was directed instead to the Michelangelo. When he arrived, he asked to see the head chef and was offered the job straight away. Two days later he telephoned home to reassure his family that he was well. His father would call him every Sunday morning.

The telephone would ring in the kitchen and Angelo would run to snatch the receiver and would always utter these words to his father that I will never forget: "God bless you, and I kiss your hands, Father."

The mentality was very old and yet, at the same time, it showed a great respect towards his father.

Angelo was a very nice and affable person. He had a good sense of humour and was fun to be with. He was of average height, had black hair swept into a parting on one side and olive-coloured skin. He had big muscles on his arms and legs and would show off like a bodybuilder. When we used to go out together he would roll up his white shirtsleeves to his shoulders, to make sure that the Roman girls would admire his big muscles! He loved the cinema. He was a big fan of the famous epics such as *Spartacus*, *Ben-Hur* or *Quo Vadis*, where there were fights amongst gladiators and chariots races.

His favourite actors were Kirk Douglas, Victor Mature and Charlton Heston. On his days off he would tour the Cinecittà film mecca of the sixties, or, as it used to be called, the Italian Hollywood hoping to be discovered by a big film producer. I think his big dream was to become an actor and play a part as a gladiator in a film. We had many good times and laughed a lot together. Then destiny parted us and after I had left the Michelangelo for health reasons and several years later whilst I was at Kensington Palace I tried to contact him through his old address. However, I never received a reply. I do not think he was ever discovered!

The pontiff at the time, in 1963, was Pope Giovanni Battista Montini, Paul VI. A rather shy, mild-mannered and kindly pope who hated upsetting others. He had laid out a plan. The plan was that he would follow in the continuation of the Second Vatican Council, initiated by his predecessor Pope John XXIII. He announced his thinking and explained that the council would look into the renewal of the church doctrine, and rapprochement with all Christian faiths. I had seen this pope once, together with my colleague Egidio, while I was still working at the Belgian Embassy and with another friend, and a school companion, Nicolino Coppola, while visiting *Piazza di Spagna* (the Spanish Steps). A large crowd of people was gathering around the piazza and the streets around. Word had spread fast that His Holiness the Pope Paul VI was going to pay a homage visit to the statue the Madonna of the Immaculate Conception on 8 December. The statue, which stands high on an obelisk overlooking the piazza requires a fire brigade officer on a very long ladder to place a flower wreath at the feet of the Virgin!

Rome was full of cardinals and ecclesiastical members from all over the world. And they needed many places for accommodation and food. The Michelangelo was not only a new and beautiful hotel with the latest facilities, but also convenient to some of the cardinals within the Vatican Walls.

A great respect was shown by our maître d'hôtel, and the sommeliers and other staff. The twenty-four cardinals that were chosen to stay with us sat around the table, which was beautifully decorated with silverware and crystal. The many courses that were served to them seemed endless and quite breathtaking.

I was sixteen years old at the time and I could not resist pushing my head slowly through the dining-room door. I wanted to see the cardinals with my own eyes and how they were dressed with their beautiful robes.

Once, on my day off, I was crossing St Peter's Square and a breathtaking flow of red cardinal-coloured silks came flooding out from the basilica's main door. The cardinals were moving slowly en masse, gesticulating with their hands, and I suppose discussing the morning events. A humming of voices echoed in the air. They were walking down from the basilica steps like a vast sea toward the pillared colonnades, which encircled the piazza, and disappearing away in every direction. In one's life one is privileged to witness such an event – something unique and special. Only time will tell when in the future another similar gathering will take place. My memories of this will never fade away.

None of the kitchen staff were given summer holidays. We were far too busy with tourists so our holidays were always given to us in the autumn months, when it was quieter. Then we were given another holiday later in the year which was called forced holidays for a month, unpaid and only to the young ones and unmarried.

I used to love it – especially that I was going home to our small village to be with my family. It was always peaceful and quiet, with the snow high on the ground, and I would meet my old school friends.

One of my greatest passions, besides cooking, has been music. My favourite instrument has always been the accordion. I love its melodic and nostalgic sound. It lifts the spirit to hear its harmonious notes. After a few months at the Michelangelo I bought my first accordion. It was very expensive at the time – about one and a half times my wages. Through a friend I found a music teacher called Luciano Merli, who lived a fair distance away from the hotel, on one of the Seven Hills of Rome. After so many years I still remember his surname, which in Italian means 'blackbirds'.

My weekly lesson was something of an adventure! With no explanation, we had more work then usual in the dining room. The customers arrived later than 2 p.m., when I should have been already out of the kitchen. In such a rush I had to change quickly, and run from the hotel and through St Peter's Square from one end to another. I caught one bus, then another. I used to arrive for the lesson exhausted. Coming back it was the same marathon. I had to return to work by five o'clock, in time for the evening shift.

During those years, catering strikes were very frequent and unions would call all members of the catering industry to strike for better conditions, more money and more-sociable hours. Some hotel owners became very unhappy with the way the unions would paralyse the hotels during the high seasons, as the hotels could not afford the high wages that the unions demanded. At the Hotel Michelangelo I am glad to say that our employer did look after us very well, and that we rarely took part in a strike. I only ever took part in a strike once, and that was because I was curious to know what it was like, and because I wanted a day off work. I decided that I didn't want to go to the union's rally to show my support for the strike, because it was a long way away, and I wasn't particularly interested anyway.

In the mid-morning I found myself out at a local bar where I used to gather after work with my colleagues, but this time I did not know where they had gone. There were only two people there that I knew, and they were older than me: Dino (a short and plump man with curly hair swept back and a round face with red cheeks) and Stefano (a skinny man with short black hair swept back like a brush, with bowed legs as if he had grown up sitting on a horse). They were both waiters, and lovely companions.

After discussing what we were going to do, we decided to leave Rome and head for the countryside. We drove out of Rome in an old Fiat 600 and arrived at a restaurant whose owners were friends of Dino's. They weren't there when we arrived, but Dino thought that they would return soon, and so after a short wait a lovely couple arrived and opened the little inn trattoria.

The woman, a beautiful Roman lady (*una bella donna*) with black eyes and long dark hair, went straight into the kitchen and cooked us a lovely meal of spaghetti with bacon, tomato, onion and garlic (*spaghetti alla Matriciana*), which wasn't even on the menu. This was followed by grilled steak with fried potatoes, fresh vegetables and a mixed green salad. The bread that accompanied the meal was crusty and the red wine was home-made, and there was fresh fruit picked from the orchards on the surrounding hills.

After the meal, the owner of the inn had to deliver some cherries, so we all went into the orchard to help him. Stefano shot up a tree like a squirrel and began to throw the cherries down to Dino and me on the ground. We picked them up and placed them into wooden boxes so that they could be delivered to the local shops. It must have been a day in June because the weather was fantastic and the cherries are ripe on the trees around that time of the year. It was a really magnificent day that will for ever be imprinted on my mind. It was as if I had found heaven!

Back at the Hotel Michelangelo, I was the youngest commis in a big kitchen, and so the senior chefs would often pull my leg. Giorgio would tell me that, when he used to work at the Grand Hotel Excelsior in Venice, the stockpot was so huge that to skim the froth on the top he used a gondola! Can you imagine that?

Picture in your own mind two chefs in whites, one rowing the gondola and another sitting on the back with a ladle skimming the stockpot. Have you heard anything as silly as that?

Sometimes, in the summer months, and on my day off, when I was looking for a lazy afternoon, I would take the tram in the sweltering heat and travel from the city centre to the outskirts, going through some old and historic parts of Rome to visit the di Tullio family. They had left our village many years before me so that their son Enisio could go to the university while his sisters were working. I had known them ever since I was a child and they were a well-known and respected family in our village. Enisio's uncle was our local blacksmith and a farrier of high regard. They were such gentle and lovely people, and they would make me feel as welcome as if I were part of their family. We usually would talk about our village and recount the latest and the forthcoming events. They owned a beautiful and comfortable apartment, with a terrace overlooking the countryside. Very kindly they would offer me anything to eat or to drink. We sat down and spent an enjoyable half day together with them. Enisio is a laureate in science and politics and his hobby is writing poetry.

We have exchanged a few letters. I asked Enisio if I could use one of his beautiful poems in my book, *Il Mio Paese,* for which he very kindly gave me his permission. He added in his letter that he wrote the poetry when he was a young student at the university; and he talked of the good old days of Rome. Since then many years have gone by. Now, sadly he said he was on the threshold of his retirement.

Back at the Michelangelo we would lower the gas on the burner and the ovens at 10.30 a.m. It was time to have our lunch. The table was laid complete with wine, bread and fruit, in the *garde-manger* area (meat section). Gino sat at the head of the table, the brigade alongside, and our four efficient kitchen porters would share the table with us.

Talking and joking before the lunch service started, Antonello, the silver-cleaner from Cassino, recounted his brief life story from this town I knew from the coach journey from Rosello to Rome. The coach would go through this town, and stop at the Bar Italia for about fifteen minutes to allow passengers to refresh themselves before continuing their journey. Cassino had been completely destroyed in the Second World War, and Antonello told us that before the war his family had been well-known and respected owners of hotels and restaurants in the town.

In the summer months, when the peas and broad beans were ripe for picking, his father would take them to the local prison, where the inmates would shell them for a few lire. When he returned later, he would find that many of them had already been eaten! Antonello would laugh heartily as he told us this tale, but sadly they had lost everything they possessed in the war and Antonello had never learned a trade. His favourite saying was that the word 'destiny' is the most absurd one in any language's dictionary. We make our own destiny, he said! Perhaps for him, though, the good life was in the hotel among the gleaming silver and the laughter there.

I have fond memories of my time at the Michelangelo, but then I left the hotel, and returned home for health reasons.

I had begun to feel unwell and so very tired, especially when I got up in the morning and my face, hands and knees were swollen. My whole body ached and I still felt so sleepy as though I had not slept all night. After a while I went to see a friend of mine who was a medical doctor – the same Dr Mario Zanna whom I wrote of in the introduction. He said I should go home and have my tonsils out. This is what I did, but still the symptoms persisted and I returned to Rome.

All the employees in the catering industry were called for a yearly chest X-ray for TB. The day I went for my X-ray I asked one of the doctors what could be wrong as the ache and stiffness of my muscles and tissues were not getting any better. Soon I had an answer and I was told I had scleroderma. I was soon hospitalised in one of the best hospitals in Rome and treatment commenced to try to stop the illness. I was in hospital for a month and eventually I was sent home to recuperate.

On arriving at home I was unable to work for about a year so I took French lessons from Rita Sammarone a beautiful caring young lady and a student at the time. I did enjoy studying the French language with her all those years ago. Rita was a very good teacher and serious with the lessons, and it came in very handy later in my life when I went to work in Switzerland.

We have remained good friends ever since, and she is helpful when I need her. She is a very dear person to me to this day. I then travelled further abroad, and I never returned to work in Rome again.

SCLERODERMA is a disease of the skin, joints and, sometimes, internal organs. Its cause is not known. Scleroderma means hardening (fibrosis) of the skin, and, due to malfunction of the vascular and immune systems, results in the overproduction of collagen (connective tissue in the body).

Currently, there is no known cure for scleroderma. It is relatively rare, and not contagious. It is not thought to be inherited.

THIS IS WHAT THE WORLD ... THINKS OF ME

Pino and Caroline are the Godparents to our youngest son, Ashley, who is now 16 years old and they have been friends to Paul and myself along with their son, Edilio and our two other children, Jason and Leanne. We have a wonderful friend ship with the family and the utmost respect for Pino, not only for his courage but also the great love he has for his family and mine. Friends good and true.

Lin Hedges, Warwick

I have known Pino for many years and never cease to be amazed by his many talents. He is a fantastic person and has always been so generous in sharing his knowledge.

Pino and Car prepared the wedding breakfast when Peter and I married and at the time Peter had a junk rig yacht which Pino created in sugar as a three dimensional model for the cake which was a complete surprise for Peter. It was absolutely magnificent.

Rhylva Holder, Ratton, Eastbourne

SPAGHETTI ALLA MATRICIANA
SPAGHETTI WITH PANCETTA, TOMATOES AND ROSEMARY

600g/1¼lb spaghetti
1 medium onion, finely chopped
30g/1oz butter
3 tbsp olive oil
250g/8oz pancetta or streaky bacon, cut into strips
400g/14oz tinned Italian tomatoes
1 small dried chilli, chopped fine (optional)
4 tbsp freshly grated Parmesan cheese
2 tbsp freshly grated Romano pecorino cheese
Salt
Freshly ground black pepper
2 tbsp of pitted black olives

Sauté the onion in a saucepan with the butter and oil until it is pale gold. Add the strips of pancetta and sauté for about a minute. Add the tomatoes, chopped chilli and salt. Cook over a low heat, uncovered. The sauce is done when the tomatoes and the cooking fats separate, after about 25 minutes, turn off the heat, adjust seasoning, and add the black olives. Now the sauce is ready to use.

Drop the spaghetti into 4 litres (7 pints) boiling water. Stop the cooking when the pasta is al dente, and drain immediately. Transfer the cooked spaghetti to a warm serving bowl, add the sauce, and mix. Add the Parmesan and Romano, mix thoroughly and serve.

Serves: 6
Preparation: 30 minutes
Cooking: 40 minutes

Chef's note: For this Roman dish I recommend the spaghetti much larger in diameter, called *bucatini,* which is hollow and has very thin sides. They quickly turn from firm to soft, but, are tastier.

UOVA ALLA FIORENTINA
EGG FLORENTINE

This is a delicious vegetarian starter that is light and tasty.

6 fresh eggs, size 1
1kg/2lb 2oz fresh spinach or rocket leaves
500ml/16fl oz whipping cream
60g/2oz grated cheese, Gruyère or Cheddar
3 tbsp fresh breadcrumbs
Salt
Freshly ground black pepper

Wash the spinach in cold water and drain in a colander. Cook the spinach in a frying pan with a knob of butter, adding salt, pepper and nutmeg. Let the spinach soak up the butter. Heat through thoroughly, set aside in an oven dish and keep warm. Poach the eggs in boiling water with a little salt and a few drops of vinegar for 2 minutes. With a slotted kitchen spoon lift the eggs out of the water, trim off some of the egg white with a small knife and place over the spinach.

In a frying pan warm up 500ml/1 pint whipping cream, and then add a little seasoning and the grated cheese. Preheat the grill at a high setting. Spoon the sauce over the poached eggs, sprinkle with the breadcrumbs and gratin under a very hot grill. Serve immediately.

Serves: 6
Preparation: 30 minutes

Chef's note: The eggs can be poached in advance and reheated in hot water (if you would like to do this, cool them quickly in cold water after cooking). This dish can also be served as a main course with a green mixed salad, for this the ingredients can easily be doubled.

ZUCCOTTO

Zuccotto is a dome-shaped Florentine speciality. It is said that the demi-spherical cupola of the Duomo of Florence, which reminds the Florentines of Brunelleschi's dome, inspired this dessert. This dessert used to be served by the long white-aproned camerieri. Now Zuccotto is served all over Italy and is a firm favourite.

30g/1oz whole almonds, skinned, roughly chopped
30g/1oz whole hazelnuts, roughly chopped
1 sponge or Madeira cake, stale
4 tbsp brandy
4 tbsp Grand Marnier or Vermouth Bianco
70g/2½oz good dark chocolate, roughly chopped
568ml/1 pint double cream
110g/4oz icing sugar
3 tbsp cocoa powder
Orange rind
1 litre/2 pint sized bowl

Brush the inside of a dome-shaped bowl with a little butter. Line it with a piece of cling film big enough to overlap at the top. Cut the sponge cake into slices 1cm/½in thick. Cut each slice on the diagonal, making two triangular pieces. You will need at least 16 good triangles already cut. Place the narrowest ends at the bottom of the bowl until the inside of the bowl is completely covered. Where the side of the piece has crust on it, make it meet the crustless side of the piece next to it so when the dessert is unmoulded it looks like a sunflower with the lines running down the sides. Put the liqueurs into a glass and, with a brush, soak the insides of the sponge pieces.

Put half the amount of whipping cream into a clean bowl. Add 60g/2oz of icing sugar and beat very lightly to form a peak. Add the chopped almonds, hazelnuts and chocolate and amalgamate the ingredients, taking care not to over mix. Spoon into the cake-lined bowl, spreading evenly over all the cake pieces. This should leave a still unfilled cavity in the centre.

Beat the remaining cream with cocoa powder, icing sugar and a little grated orange rind until it is not too stiff. Fill the centre of the bowl and smooth with a palette knife. Place a few slices of sponge cake on top, sprinkle with a few drops of liqueur and cover with the overlapping cling film. Press down lightly and place in the fridge for several hours, or overnight, to settle.

To serve: Remove the cling film and put a plate over the bowl. Turn it upside down and then lift the bowl off. Remove the rest of the cling film. Add a good dash of liqueur and serve the dessert cold. Serve with chocolate sauce (see page below).

Serves: 6 or more
Preparation: 45 minutes

SALSA AL CIOCCOLATO
CHOCOLATE SAUCE

200g/7oz best dark chocolate
300ml/10fl oz cold water
60g/2oz unsalted butter

Break the chocolate into small pieces and melt in a small saucepan over a low heat, stirring occasionally. Add the water, bring to the boil, stirring constantly and finally, whisk in the butter.

Makes: 400ml/14fl oz of sauce
Serves: 6 or more
Preparation: 5 minutes
Cooking: 10 minutes

NYFFENEGGER LAUSANNE

Dipingere e stendere la sfoglia é un arte
Painting and rolling out pastry are both a form of art

The passion that I always had for patisserie drew me to Switzerland, where famous chocolate names are known the world over for their taste, finesse and elaborate presentations. The patisserie houses were incredible for their superb quality and variety, and the displays of assorted pastries of sweet and savoury in the shop windows were well worth seeing. There were hand-made chocolate truffles of all kinds, fresh fruit flans, and delicious gateaux, flavoured mousses and pastries alongside countless other mouth-watering products, all eye-opening and very tempting.

I was very fortunate to have the chance to find work at one of the finest patisseries and restaurants, Nyffenegger's in Lausanne, where I was trained in *patisserie* and *confiserie*. This was an invaluable experience, being able to either work as a *patissier* or as a chef. The job was found through a cousin of mine, Giuseppe, who had already been working for many years as a waiter in the Nyffenegger restaurants and was highly respected by Madame Nyffenegger for his good experience. I went to see the head chef *patissier,* Claude, and asked if he could offer me a job with his team in the *laboratoire de patisserie.*

The patisserie was not spacious but very elegant. It was well planned at street level, with beautiful glass cabinets to display a large variety of chocolates, such as chocolate cream truffles and hard-boiled sweets along with a vast selection of toffees and biscuits. Two big windows, one at the front of the shop and the other on the left-hand side kept the shop bright, and both windows displayed a variety of mouth-watering delights. There were three young salesgirls that looked after the shop. An endless stream of customers always kept them busy. At the back of the patisserie was a tea room, serving breakfast with fresh pastries and croissant with butter and apricot conserve. The smell of the fresh coffee from the steaming machine and the noise and chatter of the customers broke the cold Swiss morning air.

The restaurant occupied the first floor of the building, where a very large number of people could be seated. It was a beautiful dining room with round tables, laid with long white tablecloths down to the floor and fine napkins. The waiters, smartly dressed in white jackets and bow ties and with napkins folded on their wrists, would wait to take the first order and would serve the meals from twelve o'clock onwards. In the afternoon the restaurant would become very busy and the waiters would run back and forth with hot silver pots of coffee and tea to delight a large number of customers having tea, coffee, cakes, pastries and ice cream. On a warm day the balcony doors would be opened.

Terracotta pots of red geraniums cascaded from the balcony railing, and an excess number of beautiful ladies sat at tables enjoying the view and overlooking the Place St François, a prime spot for passers-by and visitors to Lausanne. On the same floor at the back of the building was the kitchen on the right-hand side and the pastry laboratory on the other side. They were set well apart so the two were very much independent.

At seven in the morning, half a dozen half-asleep men had to start a new day. The German night baker, Herr Flick, would soon leave, looking tired and white like a bag of flour from his long sleepless night. We walked inside to a wonderful warmth and a lovely smell of fresh baked croissants, brioches, and small petits pains.

I remember one type that he used to make, which was white bread, baked in a long baking tin – a sort of tube that would open in half. Once the mould has been buttered and dusted with flour, the exact amount of dough is placed inside, the mould is closed, the dough is left to rise and finally it is baked. The loaf would come out of the mould light brown and in the shape of a cylinder. It was then left to cool, sliced and buttered, and a thin layer of mayonnaise was spread across it. Various fillings were placed on top, such as pâté, tuna with gherkins, ham, eggs with capers and so on. Finally it was glazed with aspic to seal the topping. These were my favourite; it was like eating a huge canapé.

A few years ago, I went down the Portobello Road. On one of the corners I saw a market stall selling bric-a-brac and amongst it there was an old Swiss bread baking tin. Like a fool, I was uninterested in buying it; now I wish I had.

The morning pastries were taken straight away to the shop. Certain items of *patisserie* needed to be finished off in the morning. Small butter-cream cakes needed icing, and chocolate tartlets, strawberry and chocolate truffle gateaux, and raspberry flans needed glazing before they were displayed in the shop window later in the morning. Meanwhile we had to get on with our work and replace what went out in order to have it ready for the following morning.

The *laboratoire* was not a big place to produce such wonderful *patisserie*, but we were a team of professional and dedicated people who enjoyed creating and achieving a high standard in our work. Inside the *laboratoire*, on the right-hand side as you walked in there were shelves of greased and stored baking trays, for Swiss rolls and biscuits and pastry bases. Next to these were the big electric double baking ovens. Alongside the wall facing the door was the indispensable electric pastry-rolling machine to maintain the consistency of the pastry thickness. It was in constant use to line flans and tartlets. Next there was the quintessential electric truffles chocolate machine on a stand with two large adjustable marble cylinder wheels, rolling opposite each other to keep the chocolate mixture cool. This was used for refining various chocolate fillings, before they were rolled by hand and dipped. There were also two electric beaters for whipping sponges, creams and meringues.

On the left-hand side there was the sink with two basins to wash all the utensils. On either side of the sink was a large window overlooking a huge building, which was a Swiss bank, and the street below, where we could see people walking and shopping. A heavy-duty fridge with thick doors kept the *patisserie* cold. Next to this was a finishing worktop just to decorate gateaux. In the centre of the room there was a preparation table with a thick marble top where every morning the same ritual took place for the finishing-off of confectionary creams, pastries and fancies covered in multicoloured fondant icing.

The experience was unique and memorable. With a view to moving around and working with foreign colleagues, it is very important and useful for a chef to know how to make and prepare several desserts, or at least for him to have an idea about them as it is very much part of the chef's work when planning a menu. Knowing how all the food is prepared helps to provide the best desserts in the right seasons, and also helps to balance the colours of the different courses, as the dessert is the grand finale to a meal. The dessert always plays a very significant role as the guests are waiting for something delicious to adjust the palate at the end of the meal.

Personally, I do not like too many varieties of dessert on a restaurant's trolley. I find it very distracting, and difficult to choose from. It is better to concentrate on a few good ones – this is the same at home with friends.

When I have a dinner party at home, I usually just make a soufflé and Caroline makes a fruit salad. In that situation, two desserts are sufficient, but too many could create difficulties when serving. One of my great pleasures is to make a fresh fruit flan, where I can arrange the fruit in an attractive way, allowing my imagination to take over freely, sometimes letting myself get carried away.

I think a soufflé is the easiest of desserts, it can be prepared hours in advance, it is light, interesting and always impresses your guests.

Once a week on a Tuesday evening, after I had finished work I would go to a private school to learn French. It was a beautiful old carved-stone building at the heart of town, hardly five minutes' walk from my job. This was one of my best times in Lausanne. I would join six other students of different nationalities on the fifth floor. We were all beginners and we would struggle with pronunciation while we were trying to communicate amongst ourselves. The teacher was the soul of the class – an elderly mademoiselle at the head of the large long table. She was full of beans and enthusiastic about her work, very pleasant and encouraging about my progress, which made me feel good and made every lesson enjoyable. The French language has been very valuable for my work.

Sunday was always my day of rest. At times I would contact a family who came from Rosello who had been working in Switzerland for many years up until their retirement. Giovanni and Eugenia Tartaglia had been our neighbours in Rosello and I would spend my time off with them. I would leave Lausanne Station on Saturday afternoon so I could spend the night with them. At the next stop the train was swamped by school children. The ticket collector would open the compartment door, give a look around and say, "*Ça va, ça va,*" and he would quickly shut the door thinking that I must be a teacher sitting with the children. My ticket was never punched. The train would go through the prettiest countryside and towns, to the canton of Neuchâtel, and reach the small town of La Chaux-de-Fonds, where I would be met by Giovanni, a stocky man with brown hair, and we would make our way to his home.

Eugenia, a blonde and well-dressed lady, and their small children would be waiting for me, and they very kindly offered me whatever I wanted. I was treated like a member of the family.

On the Sunday after we had lunch more Rosellani and their children would come over to see me. Giovanni's brother, Oriente, with a round face and contagious laughter, and his wife, Nina, were a lovely and friendly couple. Also Domenico and Venerina Mucilli were there – two wonderful people of whom I am very fond. Albina and her husband, Domenico Palumbo, were another gentile couple and great friends of my father.

It was such a joy and a great feeling to see these familiar faces. We would talk endlessly, laughing and remembering the people back home. We all went for a walk, window-shopping in the snow wrapped up for the cold, and then I went back to the station to return to Lausanne.

I left Lausanne in the summer of 1970 and returned home for a holiday. Meanwhile I contemplated what I would do next. I had been thinking of going to Germany, to find out what it was like, and I knew several people in the village who had worked in Germany who could recommend places of work for me. I approached Armando Falcione, whom I had always known in Rosello, who lived nearby. Armando had a brother in Germany who worked in Stuttgart and had been working in Germany for many years. "I am sure he will let you stay in his apartment and help you find a job," Armando assured me. Right! Armando was a very nice and a serious man who could be trusted.

Furnished with his brother's address and a heavy suitcase, I took the train and I arrived in Stuttgart's main railway station in the late afternoon. "Well," I said to myself, "where I am going now?" I didn't know the city or what bus to take. I got into a Mercedes taxi, and showed the address to the taxi driver, who turned out, to my great surprise, to be an Italian. I explained to him where I needed to go and he drove me to the address I had shown him.

We arrived, and the taxi driver asked a woman standing at the front door of the apartments if there was an Italian living at that address. "*Ja, ja,*" she said, and called him. The first-floor window sprang open and a young man in his thirties appeared.

"Are you Mario Falcione?" I asked.

"*Si,*" came the reply.

"My name is Pino Iacaruso. I come from Rosello; your brother Armando has given me your name and address promising me that you will help me."

"I don't know you; I don't know you from Adam," came the reply as he turned his head. "My brother has not written to tell me that you are coming . . ." He paused and then said, "I don't even know that 'you' is you! I can't help you."

Mario looked a bit annoyed; I must have disturbed him. I was not sure what to do next; I must have looked ashen-faced at this unexpected dilemma.

The taxi driver, thank God, did not leave me. He had witnessed the entire scene and felt sorry for me. "I have got an idea," he said.

I jumped back into the car and he took me to a bar to meet some other Italians. The taxi driver introduced me to a half-dozen of his friends and left. I spent the evening with complete strangers; they offered me drinks, food and friendship. At closing time we left the bar and they took turns at carrying my heavy suitcase on their shoulders. We walked through a building site where they all worked as bricklayers and labourers, and went inside a wooden shack with beds on either side. One of the men, who was older, short in stature and round, seemed to be in charge. He pointed out to me, with his chubby finger, a free bed where I could spend the night.

"In the morning we get up very early to start work," they told me. "When you leave, shut the door behind you."

I thanked them for their kindness and hospitality.

My next move was to find the job centre, where I was offered a job and accommodation at a restaurant. I lasted four days. I didn't like the country and took the next train back to Milan, where I found work at the Europe Hotel. I do think sometimes of that short-lived experience in Germany, but even if I would have liked to say 'arriverderci' to the Italians, I could never have traced them. After having gained good experience now of both *patisserie* and the French language, I was hoping to find a worthwhile job and maybe even learn another language.

Whilst I was in Milan I was contacted by a friend, Domenico Caracino, and he told me about a job in the kitchen at the Italian Embassy in London. Domenico is known to his friends as Mimi. He too is a chef, and also comes from Rosello. He has been living in England for many years now – at least as long I can remember. He was working with the Canadian High Commissioner at the time. In his heyday he worked as a chef with the famous English writer, Ian Fleming, the creator of Bond, James Bond.

It was an opportunity too good to miss, and in those days England was very fashionable. It was a new country to discover, and the language could very likely come in very useful one day.

My intention was to stay for three to four years and perhaps then go back to Italy. Well, if you look at the date I left Lausanne until now it will tell you how many years I have been in England. I am happily married to a lovely Welsh girl, Caroline, and we have a beautiful son, Edilio.

TARTUFI DI CIOCCOLATO AL RUM
CHOCOLATE RUM TRUFFLES

These are lovely chocolate truffles to serve with coffee.

400g/14oz best plain chocolate, for dipping
180/6oz best plain chocolate, melted
110g/4oz ground almonds
110g/4oz ground trifle sponge or digestive biscuits
3 tbsp cocoa powder
2 tbsp caster sugar
1 heaped tbsp apricot jam
3–4 tbsp double cream
3 tbsp rum
200g/7oz cocoa powder

All you do is place in a bowl, the ground almonds, the ground sponge, the cocoa powder, the apricot jam and the melted chocolate. Mix all the ingredients well, then add the double cream and the rum. Form into a ball and place it in the fridge to set slightly, for about 10 minutes. This makes it easy to handle. Take a good pinch at a time from the mixture, the size of small chestnut-sized balls, and roll it between the palms of your hands. Place onto a tray and continue until you have finished all the mixture, and refrigerate until firm.

Sprinkle the cocoa powder onto a small tray and melt the dipping chocolate in a bowl over a bain-marie. Make sure that the water never comes to the boil, as the chocolate would become too thick to use. Place each truffle in the cup at the end of a fork, and dip them into the melted chocolate. Tap the fork on the side of the bowl to shake off the excess and then roll the truffle in the cocoa powder with another clean fork. When the chocolate around the truffles is set, place on a tray lined with greaseproof paper and allow the truffles to set in the fridge. With a kitchen brush, dust away some of the cocoa powder before serving.

Makes: about 50
Preparation: 30 minutes, plus dipping

Chef's note: There are hundreds of different chocolate truffles, and many difficult ones for your home. This is an easy one to make – even children can make this one. If you wish, you can substitute the dark chocolate for white chocolate, and roll the truffles into sieved icing sugar.

TORTA DI FRAGOLE
STRAWBERRY GATEAU

A rich gateau flavoured with kirsch, decorated with strawberries and Chantilly cream.

1 plain sponge (see recipe on page 85)
500g/1lb 2oz fresh strawberries or wild ones, reserve some for decoration
568ml/1 pint Chantilly cream see recipe below

Sugar syrup:
6 tbsp caster sugar
12 tbsp hot water
6 tbsp kirsch

Slice the sponge horizontally into three pieces and use a kitchen brush to moisten the slices with the sugar syrup.

Place the first slice on a cake board or round dish. Moisten the sliced sponge. Spread the first slice with one third of the Chantilly cream mixture, and put some sliced strawberries on top. Place the second slice of cake on top. Cover with more cream and sliced strawberries, and place the third slice over this. Coat the top and the sides of the gateau with the cream making sure to keep the shape of the cake. Decorate with strawberries and piped Chantilly cream around the top.

Serves: 6 or more
Preparation: 30 minutes

CREMA CHANTILLY
CHANTILLY CREAM

Chantilly cream is used to lighten and enrich pastry creams. It can also be served just as it is and will complement many desserts, fruits and ice creams.

568ml/1 pint whipping cream, well-chilled
60g/2oz icing sugar
A few drops vanilla essence

Combine the well-chilled cream with the icing sugar and vanilla into an electric mixer bowl and beat at medium speed for 3–4 minutes. Do not over beat, or the cream may turn to butter. The Chantilly cream must be a little firmer but light and smooth.

Makes: 600g/1lb 5oz

PAN DI SPAGNA
PLAIN SPONGE CAKE

4 eggs, size 4
125g/4½oz caster sugar
125g/4½oz plain flour
30g/1oz melted unsalted butter

Brush the inside of a 21cm/8in cake tin with melted butter, line the base with a circle of greaseproof paper and butter this also. Sprinkle with a little flour and shake out the excess.

Melt the butter over a low heat and keep to one side, slightly warm.

Put the eggs into a large bowl and add the sugar. Set the bowl over a pan of hot but not boiling water, and beat for 10–15 minutes or until the mixture is light enough to leave a ribbon trail when the whisk is lifted. Take the bowl from the heat and continue beating until cool.

Sift the flour over the mixture a little at a time, and fold in as lightly as possible with a wooden spoon. Just after the last batch of flour, fold in the butter.

Pour the mixture into the prepared tin and bake for 25–30 minutes, or until the cake shrinks slightly from the sides of the tin and the top springs back when lightly pressed. Leave to cool in the tin or turn it out onto a cooling rack.

Preparation: 25 minutes
Oven: 170°C/325°F/Gas 3

Chef's note: An electric beater would make this work much easier and quicker of course. A few drops of vanilla essence or lemon or orange zest can be added for different flavours. Sponges are best when used the day after they are made, as they are then easier to slice.

TORTA DI CIOCCOLATA AL TARTUFO
CHOCOLATE TRUFFLE GATEAU

This is a chocoholic's dream come true!

1 chocolate sponge (see recipe on page 87)
1 chocolate cream ganache (see recipe on page 88)
1 packet of vermicelli (optional)
1 tbsp coca powder to dust
A few crystallised mimosa flowers to decorate (optional)

Sugar syrup:
6 tbsp caster sugar
12 tbsp hot water
6 tbsp rum

Slice the sponge horizontally into three pieces and use a kitchen brush to moisten the slices with the sugar syrup.

Soften the chocolate cream ganache as explained on page 88.

Place the first slice of sponge on a cake board or on a plate of the same size. Moisten the chocolate sponge. Spread the first round slice with about one third of the ganache mixture. Place the second slice on top. Moisten the sponge again. Spread some more ganache on top of the second slice and then place the third slice of the sponge on the top, and moisten the sponge once more.

Coat the top and the sides of the gateau with the chocolate cream (reserve a little to pipe on top) making sure to keep its shape. Hold the gateau with one hand, and coat the sides with vermicelli.

With the remaining ganache mixture pipe 5–6 lines with a 1cm/½in round nozzle tube on the top, dust with cocoa powder and garnish the chocolate lines with 3 or 4 mimosa flowers. Place in the fridge to set.

Serves: 6 or more
Finishing time: 30 minutes

Chef's note: To appreciate the taste of this lovely gateau, serve at room temperature.

CIOCCOLATO
CHOCOLATE SPONGE

150g/5oz caster sugar
110g/4oz self raising, flour
30g/1oz cocoa, powder
4 eggs, size 4
30g/1oz melted butter

Brush the inside of a 21cm/8in cake tin with melted butter, line the base with a circle of greaseproof paper and butter this also. Sprinkle with a little flour and shake out the excess.

Put the eggs into a large bowl and add the sugar. Place the bowl over a pan of hot but not boiling water and beat for 10-15 minutes or until the mixture is light enough to leave a ribbon trail when the whisk is lifted. Remove the bowl from the heat and continue beating until cool.

Sift the flour and cocoa into the mixture a little at a time, folding in as gently as possible with a wooden spoon. Just after the last batch of flour, fold in the butter. Pour the mixture into the prepared tin and bake for 25–30 minutes or until the cake shrinks slightly from the sides of the tin and the top springs back when gently pressed.

Leave to cool in the tin or turn out onto a cooling rack.

Preparation: 25 minutes
Cooking: 25–30 minutes
Oven: 170°C/325°F/Gas 3

Chef's note: An electric beater would make this work much easier and quicker of course.

CREMA AL CIOCCOLATO
CHOCOLATE CREAM GANACHE

300g/10oz double cream
150g/5oz unsalted butter, softened and cut into cubes
300g/10oz best plain chocolate, with high cocoa content

Finely chop the chocolate and place in a heatproof bowl. Place the cream in a pan, bring to the boil, pour onto the chocolate and leave for a few minutes, then gently mix together and stir in the butter with a whisk. If it starts to separate, put the bowl over a pan of simmering water and beat until smooth. Pour the ganache into a bowl, leave at room temperature for 12 hours.

To use: Soften the chocolate cream by placing it over a saucepan of hot water and beat continuously for 3–4 minutes with a wooden spoon. Draw off the heat, and continue to beat until the mixture is completely smooth and light, and is ready to use for gateaux, pastries and decorations.

Makes: 600g/1¼lb
Preparation: 10 minutes, plus resting time

Chef's note: For an extremely light chocolate cream ganache, place the mixture in a mixing bowl and whisk at medium speed. Use it straight away.

THE ITALIAN EMBASSY

*Enormi zabaglioni biondi, monte bianchi con vette di panna montata e
cassata picchiettata con pistacchi verde*
Huge blond sabayon, Mont Blancs topped with snowy whipped cream,
cassata specked with green pistachio nuts

There are certain things that we never forget in our lives; they stay imprinted on our minds for ever. I was crossing the Channel for the first time on a ferry to come to England. I was tired from the long journey by train from Italy to Calais. I sat quietly below deck, looking at the sea and the people around me. I was bewildered, listening to people speaking a different language, and thinking of what this new land might be like. I was thirsty, my mouth was dry and I was a little shy perhaps to go to the bar for a drink, as my English was very poor. I fancied a nice glass of orangeade. I was thinking of those lovely orange drinks, in lovely round green bottles that we have in Italy – full of taste, sparkling and refreshing. Instead, I got a plastic cup with a squirt of orange essence that was diluted up to the top with water. I half smiled and said to myself, 'Pino, where are you going?' as I looked down at the drink. From that moment on, I sensed that things were going to be different from how they always had been before and smiled. I never forgot that simple orange drink.

When I arrived at Victoria Station, Mimi and the Italian Embassy chef Gino Esposito met me and I was driven to the Italian Embassy. The embassy in Grosvenor Square is one of the most exquisitely beautiful houses in the heart of London. It is filled with the finest paintings dating back to the Renaissance period. Antique furniture and priceless objets d'art decorate every room of the embassy. A member of staff told me that at one time it was open to the public.

Gino first took me upstairs to the staff quarters on the fourth floor where my bedroom was. It was pleasant and nicely decorated, but I couldn't see much of London as the bedroom window looked out over slate roofs, and high terracotta chimney pots. I was never attracted to Grosvenor Square as it was too quiet and reserved for me, and I would often escape towards Piccadilly Circus and Oxford Street, where I discovered hamburgers, chips, peas and tomato ketchup served with a cup of tea or a glass of Coca-Cola.

Gino Esposito, a Southerner from the Neapolitan region, who was in his thirties, had lived in England for many years. He lived in the embassy with his wife, Margherita. He was a very kind person with a good heart, as all Neapolitans are. Gino and I catered for many official parties and kept the tradition of serving classic Italian dishes with the approval of His Excellency the Ambassador, Raimondo Manzini, who lived in the residence with Signora Manzini, his mother. They both thoroughly enjoyed their everyday meals, and on Gino's days off they would recognise my cooking, and would ask the *maggiordomo*, "Is it the young chef who cooked it?"

The starter could be anything, such as *lasagne alla Bolognese; spuma di pomodoro con salsa di peperoni* or *risotto con radicchio Trevisano* and the main course could be *anatra al cedro, filetto di bue con porcini, petti di pollo con legumi* or a simple grilled Dover sole with a salad and a *pannacotta* as a dessert. For the staff lunch, pasta dishes and *pomodoro* were a daily affair.

My wage was £11 a week clear, and it was quite a lot of money at the time – especially as the Ambassador provided us staff with food, accommodation, two bottles of red wine weekly, two cartons of Italian cigarettes monthly per person and all the comfort. After work, I would meet my new friends in Regent Street and spend the evening out.

As soon as I had settled down to my new life in London, I decided to phone a friend of mine, Giuseppe Colaizzo, known as Peppino. I knew Peppino and his family when I was growing up. When I used to walk along our street, his mother – Aunty Fiorentina – who would always be sitting out on her veranda catching the sunshine, would call me over for a chat and ask me where I was going, interested in my everyday life. She was a large lady, with white hair which she pulled back into a bun. She had a wonderful warm presence. She wore a navy-blue dress dotted with delicate white flowers and over it a long black apron as though it was part of a national costume, and a thick silver chain around her neck, upon which hung a pendant in the shape of a casket. She lived in a house with her sister, Aunty Giovannina.

I met Peppino one day whilst I was visiting the de Tullio family. He had been a good friend of my father's since they were young. I was introduced to him and we started talking together about our life and work. He was interested in me, and wanted to know all about my work in the kitchens. Before I left, he gave me his address and telephone number. I never thought I would come to use it.

In the 1950s, Peppino had travelled to England to work at the Savoy Hotel, one of the most prestigious hotels in the country, even to this day. He had written a letter to the Savoy from La Chaux-de-Fonds in Switzerland, where he had been working in the Hotel de la Paix for a while. In this letter he asked the head chef for a position, for which he was accepted, partly due to his excellent references. As a young man, he had worked in grand hotels in Rome, on the Via Veneto.

When we used to meet, he would recount to me over a drink his experience of the kitchens in the Savoy. All of the kitchen brigade were continental – there was not a single English worker at all. They wore tall white hats and jackets whilst they bustled around the busy yet disciplined kitchen. The head chef was a Frenchman named Monsieur La Planche.

One of his proudest moments happened when the mâitre d'hôtel burst into the kitchen one day, and demanded, "Who can make an omelette soufflé?" – a request from a customer.

Peppino promptly raised his hand and replied, "I can make it, *Monsieur le mâitre!*"

He swiftly went to the stove and proceeded to cook it. It turned out that Sir Winston Churchill was dining there with his wife, Lady Clementine, and their children. He had requested the dish and when he dined at the Savoy that was his favourite. He also loved the millefeuille.

After he had worked there for a while, Peppino was made senior sous-chef, due to his expertise being recognised. He carried on in this position for many years, until he left to marry. We kept in touch every Christmas, and occasionally through phone calls. There was a lot of affection between Peppino, myself and Caroline. He moved on from cooking to run a wine cellar with his wife in London. After a while, he fell seriously ill, and was forced to retire. As a young man, he had been very handsome, with the looks of a film star, and this illness had a big effect on him. In 2004, Peppino passed away. It was a great loss, both to us and the world of cuisine.

The embassy kitchen was in the basement at the far end of a long corridor. A painted white door would open on the left-hand side, and we would gasp for air. Our eyes would focus on a large rectangular preparation table with a white Formica top, in the middle of the kitchen. I was told, by the embassy staff that before me another young chef, called Cosimo, would sprint from the corridor, somersault the table and land on his feet on the floor like an acrobatic. He was such a little devil, they would say!

Deep drawers on both sides of the table were full of charlotte moulds, large and small, and flan rings of all sizes. Knives and other utensils were also kept there.

Facing the wall was a large and fairly new gas stove that sometimes failed to light properly and the oven would go off. To my horror one morning, I thought I was going to blow up the embassy. Next to it there was a very old-fashioned cast-iron coal stove with brass knobs on the doors. It was unusable. To the left, there were wide shelves containing various sizes of copper saucepans and underneath was a small wooden table where we could sit and eat. Next on the left of the shelves was the entrance to the vegetable store and a very large washing-up sink. On the other side of the kitchen were two doors. One door led to the larder with a *patisserie* oven that had seen better days and had not been working for years, and the other led to a long room with two fridges and two freezers. I discovered that this kitchen, although it was outdated and archaic, was well equipped. The light from the skylight above in the ceiling filtered through dirty glass onto the kitchen table. Opaque and dull light meant cloudy. Bright and clear meant sunny. Years later my colleague Filippo would refer to the skylight as high and low pressure.

The Ambassador would often give official parties and never interfered with kitchen matters. He put the Chancellor in charge of discussing menus with Gino. Often it would be members of the royal family, government officials or Foreign Office civil servants and, of course, other embassy ambassadors and colleagues. Great Britain was about to join the Common Market, and it was a really exciting time for European affairs; and for me it was something new and different.

It was especially exciting for me to cook for the first time for the royal family and other important guests, and I gradually grew accustomed to the English way of life. It was a happy household and I was very proud to be amongst other Italian staff, and to take part in looking after our Italian Ambassador. The embassy had a staffroom with a pool table, and in the evening after work we would sit down and have a chat over an espresso coffee. As everything in life comes to an end so did this job, and after five months I moved on to Kensington Palace. I did lose contact with Gino, and he was most upset at my departure.

Several years later when I was working at the Finnish Embassy in London in Kensington Palace Gardens I was called to the telephone. It was a dear family friend, Filippo, from the same village as me who had arrived from Austria with the new Italian Ambassador and his wife to take up his new post at the Italian Embassy in London. The Italian Ambassador, His Excellency Andrea Cagiati was a career diplomat who kept the embassy especially busy so that he could introduce himself to his new colleagues, Members of Parliament and other VIP guests.

The last I heard of Filippo was that he was working at the Italian Embassy in Libya. I was little more than a child when I first knew him, when he would come back home to Rosello with his wife, Nelida, and their two children on holiday. All smartly dressed and suntanned, they looked somehow different from the rest of us. I remember Filippo sporting a light-blue summer suit, white shirt and tie. He was slim, with glossy hair slicked back, dark rectangular sunglasses with thick frames and a newspaper folded under his arm. He could have been anybody – even a director of a Swiss bank. I always assumed that they were strangers, and I never thought one day we would become good friends, and I would give him a hand when he needed one.

He had phoned me because he wanted to see me as soon as I could go over to the embassy. I had hardly walked in the kitchen door when, with a straight face, he said, "Do you want this job, Pino? I don't like it here. I feel so much out of place, this house is too big for me and there is far too much for me to do."

I was nodding my head in agreement. My reply was that I couldn't accept it; I had the most magnificent job in London with the most fantastic employer in the world. I knew from my previous years of working there, that to run that embassy was to have a headache and a half, to say the least! But I did promise to go and help him any time he wanted me when he had large functions on. I must say that we did do some nice functions together.

One Saturday afternoon, my wife and I met up with our dear friend, Janie, and decided to go with our children to Oxford Street. So there was myself, Caroline and Edilio, and Janie with Annabel and Jamie. As we were window-shopping, we wandered around and eventually ended up in Grosvenor Square. I suggested going to see Filippo at the embassy. We were all a little tired and in need of refreshments. He warmly greeted us, but before I introduced him to my family and friends, Caroline told me to tell Filippo that she was my wife and Edilio our son, but also that Janie was my mistress and Annabel and Jamie were my children. Filippo's eyes were like saucers, and he became quite excited with my confidences as he congratulated me several times over on my lovely large family! He was completely overwhelmed and was patting the children on their heads and spooning out delicious home-made ice cream, while Caroline and Janie were laughing away in the corner and both demanding ice cream too! We all remember that day so well, but I did admit to Filippo before we went that we had pulled his leg. On reflection it was good that I had eventually told the truth as news can travel very fast. The village of Rosello would have been agog with this news.

It was good news to hear that His Excellency put Filippo's name forward to be knighted and to receive the *Cavaliere del Lavoro* for dedication and service to the Italian Government. Caroline and I were invited to the embassy for a drink in the grand salon amongst his friends and staff, while the Ambassador made a nice speech and presented the medal to Filippo.

I was asked once on one afternoon when he had ninety VIP guests to cater for at a dinner party and there was a lot of work involved. But it was something that I found very interesting. I had never thought of it before and I never thought you could do it either. On the menu as a main course there were saddles of venison. In the morning another great chef and a friend of us both, Michele Maranzano, also from Rosello, told me that when he had worked there, there had hardly been any equipment at all and that he had written a letter some forty years earlier to the Italian Foreign Office asking for kitchen equipment. Michele Maranzano was a rare man with lovely qualities who cared about his family and food. He was an old master of the kitchen, very precise with his work and economic with the ingredients and careful with very little waste. His long career started at a very young age in the kitchen at the home of the Prince Sciarra in Rome. His father was the chef, and Michele the kitchen boy.

One of his delightful tales that I always remember was that when he later worked with another chef he had the habit of roasting a chicken until completely burnt, then he would add water to make a sort of syrupy black stock and save it to darken sauces and for other uses. Michele would nod his head remembering those early days in his life. What a waste! What a waste!" he would utter.

He suggested to Filippo that the saddles (after they had been marinated in the proper manner) should be roasted late morning, left to cool down, then the meat should be carved and put back on the saddle bones, complete with toothpicks to hold it in place. All the saddles looked beautiful and very professionally done – they were going to be reheated in a hot oven just long enough not to spoil the meat. I must say it was a worthwhile cookery lesson.

Eventually, the Ambassador was recalled to Rome and posted to the Italian Embassy to the Holy See. Filippo worked with His Excellency until his retirement.

THIS IS WHAT THE WORLD ... THINKS OF ME

I am very proud of my brother in law, Pino. He is an amazingly creative and generous Chef, and is multi talented in many other directions, including being a very competent artist, carpenter and musician, and has a beautiful garden which contains many exotic plants and water features which are quite out standing.

He is a loving husband and father who has faced his illness with the utmost fortitude. He is truly an inspiration to all who know him.

Charlotte Iglehart, Kircudbrightshire, Scotland

LASAGNE ALLA BOLOGNESE

Bolognese sauce (see recipe on page 95)
1400ml/2½ pints milk
18 lasagne sheets of fresh pasta
60g/2oz freshly grated Parmesan cheese
1 mozzarella cheese, cut into small cubes
110g/4oz butter
90g/2½oz plain flour
Salt
Freshly ground black pepper
Freshly ground nutmeg

One ovenproof dish measuring: 36cm/14in long by 25cm/10in wide.

Make the Bolognese sauce and keep warm.

Make the béchamel sauce: In a heavy medium-sized pan, heat the milk and bring to the boil. Melt the butter in a small saucepan over a low heat and add the flour, stirring constantly with a wooden spoon. Leave to cook for 2 minutes. Now lower the heat under the milk and add to it the flour-butter mixture. Mix with a whisk. Beat from side to side to thicken the sauce and to keep it smooth. Add salt, pepper and nutmeg, being careful not to overseason the sauce. Keep stirring as it can burn very easily. Add two tablespoons of grated cheese. If the béchamel is too thick simply add a little more milk, if it is too thin make a little more flour-butter mixture and add to the sauce. Leave to boil for 2–3 minutes and then taste for seasoning.

Pour two small ladles of béchamel sauce at the base of the dish. Lay six sheets of lasagne so that they are slightly overlapping. Add two ladles of Bolognese sauce and spread over the pasta sheets, then add two ladles of béchamel over the Bolognese. Sprinkle with some Parmesan and mozzarella cheese. Repeat this sequence twice. Coat the third layer with more béchamel to cover the dish evenly. Sprinkle with the remaining grated Parmesan and mozzarella cheese and bake.

Serves: 6
Preparation: 30 minutes
Cooking: 40 minutes
Oven: 180°C/350°F/Gas 4

Chef's note: Both sauces must be warm and runny, as a thick sauce would be difficult to spread on the pasta sheets. You can buy very good non-boiling dried pasta to use for this lasagne dish.

SALSA BOLOGNESE O RAGÙ

The union of any kind of pasta and ragù is a marriage made in heaven! Such as tagliatelle, it is indispensable in lasagne dishes, and it is excellent with spaghetti, penne, rigatoni and many others. When a menu lists *alla Bolognese* that means it is served with ragù.

1 small chopped onion
2 clove of garlic crushed
4 tbsp olive oil
2 tbsp finely chopped or grated celery
2 tbsp chopped or grated carrot
700g/1½lb minced beef (not too lean)
Salt
Freshly ground black pepper
100ml/3fl oz dry red wine
2 whole cloves
1 bay leaf
1 tbsp tomato purée
800g/1lb 12oz tinned Italian tomatoes chopped, with their juice
2 tbsp corn flour mixed with 2–3 tbsp of water.

In a heavy-bottomed saucepan put the chopped onion, garlic and the oil and sauté briefly over a medium heat until transparent. Add the celery and carrot and cook for a further 2 minutes.

Add the minced beef, and stir to separate the meat. Add salt and pepper and cook until the mince has lost its raw, red colour. Pour in the wine, turn the heat up and cook, stirring until all the wine has evaporated.

Add the cloves, the bay leaf, tomato purée and the tomatoes with their juice, and stir thoroughly. When the mixture has started to bubble, turn the heat down and cook the sauce by gently simmering. Cook uncovered, making sure to stir every now and then as the sauce could stick and burn easily. Thicken the sauce lightly with the cornflour to concentrate the taste. Taste and adjust seasoning.

Makes: 1kg 400g/3lb 1oz
Serves: 6
Preparation: 20 minutes
Cooking time 1½ hour

Chef's note: Ragù can be kept in the fridge for up to a week, or frozen. Reheat and simmer for about 15 minutes before using.

RISOTTO CON RADICCHIO TREVIGIANO
RISOTTO WITH RADICCHIO

For this classic risotto use Italian rice as the grains will swell in the stock and become sticky and tender, yet will also remain firm.

60g/2oz butter
4 tbsp olive oil
1 medium onion, finely chopped
250g/8oz fresh radicchio, sliced across
500g/1lb 2oz Italian rice
100ml/3fl oz dry red wine
1½ litre/3 pints hot chicken stock or vegetable stock
110g/4oz mascarpone cheese
4 tbsp fresh grated Parmesan cheese
Salt
Freshly ground black pepper

In a heavy-based saucepan heat half the butter and the oil. Add the finely chopped onion and fry until transparent but not brown. Add the rice, stir with a wooden spoon and fry for 2 minutes over a brisk heat. Add the wine and leave to evaporate. Add the sliced radicchio, stir well and then add 1–2 ladles of hot chicken stock.

Simmer gently and stir with a wooden spoon to loosen the grains of rice. When the stock has been absorbed, continue simmering and add further hot stock every 5–6 minutes. Stir occasionally to free the rice from the bottom and the sides of the pan. The risotto is done when the rice is tender and firm to the bite, but the risotto remains runny (in Italian it is called all'onda). Add the remaining butter and the mascarpone cheese and mix thoroughly. Spoon into a hot dish and serve with Parmesan shavings or freshly grated Parmesan cheese.

Serves: 6
Preparation: 10 minutes
Cooking: 20–25 minutes

As a young apprentice at the Belgian Embassy in Rome, the chef Eduardo Coletta often used to make the risotto for the Ambassador and his family. The first thing that I was taught was to make a good chicken stock that is full of flavour. This is essential for a good risotto. Of course, it goes without saying that you need Italian rice such as Vialone, Maratello or Arborio, which is the best-known rice in Italy. Other ingredients can be added to the risotto, such as cooked diced vegetables for a delicious risotto primavera, or prawns towards the end.

Chicken pieces should be added to the saucepan with the onion and sautéed until light brown before adding the rice.

Chef's note: Alternatively, dried porcini mushrooms (Boletus) can be used but the quantity of mushrooms should be reduced to 30g/1oz. Follow the recipe as before. Reconstitute the porcini mushrooms by covering them in hot water in a bowl, leaving to soak for 20 minutes, and then squeezing out the water so that they are ready for use. Keep the water and add 1 ladle to the risotto while it is cooking.

FILETTI DI BUE CON PORCINI
FILLET OF BEEF WITH WILD MUSHROOMS

This fillet dish has a good robust flavour and makes a splendid meal for a dinner party. The croutons and the mushrooms will dress the meat for a fine main course.

6 tournedos cut from the fillet of beef, each weighing about 140–160g/6oz
6 bread croutons, same size as the fillet, fried in butter until golden and set aside
110g/4oz butter
1 small onion, finely chopped
3 tablespoons olive oil
30g/1oz dried porcini mushrooms (cèpes)
400ml/12fl oz chicken stock
400ml/12fl oz red wine or port
1 bay leaf
1 pinch ground cinnamon
2 tbsp double cream
1 pinch of caster sugar
Salt
Freshly ground black pepper

Beurre Manié:
15g/½oz butter, softened and mixed with
15g/½oz flour

Garnish:
1 tbsp chopped parsley

Place the dried porcini mushrooms in a bowl and pour 100ml/4fl oz hot water over them. Leave to soak for 20 minutes. Drain them and set aside, reserving the liquid.
   For the sauce: In a saucepan melt a little butter with the olive oil and fry the mushrooms for 2–3 minutes. Remove them and keep aside. In the same pan gently fry the onion until transparent, but not brown. Add the wine and the bay leaf and reduce by half at a high heat for about 10 minutes, then add the stock and boil to reduce again also by half. Add the mushroom water and thicken the sauce by adding the beurre manié, stirring with a whisk. Add the cinnamon, the double cream and sugar, and sieve. Adjust the seasoning, add the mushrooms and keep warm. The sauce must taste slightly sweet with a taste of wine.
   Sauté the tournedos very quickly in a small amount of butter and 2 tablespoons of oil over a high heat until both sides of the meat are golden. Cook the meat according to taste and add seasoning.

To serve: Place the croutons on warm plates or a large serving dish and place the tournedos over them. Divide the mushrooms and pour over the hot sauce. Sprinkle with parsley and serve.

Serves: 6
Preparation and Cooking time: 30 minutes each

Chef's note: You can use this lovely red wine sauce with any red meat.

PANNACOTTA

Pannacotta means cooked cream in Italian and it has become a very fashionable dessert in many smart restaurants. It can be served with fresh fruit, such as mango, raspberries or pineapple, all arranged around the unmoulded pannacotta.

250ml/8fl oz milk
3 tbsp powdered gelatine
675ml/1½ pints double cream
1 vanilla pod or ½ tsp vanilla essence
2 zests of one lemon
6 tbsp granulated sugar

You will need 10 ramekins of 100ml/4fl oz. Place them onto a tray and put in the fridge to get cold. Alternatively to make it easier use a 1 litre/2 pint soufflé dish.
    Pour the milk into a medium-sized saucepan, sprinkle over the gelatine and leave for 10 minutes to soften. Meanwhile, with a small knife scrape the seeds from the vanilla pod into the cream, then add the scraped pod to the cream also and the zest of lemon. Heat the milk over a low heat, stirring for a minute or two until the gelatine dissolves. Take off the heat, add the sugar and a pinch of salt and stir until dissolved. Bring the double cream to boil and pour into the milk mixture, stir well and sieve into a clean bowl. Remove vanilla pod and save for another use. Leave to cool, which can take a little while. Stir the mixture occasionally.
    With a large jug fill all the ramekins with the mixture. If you want to unmould the desserts, dip each ramekin in hot water, invert a plate over it and turn out, and serve.

Serves: 6 or more
Preparation: 20 minutes

PRINCESS MARGARET

Credo molto all'uso delle erbe aromatiche
I believe very much in the use of fresh herbs

From the Italian Embassy, another telephone call was to change my direction once again. Princess Margaret's chef, Renato, a family friend, was looking for a second chef at Kensington Palace, and he contacted me. I hesitated a little at first about giving in my notice at the Italian Embassy; they had been very kind to me and, when I was new in England, they had helped me to settle down and had made me feel welcome. After a lot of thinking, I plucked up courage and prepared my small 'speech' of what to say to the Ambassador's secretary, Signora Fiermonte. Although she was very disappointed, she eventually accepted my notice with a sad face. They were all sorry to see me leave.

I arrived at Kensington Palace with courage and looking at a new horizon. This was my chance to be part of this well-known English household. Renato and his wife, Daphne, greeted me and they were both delighted. He said how pleased and happy he was that I was able to join him, after all. I was taken on a tour to the spacious kitchen, where it was well lit and comfortable to work in. There was a larder at the back, well furnished with plenty of everything, from apple juice and cornflakes to zucchini.

I was introduced to the other members of the staff, who were mostly elderly and kind ladies.

I was accompanied upstairs by Miss Follies, the housekeeper, and she showed me my bedroom. The corridor leading to the staff quarters was of an old style, but beautifully decorated and very, very quiet – as if nobody lived there. You could hear the floorboards creaking under your feet at the slightest movement, and when I used to go back to the palace very late at night after being out, it was spooky. I would turn my head and look back over my shoulder. I was told that there was a ghost in the palace, but I have never seen it!

The room was very bright and airy, beautifully decorated and spacious with dark old beams in the ceiling, a wardrobe, and a big and comfortable armchair in a corner of the room where I would sit and look out of a large window overlooking Kensington Palace Park and the palace's private gardens. I saw Princess Margaret many times, sitting out on a long chair enjoying the solitude and admiring the flowers.

Many years later I saw the same window many times on television, when people were laying flowers for the late Princess Diana. From that very bedroom I took up painting. I bought my very first set of oil colours and a canvas and I discovered that I could paint – not very well, but it was a start. Although I had the window wide open and was looking at a beautiful park under my nose, I was painting still life, but still life from my head! I never thought to paint the park or the Princess's garden. I am sad to say that I never did paint the garden, even for a keepsake. That would have been wonderful and priceless to me, but it is too late now.

Renato and Daphne have two or three of my paintings, and I don't know what happened to the others. I have pursued my painting ever since and I find a great satisfaction at the end when I put the paintbrush down. Later on, when I married, my sister-in-law Charlotte liked my still life so much that she has described my watercolour paintings as primitive.

I felt privileged to be living in such a beautiful place in those lovely surroundings. The palace had a very happy and relaxed atmosphere, and everybody was helpful and aware that I was new and had not been living in England for very long.

The kitchen had been renewed and redesigned by Lord Snowdon with all the latest equipment at the time. Two kitchen windows were overlooking the old and uneven worn cobblestone courtyard in the heart of Kensington Palace. At the main entrance was a big white arch and a tall clock tower, which never failed to strike the time, with its impressive round gold cupola on the top. There were various grand-style apartments with endless white panelled glass windows complementing the courtyard. Here lived Princess Alice, Countess of Athlone, the Duke and the Duchess of Gloucester, the British Museum, and, on the ground floor at the far end of the courtyard, the chef, Renato, and his wife, Daphne, with their daughters, Corinna and Sonia.

Kensington Palace's main front door was panelled in black, with a large glass veranda entrance, for protection from the rain and the wind, raised from the ground with a few stone steps. As soon as you walked through this door, into the hall, there was a most beautiful portrait of HRH Princess Margaret at a young age on the right, with the bluest shining eyes you have ever seen. It was painted by the well-known Italian artist Pietro Annigoni, famous for his portraits of European royalty.

The grand salon was where the Princess would welcome and entertain close friends and family and where she would relax with a drink and a cigarette in a holder in the quiet and peaceful surroundings of her own home. The salon was furnished with exquisite decor, comfortable sofas, fine paintings and signed photographs of friends and family in silver frames placed on the grand piano as mementos. The Princess loved to entertain.

Princess Margaret did not like her guests turning up late. She would get annoyed and walk into the dining room followed by the other guests. They would proceed to eat, and the latecomer had to eat whatever course was brought in. (Comment from Caroline: "Quite right too!")

The table was laid to perfection by the Italian butler, Alberto, and was heavy on the silver, sparkling crystal glasses and very fine old porcelain. Princess Margaret enjoyed good food that was well prepared, tasty and beautifully presented.

Renato, a very fine chef, had started at an early age in the kitchen at the villa Aldobrandini, many years before his brother Nicolino, which I mentioned earlier. He worked alongside the master chef Umberto di Tullio, a friend, also from our village with the Prince and Princess Aldobrandini, in the picturesque town of Frascati, near Rome.

Renato and I prepared delicious meals for the Princess and Lord Snowdon at the time while we were there. From the kitchen windows we could see Princess Margaret being picked up by the chauffeur in her maroon Rolls-Royce, David and Sarah leaving for school in the morning and guests arriving at the palace.

Renato was a dear friend, a perfectionist and an explorer in the kitchen. I worked well with him as a team member, not as head chef and sous-chef. We made our job enjoyable by creating new dishes and new menus for the Princess and Lord Snowdon, which they both enjoyed.

Working at Kensington Palace was, for me, one of my best years in a kitchen. I was young and Renato, who had worked in many households, talked to me about the English cuisine.

Many dishes were truly English recipes with the freshest ingredients. They were wholesome and healthy and interesting. I enjoyed preparing and eating them. I would never turn down a good cottage pie.

The Princess would often be away on tours or on holiday on the island of Mustique, where she owned a villa. Or she would take the children, Sarah and David, to Windsor Castle to spend the weekends together with the Queen and other members of the royal family. This gave me a lot of free time to enjoy myself and to pursue my hobby of painting. I was young and we lived in a less dangerous world, and after so many years I still have the fondest memories of the time I worked at Kensington Palace.

Princess Margaret and Lord Snowdon would unexpectedly come into the kitchen to see us and would bring their friends to thank us for their meals. The children, David and Sarah, used to come in too with an excuse to see us, but always in a hurry as their nanny, Miss Summer, did not want them in the kitchen. She was very protective of them and it was obviously her responsibility to make sure they did not get hurt. When the Princess was at home, she would pop into the kitchen to say hello and ask if all was well. If there were saucepans on the stove she would ask what we were cooking, and stir and smell the contents, sometimes tasting them too.

At Christmas time, when we used to make the traditional English Christmas pudding, we would all get excited and tidy up all round the kitchen. The Princess would come down to the kitchen especially to stir the pudding, holding the wooden spoon, closing her eyes and making a wish. It was all beautiful and merry. The Christmas staff party was magical when all the staff could all get together at the downstairs staff dining room. The kitchen was closed for the evening so Renato and I did not have to cook. The food was brought in, and served by a catering company. The Princess wanted everyone to have a good time and enjoy themselves. You could bring along a relative or a friend. Members of other royal households would join us, and food suppliers were invited too.

The Princess and Lord Snowdon would come slightly later to join us for a drink. We would form a circle all around the room so they could shake hands, and say a few words with a courteous smile and ask questions. They loved meeting people and wanted to wish everyone a very happy Christmas. The

Christmas present was not really a surprise in the true sense of the word. We had to buy something that we liked, and to spend no more than so many pounds, which were then reimbursed by the secretary (I can't remember how much now). Then I had to wrap it up, write the little card with my name on it and give it to the housekeeper.

On 23 December, before the Princess left with David and Sarah to spend Christmas at Windsor with the Queen, we were called one at a time to the grand salon where Princess Margaret would hand the gifts out. I walked into the salon and bowed. Then I approached the Princess and while she handed me my present we smiled at each other. As I had been in England for only a short time I could not remember all the Christmas wishes. On my first year at Kensington Palace I bought a pair of green trousers, which I didn't like that much after all – they were a funny colour; and the second Christmas I chose a jumper.

In spite of their lifestyle, with the very best and finest of everything, their simple and favourite dishes were prepared and served. Princess Margaret loved egg dishes cooked in various ways. Avocado with egg and Béarnaise sauce was a favourite of hers, and Lord Snowdon's favourite dishes were shepherd's pie and fishcakes – all freshly made, of course. The Princess always checked the menus weekly.

The butler, Alberto, would take the menus to her. She would sometimes amend the chef's suggestions. However, on one occasion during my time there, the Queen came to lunch and on this occasion the menu certainly met with her approval – fresh corn on the cob with butter, best end of lamb with vegetables and vanilla ice cream to finish. The menu looked like this:

Fresh Corn on the Cob
with Melted Butter

***

Rack of Lamb
with Blackcurrant Sauce

***

New Minted Potatoes
New Glazed Carrots

***

Vanilla Ice Cream

Three big events took place whilst I was at Kensington Palace. Her Majesty Queen Elizabeth, and the Duke of Edinburgh celebrated their 25th wedding anniversary. A collection was raised from every member of staff in the royal household towards gifts, which were a portrait of Prince Edward, a harness, a birdbath and trees for Windsor, Balmoral and Sandringham. They were both very touched by this lovely gesture and thought. A photograph of the Prince Edward portrait and a thank-you letter were sent to everyone, and mine are very much treasured.

The second event was the marriage of Princess Anne to Captain Mark Phillips. A red Spode Stafford dinner service was given as a wedding present from contributions given by every member of staff in the royal household. Before the wedding ceremony I had sadly left the palace after so many happy events to find my own way as a head chef and to run my own kitchen at a private house in Chelsea in London, but I had already given my donation towards the cost of the gift. I went back one day to see the chef and a thank-you letter was waiting for me. Then I was given a small blue packet, and I could not imagine what it contained. I opened it, and, to my surprise, it was a piece of the wedding cake from the newly married royal couple.

The third event, which to me has to be the most important of all, was meeting my future wife, Caroline.

In the evening after work, I would go down to Kensington High Street to a discotheque called Lulus to dance, spend a few hours out, and have a drink. One night they had a special champagne party and Caroline was there with Kim, her great friend whom she worked with at the Royal Academy of Dancing in Knightsbridge. As it happened, I first asked her friend Kim to dance, and I got a very definite no; so I turned round and asked Caroline to dance, and her reply was a clear yes. We started to dance and chat and I discovered that she had been trained in hotel management, but at the time we met she was working at the Royal Academy of Dancing. When I told her that I was working at Kensington Palace, she thought I meant the Hotel Kensington. I even told her on our first meeting that she was the kind of girl I would like to marry, and she laughed. I liked everything about her, with her one hundred lovely qualities. We were eventually engaged on St Valentine's Day 1975, married on 19 July, and thirty-two years later we are still on our honeymoon.

THIS IS WHAT THE WORLD . . . THINKS OF ME

Pino's generosity and enthusiasm knows no bounds. He is to be admired as a source of inspiration to others and his plum tarts are pretty good as well.

Joley Malby, Ladbroke

(Explanation: Some years ago Joley attended a fair at Ragley Hall, organised by Lady Kilmaine. Take Two Cooks had a stand there and Joley brought some plum tarts and liked them so much she called and made an order for a dozen the following weekend and her husband, Tim, collected them.

So this is how I came to know Tim, and I met him at the Whitings' dinner a while later. I asked him to help me with my book, and it is because of Tim's help and enthusiasm that *Flavours of Rosello* was printed.)

Energy and enthusiasm are only two of the many adjectives to describe Pino's infectious driving force he has in the kitchen and in his private life and I admire him very much.

Jo MacDonald, London

I have known Pino for over seventeen years and have spent many hours talking and watching him while he worked in his kitchen, walked in his garden enjoying with him the amazing variety of plants and wild life in it, and listened while he enthused over his love of painting, his writing, or of playing his beloved Accordion. He is an inspiration to us all with his enthusiasm for learning new skills.

His bravery during his long operation and recovery from Cancer was truly memorable, and when tragedy hit my family he was immediately helping in the way that came naturally to him, bringing welcome meals when we were at our lowest ebb.

Pino is a true friend and a gentleman.

Janet Moore, Ladbroke

UOVA AFFOGATE CON AVOGADO PERA
AVOCADO WITH EGG AND BÉARNAISE SAUCE

This is an original starter of warm avocado pear halves. The sharpness of the Béarnaise and the poached egg make a nice contrast.

3 avocados, ripened
6 eggs, size 1
300ml/10fl oz warm Béarnaise sauce see recipe

Peel each avocado, cut in half, remove the stones and place in a saucepan with hot water until they are warmed through.

Poach the eggs in a pan of boiling water with a little salt and a few drops of vinegar for 2 minutes.

Lift the avocados out of the hot water and cut each one into a fan shape. Place each prepared avocado half onto a plate. With a slotted kitchen spoon lift the egg out of the water, trim off some of the egg white with a small knife, place it next to the avocado and coat with Béarnaise sauce.

Garnish with a few sprigs of watercress. Serve immediately.

Serves: 6
Preparation: 5 minutes
Cooking: 5 minutes

Chef's note: The eggs can be poached in advance and reheated in hot water. (If you like to do so, cool them quickly after cooking in cold water).

SALSA BERNESE
BÉARNAISE SAUCE

250g/8oz butter
4 egg yolks
2 tbsp water
2 tbsp Worcestershire sauce
4 tbsp white vinegar
1 tbsp chopped fresh parsley
1 tsp chopped onion
A few slices of carrot
A few sprigs of fresh tarragon
A few whole black peppercorns

Melt the butter in a pan, skim the froth from the surface and allow it to cool a little.

Beat the water and egg yolks in a medium Pyrex bowl. Put the Pyrex bowl over a small piece of cardboard (this will prevent the sauce overheating) into a large pan half filled with water (a bain-marie), and whisk the mixture constantly until it is creamy and thick enough for the whisk to leave a trail on the base of the bowl. It is important to ensure that the base of the bowl does not become too hot.

Remove from the heat and whisk in the tepid butter a little at a time – not too fast or the sauce will curdle. Keep to one side.

Combine the white vinegar, tarragon, carrot, onion and peppercorns and boil down to 2 tablespoons. Strain into the sauce with the Worcestershire sauce and add the parsley. Adjust seasoning and serve warm.

Makes: 300g/10oz
Preparation: 15 minutes
Cooking: 15 minutes

Chef's note: This is perhaps one of the greatest sauces of the French Art Culinaire. It is the best possible accompaniment for a tender Scotch fillet of beef, or for Eggs Benedict.

PASTICCIO DI CARNE DEL PASTORE
SHEPHERD'S PIE

I have been living in England for more than thirty years now, and it was Renato, the head chef at Kensington Palace, who introduced me to this dish while I was working with him. It is still one of my favourite dishes, but I have slightly changed the recipe. It is best to make this dish with fresh minced beef for cottage pie, or fresh minced lamb for shepherd's pie. I personally don't like to use leftover meat from a cooked joint although this option is perfectly viable. I find the taste is not quite the same, and the meat has lost some of the goodness and flavour.

1 medium onion, finely chopped
4 tbsp olive oil
1 medium carrot, grated
700g/1½lb minced lamb
100ml/3fl oz red wine
2 x 400g tinned tomatoes, roughly chopped, with their juice
2 sprigs fresh, thyme
1 tbsp chopped parsley
Salt
Freshly ground black pepper
90g/3oz oats

For the topping:
1400kg/3lb potatoes
60g/2oz butter
300ml/½ pint milk
Salt, pepper, and nutmeg
110g/4oz grated cheese
2 tbsp chopped parsley

One ovenproof dish measuring: 36cm/14in long by 25cm/10in wide.

Put the oil in a large saucepan and fry the chopped onion on a low heat for 3–4 minutes. Add the grated carrot and cook a little further. Turn the heat higher and add the meat. Stir to help to break up the mince and get it nicely browned. Season with salt and pepper. Add the thyme and parsley or mixed dried herbs. Add the wine and leave to evaporate for 1–2 minutes. Add the tomatoes, stir and turn the heat right down, put a lid on the pan and let it cook very gently, stirring occasionally. Towards the last ten minutes add the oats and stir well. Don't be tempted to add more oats if the mixture looks quite thin, you will find that in a few minutes the mince will become thicker. Taste for seasoning. Spoon the mince into the ovenproof dish and leave to set.

While the meat is cooking, peel the potatoes and cut them into small cubes. Put the potatoes in a pan with enough cold water to cover them. Add salt, put the lid on and cook until soft (about 15–20 minutes). When the potatoes are done, drain them and press them through a sieve or a vegetable mouli. Bring the milk to boil. Add the butter, salt, pepper and nutmeg to the mash and stir. Then gradually pour in the milk and beat vigorously with a wooden spoon for a few minutes to fluff and lighten the potato purée. Adjust the seasoning and pipe the purée over the mince with a piping bag fitted with a star nozzle to give a nice presentation, or simply spread the mashed potatoes evenly all over the meat with a palette knife and draw lines with the back of a fork. Bake in the oven on the middle shelf for 35 minutes. Take the dish out and sprinkle the grated cheese and parsley on top. Return to the oven for the last five minutes to melt the cheese to a delicious crusty dish.

Chef's note: The recipe above for the potato purée can be used to cover other pies, and makes a perfect marriage with dishes like chicken casseroles, turkey escalopes and sausages. For a smooth and tastier mash press through a sieve. If serving with a main course, you can prepare this up to one hour in advance. Just before serving, warm in a bain-marie and spoon over 3–4 tablespoons of milk to prevent a crust forming. Beat with a spoon and serve.

Serves: 6
Preparation: 20 minutes
Cooking: 35–40 minutes
Oven: 180°C/350°F/Gas 4

PICCOLE TORTE DI PESCE
FISHCAKES

500g/1lb 2oz cooked salmon
500g/1lb 2oz mashed potato
2 tbsp fresh chopped parsley
2 tbsp finely chopped chives
2 tbsp lemon juice
A good pinch cayenne pepper
Salt
Freshly ground pepper
Freshly grated nutmeg
60g/2oz butter

For the coating and frying:
2 eggs, size 4, beaten
200g/7oz fresh white breadcrumbs
568ml/1 pint cooking oil

To garnish:
fried parsley,
lemon wedges (optional)

Place the salmon over a piece of silver foil, skin side down. Sprinkle with salt and pepper, and then add a squeeze of lemon juice and two tablespoons of olive oil. Wrap up the salmon in silver foil and bake in the oven for twenty minutes. Leave to cool.

Peel the potatoes, cut them into cubes and boil for 15–20 minutes. When they are done, drain and press them through a sieve or a vegetable-mouli over a bowl. Add the knob of butter, salt, pepper, nutmeg, parsley, chives and lemon juice. Mix well and taste the mash. Flake the salmon and mix with the potato mash, combining all the ingredients for the fishcakes together thoroughly. Taste to see if more seasoning is required. Lightly flour a working surface, turn out the fish cake mixture and divide into twelve equal-sized portions. Roll each part of the mixture into a ball and gently squash each ball into a round flat shape. Dip the fishcakes, one by one, first into the beaten eggs and then into the fresh breadcrumbs. Pat the fishcakes lightly with a small palette knife to tidy up the loose crumbs. Heat the oil in a shallow pan and fry the cakes until golden brown on both sides. Place onto kitchen paper to drain, and serve. ̄

Chef's note: These delicious fishcakes can be accompanied by fried parsley. If you wish to do this, the parsley must be thoroughly dried, quickly fried in hot oil and then placed onto kitchen paper to soak up the oil. The sabayon sauce below also complements the fishcakes beautifully. If these accompaniments are required, fry the parsley before you fry the fishcakes on both sides and make the sauce after these are both cooked. The fishcakes can easily be kept warm in an oven.

Serves: 6
Preparation: 1 hour
Oven: 190ºC/375ºF/Gas 5

SALSA ZABAGLIONE
SAVOURY SABAYON SAUCE

6 egg yolks, size 4
4 tbsp white wine
A little seasoning, salt and freshly ground black pepper

In a heatproof bowl, combine the egg yolks, wine and seasoning. Whisk until the mixture expands to four or five its original volume and becomes light and foamy. Stand the bowl in a pan of hot, but not boiling water, and place it over a moderate heat. Continue whisking for 5 minutes, taking care not to let the water boil. When the mixture is firmer and has the consistency of lightly whipped cream, remove from the heat and keep warm.

Serves: 6
Preparation: 5 minutes
Cooking time 10 minutes.

Chef's note: This light and fatless sabayon sauce is ideal for serving with poached or grilled salmon and asparagus.

GELATO ALLA VANIGLIA
VANILLA ICE CREAM

An extremely good vanilla ice cream, delicious served with langue de chats biscuits.

500ml/16fl oz milk
500ml/16fl oz double cream
1 vanilla pod or ¼ tsp vanilla essence
2 zest of lemon
6 egg yolks, eggs size 4
200g/7oz caster sugar

You will need an ice cream maker.

Bring the milk, cream, the vanilla pod (or vanilla essence) and the lemon zest to the boil and leave to infuse for 10 minutes, scraping the pod to release the full flavour.

Beat the egg yolks and sugar until light and white. Pour into the milk mixture and replace on a medium heat. Stir with a wooden spoon all the time until it coats the back of the spoon, ensuring the mixture does not boil. Strain through a fine sieve and stir a few times. Leave until cold. This stage of the making can be done well ahead and will keep in the fridge until you are ready. Put the mixture into the ice cream maker and churn until set. Place in the freezer.

Serves: 6 or more
Makes: 1¼ litre/2¼ pint
Churning time: 30 minutes or longer
Different flavours can be added to the mixture before churning.

Variations:

Pistachio ice cream: Add 100g/4oz finely chopped pistachios. You can make a natural green food colouring for this by blending a few leaves of chopped spinach and straining through muslin. The pistachios should be added after you have strained the mixture through the sieve.

Chocolate ice cream: Melt 200g/7oz of good quality chocolate in the milk before sieving.

Coffee ice cream: Add 2–3 tablespoons of instant coffee to the milk before sieving.

Chef's note: When I make my own vanilla ice cream, I prefer to leave the ice cream mixture in the fridge overnight for a better flavour before churning.

My niece, Anna.

Joanna MacDonald – a great friend of Car's since the late 60s.
Jo is an imaginative cook and has helped me many times over the years.

My sister-in-law, Charlotte Iglehart, cousin, Anthea Jones and dear friend, Anne Thomas at the Get-A-Head Ball in Birmingham.

My dear friend from Rosello, Rita Candolfo.

Lin Hedges – a close family friend.

*Teresa Barclay –
the dearest of friends and the most
unique giver of Christmas presents.*

*Maureen Baker – my best admirer of everything I do
and gives me so much encouragement from New York City.*

Hilary Hakim and Janie Wingfield-Stratford – both glamorous grandmothers.
Hilary and Car both Bay Tree Girls. Janie and Car old Homefieldians from the
late 40s.

My sister-in-law, Franca.

My cousin Lucia.

Ann Boughton-Leigh with Tao. Ann and Car, best friends since childhood.

Julia Cheetham – a dear close family friend.

Me and our son, Edilio.

The Spanish Embassy: The table is set to receive the royal guests.

Giving a hand at the Spanish Embassy with a friend Nicola Perella and two helpers during the official visit of King Juan Carlos and Queen Sofia to England.

*Bruno, me and his brother, Antonio De Lucia,
at the Baron Heini Thyssen's home in the Cotswolds.*

The Finnish Embassy: with a dear friend, Renato Percario.

Annabel, my god-daughter with Charlotte, my sister-in-law and Tom, my nephew.

His Excellency Ambassador Dr Richard
and Ambassadress Madame Camilla Tötterman of Finland.

At Kensington Palace:
Alberto the butler, Linda, Lucio, Lord Snowdon, me and Peter Sellers.

My parents, Edilio and Lina, sitting on the steps next to our house.

On the day of my exhibition.

A family group in Rosello: Edilio, me, Caroline, my sisters, Savina, Giovanna and her daughter, Paola, Umberto (Giovanna's son-in-law), and my brothers-in-law, Edmondo and Francesco, on the day of my watercolours exhibition.

My nephew, Jacopo.

My brother, Lucio, who now lives in our family home in Rosello.

My brother, Mario.

My first English Christmas was spent with Daphne Renato,
Corina and Sonia at Kensington Palace. A kind and happy family.

My parents, Lina and Edilio, on their engagement in 1947.

My ID photograph taken a few weeks before I went to Rome, 1963.

Us as children: Me, Savina, Lucio and Giovanna.

My nephews, Mario and Andrea, and my neice, Milena.

Angelo and me at Villa Borghese, Rome, 1964.

My Uncle Luigi and my father, Edilio, working in the navy.

A PRIVATE HOUSE IN CHELSEA

Mettete il vostro cuore per cucinare
Let your heart go with the cooking

Eventually, I left the palace in order to run my own kitchen in a private house, my training now being complete. I had come to England primarily for three years, but never imagined that I would make it my home. I began my new post as head chef at a private house in Chelsea, a very beautiful residence with tasteful decor, a burgundy Rolls-Royce, with a chauffeur dressed in the fifties uniform, a heated swimming pool and a fine English garden.

My employers were an English couple with two lovely young children. He was a businessman, a self-made millionaire, full of ambition and drive for the best, with a taste for good food and fine wines – a bon viveur. His wine cellar in the basement was impressive: row upon row of very old bottles of fine champagne, and wines of well-known French chateaux (Lafite, Latour, Mouton-Rothschild, Margaux, white Puligny Montrachet and many others). After a dinner party once there was a half-bottle of Montrachet left over so I decided to make use of it by making a dish of Dover sole in white wine sauce. The smell and the taste were unbelievable! The wine collection that extended for many years was a breathtaking experience. The minute you walked inside the cool cellar you felt a light chill on your shoulder, and a smell of old, musty air. You wished you had a corkscrew and an empty glass in your hands.

The bottles were all kept lying down and at the correct temperature, and the butler, George, had the keys and was responsible for keeping a record of every bottle of wine that was taken from the cellar. It was then uncorked and left to breathe at room temperature (*chambré*) to develop the natural bouquet. The old bottles of port were always decanted with a special silver funnel and fine muslin was used to filter the liquid.

George was a truly professional butler of the old school. He worked for the grand houses of the old aristocracy. He would often recount to me tales of how he had to iron newspapers in the morning so that the ink would not blacken the employer's hands, and how they used to make the ice in the earth of the cellar.

The kitchen was modern with a blue tiled floor, Formica tops and cabinets, four gas-ring hobs and the latest self-cleaning oven. Magic! Well lit and overlooking the garden, it was fitted with all the latest equipment a chef could want. My employer had designed the inside of the house himself, and had managed to create a beautiful interior. He changed his mind several times until he got it right. He was a perfectionist and only the best would do.

Every morning, before going to the office and whilst having breakfast, he would choose the menu for the day. He had four large photo albums that were filled with recipes of his own choice. These were all cut out or photocopied from cookery books – starters, main courses, vegetables and puddings, all numbered. He would write them down and hand them over to the butler.

George would appear at the kitchen door already half exhausted, with these books under his arm, looking more like a university tutor than a butler, and he would pass them over to me. I would check the recipes for the day, write down the ingredients and then set off to do my shopping. I could walk miles to look for certain ingredients I needed and to make the housekeeping money last as long as I could. I would then return to the house and start cooking for the staff, then for the hostess and guests. This was good experience for me to learn what to buy and how to choose. In this private house I learned even more about food. The selection of a perfect pear, the sweetest melon, the best piece of Brie, the freshest butter and the highest quality creams was as important as the way the food was going to be served and cooked. The house was full of staff, including a chauffeur, maids, a nanny, and myself.

A large collection of cookery books were placed on the kitchen shelves. It was here that I was introduced to, and encouraged to discover, the renowned English cooks of the time such as Elizabeth David, Marguerite Patten, Mary Berry, Robert Carrier and many more. The Cookery Year book was one of my favourites, and was my most used collection of recipes. It had a selection of traditional and new English recipes, written by several cooks, and beautifully illustrated. Before we got married, Caroline bought me a copy as a Christmas present, which I very much treasure.

On the occasion of one dinner party, the hostess rang for coffee and petits fours after the meal, but in my haste, and after a long day in the kitchen, I did not realise that I had sent the butler out of the kitchen with the silver coffee pot empty. It was soon rectified!

There was always something going on, the front doorbell never stopped ringing. There were guests for lunch or large dinner parties, the children's friends for tea, and busy weekends. I would start the day by cooking breakfast, then return to the house after shopping to prepare lunch for everyone. Then I would clean the kitchen and the pots and pans, before leaving for a rest in the afternoon, ready to begin again in the evening.

The evening menus always consisted of three courses such as chicken liver pâté, followed by sole fillets stuffed with smoked salmon or farmhouse chicken with mushrooms, and maybe finished with a cold lemon soufflé with crystallised tangerine. The host would get very upset if the meals were not absolutely right. I could never make or suggest serving ice cream for a dinner party; he would tell me that it spoiled the palate. On one occasion he came shouting into the kitchen to reprimand me. I should have served black-cherry conserve with rice pudding and I forgot to buy it. On another occasion he was so infuriated that he was kicking the vegetable baskets in front of me. I was scared! But I knew that certain things didn't always go the way we wanted them to. I knew this was rude and unprofessional of my employer, and, on one occasion, I was amazed at his attitude; but, on reflection now, I believe it was good for me. I paid more attention and made better use of my abilities because I knew what would have happened if the meal was not of the highest standard.

One year, at around Christmas time, he had just returned home and still wearing his heavy winter coat he came to see me. He appeared at the kitchen door and not looking at all pleased he barked at me, "Chef, I will kill you!"

"Why, sir?" I replied, feeling a bit frightened and wondering what I had done.

"You have left the kitchen door wide open and the smell is all over the house. Please don't do it any more."

I did not feel I should tell him that it was not my fault. George had left it open! As usual, the butler did it!

I had just finished stuffing two turkeys for the next day – one for the family and their guests and another for us staff. I must say his idea was very clever. On Christmas day, while they were eating the goose-liver pâté bought from Harrods (one of his favourite dishes), I was carving their turkey ready to be served. Beforehand I had dressed our turkey, whole with all the trimmings and holly leaves on a silver tray. Then the butler would swiftly lift the tray up and take it into the dining room to show this beautiful presentation to their guests – a succulent roasted bird. And – a delightful noise to my ears – they would shout at the top of their voices, "Ooh!" and "Ah!" It was the pièce de résistance.

He was a gourmet and he really gave me a good opportunity to develop my own skills and dishes at an early stage in my career – his criticism actually made a better chef out of me. He was a good person and was very generous when I left to get married.

One story I want to mention is that in spite of his demands he was also a fair man and, as I have said, George was an excellent butler. However, George had a drink problem and was a gambler. He loved the horses and studied form every day. It was always great when he won as he would bring us lovely gifts from his winnings. However, one evening when George had a night off my employer went to the bar. This bar was in a small room on the ground floor and alongside one of the walls were row upon row of vodka bottles slotted into racks that had been specially made. First he opened one bottle, then another, then a few more and he discovered they had all been opened and put back filled with water. Oh dear! George was in trouble. The next day George admitted what he had done and nothing more was ever said.

THIS IS WHAT THE WORLD ... THINKS OF ME

Pino is the epitome of a family man; family well being first and cooking comes second or are the two inextricably linked? He is also an artist who enhances life with his dedication to cooking and painting. What more can you expect from a great Italian Maestro? It has been a privilege for me to have one of his paintings hanging in my home and to have marvelled at his cooking prowess.

Pino is a man of great passion whose courage is boundless and my family and I are passionate in our high regard of a truly remarkable and much loved friend and relative.

Anthea Jones, Swansea

Pino, a highly talented chef in all aspects of culinary cuisine who has enriched our lives and that of our family with his courage, strength and friendship.

David and Pat Owen, Birdingbury

Caroline and I worked together at The Royal Academy of Dancing and have always been great friends. One evening we went to a champagne reception at a club off Kensington High Street and so together we met Pino the first time. Through the years I have known Pino he is a warm hearted and generous man and not only a superb chef also a perfectionist. When I married Dieter he made our wedding cake and last year he made the wedding cake for my son, Han Lee and my daughter in law Nicky.

Kim Paech, Curacao, N.A.

BURRO CHIARIFICATO
CLARIFIED BUTTER

Heat the butter gently until it melts and all the bubbling stops. Remove the pan from the heat and let it stand until the salt has sunk to the bottom. Carefully pour the fat through a sieve and pour over the terrine. Clarified butter is often used specifically in a dish for frying food – it will prevent burning when frying at high heat.

TERRINA DI FEGATINI DI POLLO
CHICKEN LIVER PÂTÉ

This is a lovely and tasty terrine de campagna that is ideal as a starter, buffet or for picnics.

600g/1¼lb chicken livers
½ tsp of salt
10 rounds of freshly ground black pepper
2 sprigs thyme, stalks removed
2 tbsp red wine
2 tbsp brandy
284ml/½ pint double cream
50g/2oz melted butter
1 bay leaf
250g/9oz clarified butter (see page 132)

You will need a 1.100 litre/2 pint round soufflé dish.
Roasting tin for bain-marie

Clean the livers, cut out the veins and rinse under running water. Dry with kitchen paper. Blend the livers in an electric blender and sieve them to give a smooth consistency. Add the rest of the ingredients, mix well and then poor into a soufflé dish. Place the bay leaf in the centre, on top of the terrine. Cover with foil, but pierce the top to allow the steam to escape. Place the dish in a deep baking tray over a piece of cardboard and pour boiling water into the tray until it is three-quarters of the way up the side of the dish and bake. Make sure that the water does not boil. Leave to cool and seal with clarified butter.

Serves: 6–8
Preparation: 15 minutes
Cooking: 25–30 minutes
Oven: 130°C/275°F/Gas ½

Chef's note: After several trials, I have found the perfect terrine – it does not require sophisticated livers, it is not too expensive, it is easy to prepare and gives a good result. It is smooth, light and rose coloured, and can be used spooned onto plates by dipping a spoon in hot water. Decorate with a little green salad and serve with buttered slices of toasted granary bread.

SOUFFLÉ FREDDO AL LIMONE E MANDARINI CRISTALLIZATI
COLD LEMON SOUFFLÉ WITH CRYSTALISED TANGERINE

This is a very attractive sweet with a light and refreshing taste.

150g/5oz caster sugar
6 large free-range eggs, at room temperature, separated
4 large lemons
5 leaves of gelatine, soaked in cold water or ¼oz gelatine powder
300ml/½ pint double cream lightly whipped
60ml/2fl oz milk

To decorate:
150ml/5fl oz whipped cream
3 tangerines
200g/7oz sugar
100ml/3fl oz water
Some toothpicks

You will need a 1.100 litre/2 pint soufflé dish.

Tie a double fold of greaseproof paper around the soufflé dish so it comes up to 5–7cm/2–3in above the dish. Secure with sticky tape or string. Grease the inside of the collar paper with a little olive oil. With an electric beater, whip the double cream and keep aside in the fridge. Whisk the egg yolks, sugar, one egg white and lemon rinds until the mixture is light and pale straw in colour. Pour into a fairly large bowl.

Drain the water from the gelatine and melt over a low heat. If using gelatine powder, dissolve in 100ml/4fl oz cold water in a bowl placed over a pan of simmering water. Add to the lemon custard once it has melted and is clear, and stir with a whisk. Whisk the egg whites, not too stiff, and keep aside. Add the whipped cream with a rubber spoon, then the egg whites and fold together gently. Pour into the soufflé dish and leave to set for 3–4 hours or leave overnight.

To decorate: Peel the tangerines, remove the white pith and insert the toothpicks carefully into the segments, ensuring that the juice does not spill out. Pour a little oil over some silver foil.

Melt the sugar and water to form a light caramel. Dip the pan in cold water to cool the caramel, reheat gently by stirring with a wooden spoon. Dip the tangerines into this before placing on the oiled foil to set. Decorate the mousse with piped cream and these crystallized tangerines.

Serves: 6 or more
Preparation: 30 minutes

Chef's note: The lemons can be replaced with oranges or limes for a nice, tangy taste.

SOUFFLÉ AL FORMAGGIO
CHEESE SOUFFLÉ

The Ambassador, Dr Tötterman, loved soufflé and often I would make this favourite cheese soufflé.

90g/3oz butter
90g/3oz plain flour
400ml/12 fl oz milk
60g/2oz fresh Parmesan cheese, grated
60g/2oz Gruyere or cheddar cheese
A good pinch grated nutmeg
Salt
Freshly ground black pepper
5 egg yolks, eggs size 4
7 egg whites
4 tbsp fresh breadcrumbs

Soufflé: Butter the sides and base of a 1 litre/2 pints soufflé dish and sprinkle with breadcrumbs, shaking off the excess.

Melt down the butter, mix in the flour, and cook for 1–2 minutes. Add the milk and bring to the boil. Add the nutmeg, salt and pepper. Simmer for 2–3 minutes, stirring with a wooden spoon and whisking to ensure that the mixture is smooth. Add the two cheeses and mix well. Taste and adjust the seasoning. Add the egg yolks one at a time, making sure that you stir well. A little cold milk can be added if the mixture is too stiff.

Beat the egg whites with a pinch of salt until they are firm, but not too stiff. Fold one third into the mixture stir well. Then add the remainder by folding gently and pour into the prepared soufflé dish. Bake for 40-45 minutes.

Serves: 6
Preparation: 20 minutes
Cooking: 35-40 minutes
Oven: 200°C/400°F/Gas 6

Chefs note: The cheese soufflé is perhaps the best-known dish of classic French Cuisine. The variations are simple. Follow the recipe above and change the flavour if you prefer. For a ham soufflé – add 250g/9oz. Prawns – add 100g/4oz. Chicken – add 250g/9oz, cut up into small pieces. Spinach – 200g/7oz blanched. Watercress – 2 bunches. Sorrel – a handful, all chopped. Asparagus – 250g/9oz cut up. Vermicelli 100g/4oz. Try and be adventurous with these soufflés. You can serve this soufflé also in 6 small ramekins dishes of about 8cm/3 in diameter and 4cm/2½ in deep.

INSALATA RUSSA CON TONNO
RUSSIAN SALAD WITH TUNA

1 can tuna fish in olive oil, drained
1 tbsp white wine vinegar
110g/4oz french beans
3 medium potatoes
3 medium carrots
60g/2oz frozen peas, thawed
2 small gherkins in vinegar, cut up
3 tbsp olive oil
Salt
Freshly ground black pepper
400ml/12fl oz of mayonnaise

Snap the ends off the French beans, rinse them and drop them into boiling salted water. Cook for about 8–10 minutes. Drain and refresh under cold running water and keep to one side.

Rinse the potatoes and boil them with the peel on until they are easily pierced with a fork. Drain and peel them whilst they are still hot. Peel the carrots and drop them in boiling salted water. Do not overcook. Drain and set aside. Cook the peas in boiling salted water and cook briefly, not more than 2 minutes. Drain and set aside. Cut the green beans into pieces 9mm/⅜in long; the potatoes and carrots diced into 9mm/⅜in cubes. The peas, of course, stay whole. Put all the ingredients, including the tuna and the cut-up gherkins into a mixing bowl. Season with olive oil, wine vinegar and salt. Add 250ml/½ pint of the mayonnaise and mix thoroughly. Turn the mixture onto a shallow serving dish and spread with the remaining mayonnaise, decorate with a few flat parsley leaves and serve.

Serves: 6
Preparation: 30 minutes
Cooking: 20 minutes

Chef's note: If you wish, you can serve this delicious salad with an antipasto of assorted salamis, olives and hard-boiled eggs on individual plates, or serve by filling tomatoes with the Russian salad. One of our family favourites in the summer!

IL MIO MATRIMONIO
MY MARRIAGE TO CAROLINE

Questo é amore
That's amore

On a previous occasion I had met Charlotte and Edward Iglehart, my future sister- and brother-in-law at Caroline's birthday party – the first that we had spent together. They were both friendly and charming.

Ed, as he is known, is six foot four and a little bit more, American (from Florida) with a lean and robust body. I have a much smaller frame. We got on well and we felt comfortable in each other's company. I had been in England for four years, and I was recounting my life journey. He told me that he had majored in English, chemistry and physics and was a postgraduate in human ecology. Culturally he is a Virginian, but he was born in Maryland, and raised in Canada and Florida. He is a lineal descendant of George Washington and a direct descendant of Pocahontas and Ed's great-grandmother was named after her.

He had met Charlotte in Greenwich Village in New York at Washington Square in the sixties.

The first visit in England after they married, Ed fell in love with this country and they both eventually moved to Scotland to be very close to nature. He set up a workshop as a glass-blower, creating some beautiful artwork in the form of beautiful glasses, coloured glass bottles, mushrooms, and oil lamps. He opened his own gallery and became very well known in his new adoptive country, and through exhibitions and other art galleries too. We have been very fond of each other since our very first meeting. He sees me as the hero of our family. The sad thing is, I have never visited his birthplace and he has never visited mine. I suppose we never thought to see each other's origins and family roots with our own eyes.

My sister-in-law, Charlotte, a fun-loving person with a huge personality, welcomed me into the family bosom. She is a kind and caring lady, always interested in what I am doing and wanting to know about myself. She encouraged me to paint and to continue with my hobbies. She is a lover of museums, the arts and beautiful things. In her teens she studied French at the famous Sorbonne University in Paris and discovered the Impressionist painters. Her favourite is Gaugin. She loves Scotland and lives in a lovely home with a magnificent view. Through the years she has made many friends. She is well respected in the community and is the local JP. They have two children, Tom and Annabel.

I had known Caroline for over four years, and it was time to meet my future mother-in-law, Blodwen Thomas. I had spoken with her many times when Caroline was living in New York and after I had spoken with Caroline in New York I would then ring her mother to send any messages and also to share my joy that it was time that Caroline should be coming home.

So one Saturday early in November 1974 I bought a bottle of brandy and some flowers, and I made a gorgeous chocolate gateau. On the Sunday morning Caroline and I left London and we travelled on the M1 for Dunchurch. It was a very cold day – the one day when I wanted everything to be perfect.

I was introduced and then I was warmly embraced by Caroline's mother. She smiled and looked calm. She had a warm personality and I felt very pleased to have met her. She made me feel very welcome in her home – a 14th-century old forge with a thatched roof. There was beautiful old family furniture, family paintings hung on the walls, and other objects which she loved to collect. I sat in the drawing room, where I believe the blacksmith would have worked. It was a beautiful cosy room, warmed by a fire that was in the centre of the room, full of charm. A fabulous Bechstein grand piano stood next to the window overlooking the village square.

She loved her garden. It had a well-kept lawn and an apple tree, a damson tree and a delicious Victoria plum tree. She grew many roses and always had an eye for beautiful flowers. At the top of the garden was a beautiful summer house, which was a little haven; and during the summer we would have tea there and sit amongst all these beautiful borders of sweet-smelling flowers. It was a wonderful English country garden. But her greatest passions were her music, the theatre, and books. She was a good cook, and was already in those days into herbs, garlic and the Mediterranean cuisine.

On that day she couldn't resist playing the piano. She played 'Back to Sorrento' for me and wanted me to stand next to her and sing with her. We had a lovely lunch followed a bit later by tea; and my presents were a big hit. I asked for Caroline's hand, and from that moment onwards I was accepted into the family.

She wanted to know all about my family in Italy and especially about my mother. Gesticulating like an Italian, I was trying my best to describe her, her shape and height. I recounted the family history. It was a pity that I didn't think to take some photographs to show. She was a lovely person, very kind, and she loved the simple things in life. I couldn't have wished for a better mother-in-law.

The following year, 1975, Caroline and I made our wedding plans. We got engaged on 14 February and we were to get married on 19 July. I always wanted to marry Caroline, so it was like a dream come true. On 14 February, on St Valentine's Day, our engagement was announced in the *Telegraph*. We celebrated our engagement with a candlelit dinner for the two of us at a well-known Italian restaurant in London, called La Concordia Notte. I recall the menu and it was such a wonderful evening. We had lobster cocktail followed by chateaubriand with Béarnaise sauce and then a wonderful chocolate mousse.

That Easter I took Caroline to visit my family in Rosello. We flew to Rome and were met by Papa and we then took a coach to the village. It was a very happy time for us both and Caroline straight away called my parents Mamma and Papa. They loved her very much and there was a lot of smiling. That was it – Caroline did not speak Italian and none of the family spoke English. It is still the same to this day but we have always loved our journeys back to Rosello, especially when Mamma was alive. On that first meeting Caroline met Savina, my sister, and her husband, Edmondo, who worked for the forestry commission. They had two children, Mario and Milena, and later on had another son, Andrea. Then came Lucio, who was working by this time in Rome, also as a chef. Then came Giovanna, who was married to Francesco, also in the forestry commission. They had two daughters, Anna and Paula. Finally came my youngest brother, Mario, who was fourteen at the time. He too is now a very good chef and he eventually married Franca. Their gorgeous son, Jacopo, is the second Iacaruso after our son, Edilio.

My memories of my brothers and my sisters go back to our childhood. I left home when I was too young. We all missed my teenage years of talking and discussing our future perhaps while we were sitting in our kitchen, around a fireplace with a roaring fire. We never talked about what we would like to do in our lives, which university we would like to go to and in what profession we would like to be. In our house there was never this type of talk because none of us liked to study, although there was the possibility to do so. And we have all flown the nest in different directions.

I was the first to go to Rome, as you have read earlier. Years later my sister Savina took a course in dressmaking and qualified. She has a warm personality and is a loving sister. She got married fairly young to the man she loved and they are still together after thirty-eight years. Savina left the village too and moved away where her husband Edmondo Chicarella had been posted, as a forestry commissioner in different towns through his career. She has a lovely family and a beautiful home with a long balcony, which is a suntrap with baskets of hanging geraniums. She is a great cook, and passionate about food, which she has learnt about from our mother. Sunday without a dish of fresh home-made pasta or gnocchi is like a day without sun!

A few years back in the hottest month of August, Edilio and I went to visit her and the family. It was a big get-together where they live at a village called Santa Maria in Imbaro, not far from the Adriatic Sea. No less than two types of home-made pasta – ravioli and tagliatelle – with tomato sauce were made a few hours earlier, and were placed on the table. Wine from her daughter-in-law, whose father had a good wine cellar, accompanied the meal. This was followed by meat, grilled aubergine, salad and fresh fruit. She went to all that trouble to welcome us and to make it a memorable day.

Lucio finished school and went into the kitchen. A calm and quiet man, he was very strong in his younger days. His first job took him as far as the north of Italy, where a relation of ours, Salvatore, found him work in a restaurant. Then he went to work in Milan, in the busiest restaurant in the luxurious Galleria Vittorio Emanuele. It was a hard workplace with long hours. Eventually he went to Rome and worked at the Dutch Embassy. He was called to the army where he spent fifteen months working in the soldiers *Mensa*. The Dutch Ambassador sent him a gift to buy himself a drink. Eventually he settled in Rome, the city he always loved.

One of his favourite jobs was to work at Harry's Bar in Via Veneto. In the late nineties he became ill with non-Hodgkin disease. He felt very sad when he had to give up his hotel job, which he so much loved. He hoped that one day he would be well enough to return to Rome, but sadly it has not happened. Now he lives at home with our father. He misses Rome very much. Life has not been so kind to him, but Lucio is a good man. He has always been shy and was our mother's favourite son. He has never married.

My youngest sister, Giovanna, after finishing school also took a course in dressmaking. She also lived at home with our mother and grandmother, whom she has taken after. She is slim and quick on her feet with a good sense of humour. She got engaged quite young and married in 1972. She left our home and has lived in a village called Tocco da Casauria near the town of Sulmona ever since, and loves the place. She and her husband, Francesco D'Amico, also in the forestry commission, have built a wonderful villa with all comforts and marble floors. The panoramic view from the balcony is magnificent, overlooking open fields and silvery olive trees, with the most breathtaking wooded mountains beyond. You could almost be in Switzerland. They have two lovely daughters. Giovanna is a natural cook without a diploma; she has a big passion for creativity and can turn her hand to anything.

My younger brother, Mario, has spent more time at school than the rest of us. He stayed three years longer. But Mario couldn't resist our family vocation; he too ended up in the kitchen and has worked with good chefs. He also worked at the Belgian Embassy, which I mentioned earlier.

He was also called into the army, where he too spent a year cooking. He was posted to the town of Avellino, in Southern Italy. When the town suffered a massive earthquake, they felt the tremor in Rosello. Thank God he was on leave, otherwise our mother would have died of fright. He is happily married to an attractive Roman girl, with a slim figure and dark hair. They have a beautiful little son. They live in a lovely apartment near Rome, which they have bought; and when we go home our first Italian meal is at their house. They are a very hospitable and generous couple! Mario is a quiet and gentle person with a very good heart, and he resembles our mother. He is a wonderful chef and has been in charge of *Mensa* and cooked for hundreds of people a day. I like his food very much. It is always fresh and tasty, and he knows how to make good use of the lovely colours of the Mediterranean ingredients blessed by the sunshine.

We see one another only when I go back home, which is once a year. We kiss, we talk, we eat and we exchange news. Not once have we fallen out with one another. We now grow older together and not a day goes by without my having them in my thoughts. I love them all.

Caroline also met Nonna, my paternal grandmother; my aunt Concettina, an affectionate lady with her vegetable garden; Concettina's daughter, my first cousin Lucia; and my Uncle Luigi, whom I liked very much for his sweet soft smile and amiable ways.

Luigi's thick black hair was always swept back and in the winter months he always used to wear a French beret. On entering the house he would lift up his right hand to his forehead, and swiftly he would remove his beret without having his hair spoilt. He too is a great chef. He worked in his youth for the *grandi signori* of Italy. He was on leave, and still working with the Italian Navy as a chef for the *Mensa* officers. Caroline also met his wife, Alba, a tall and lovely friendly woman with black curly hair and their daughters, Maria and Berta. My Aunt Alba never travelled away from Rosello, always waiting for her husband to return home.

My Uncle Domenico's wife, Anita, was on a visit from their home in Argentina. Caroline was very attached to Zia Anita because of her elegance and lovely manner. She has always admired this lady who has had a tragic life, losing her husband and only son, Nicolino, just a short while ago.

After our Easter break in Rosello, Caroline went home to talk to Dorethia Miller, the vicar's wife, to enquire what were the possibilities of a quiet wedding. When her mother asked when the wedding was going to take place, on that same day she made the wedding list of more than 250 people! And that did not include the Italians! Things had to be organised – invitations, wedding dress, food and drinks and so on.

I also wanted to meet more of Caroline's family, especially Nuna and Uncle Tom Beresford. They were retired and lived on a small farm called Bloomfield, in Mid Glamorgan, South Wales. They had no children. Nuna was my future mother-in-law's sister, and she was the matriarch of the family. She and Uncle Tom treated Caroline, Charlotte and John as if they were their own children. They were both very much loved by Caroline and it was decided that Uncle Tom would give Caroline away at our wedding. In fact this was with very short notice as John had been going to give his sister away and Renato was to be my best man. All I can say is that Uncle Tom, the day before the wedding, plucked up courage and wanted to give Caroline away, so my future brother-in-law, John, was my best man.

We then met many members of the family over the next few days. Aunty Dolly, Uncle Wyndham and their son Gareth gave us a wonderful welcome, but sadly they could not come to our wedding. Another cousin, Girlie, was married to an Italian called Dominic and they had three lovely girls. I later found out that Nuna had called Girlie to enquire about Caroline's marriage to me, being yet another Italian joining the family. When we found this out we laughed because we know what a happy marriage they have. They have several grandchildren now. Then we met Aunty Kate, who came to the wedding with her son, who is a doctor, Gwyn, and his wife, Anthea. They also had two children, Charlotte and Edward. Then there was Aunty Maud who was mother to Mary and Owen, who lived at a lovely farm at St Mary Hill. Also we met Aunty Dilys and her children Blair and Primrose, both married with children.

Finally we met Caroline's godparents, Dorethie and Godfrey Lewis from Wenvoe. Her godfather was asked to make a speech at our wedding.

For the wedding cake, I borrowed the baking tins from the head chef, Bruno De Lucia, who worked at the Dutch Embassy. He remains a great friend to this day and a wonderful chef. The cake was made and baked at the Australian High Commission with Tony Ricci, another fine chef and close friend, who worked there at the time. Renato, who was working at Kensington Palace with Princess Margaret, helped us too. Eventually the five baked fruit cakes found their way to Kensington Palace, where Renato and I iced them. Princess Margaret came to see our five-tiered wedding cake and met Caroline when she came to collect them in her car.

Caroline and I left London at the end of June 1975 to prepare for our wedding. We stayed with my future mother-in-law and she and Caroline decided to visit Wales to collect the wedding dress and visit relations.

I was left in charge of The Old Forge, and I had strict instructions to keep the garden well watered so that it would look wonderful for the wedding day. I was at pains to water everything and was told to count to ten slowly at each stop. My patience was running out but I did what I was told and it was really worth it. The garden looked fabulous and now I realise that I must tend my own garden so very carefully too.

The day was drawing nearer and I went to Heathrow to collect my parents, and my brothers Lucio and Mario. I remember asking my mother what she thought of the flight. She calmly replied, it is like a coach with wings – it takes off! They spent the first night in London and we travelled down to Dunchurch.

The next day the preparation for the wedding breakfast began with my parents, Lucio and myself. Mario was too young to help. We had already made preparations for the wedding to take place at St Peter's Church in Dunchurch and the reception was to be held at Bilton Grange School in the hall. Caroline's mother had wanted to decorate the church with flowers, and she had asked her friends to help, headed by a dear friend, Edna Treen.

It was a wonderful venue and we were very privileged to be able to have the use of it. Charlotte and Caroline had both attended Homefield School, the sister school to Bilton Grange and my mother-in-law was always on good terms with both of the schools.

Caroline had several friends headed by Pearly Gates, who were to do the waitressing on the day. The wedding was to be a complete family affair and 300 people attended the reception. The food was a fabulous display and Julia (Cheetham), a dear family friend, prepared the lovely flower displays. I had made a huge sugar-paste swan and I have pictures of the flowers that Julia decorated it with. We took the wedding cake the day before to the hall, and I thought to myself, 'I may as well assemble it; it is going to be one thing less to worry about.' Sure enough, we celebrated the night before with a big family dinner party at the Dun Cow.

It was a sunny morning on my wedding day and, whilst I was getting dressed – as they say bad news travel fast! – somebody said to me that the fourth and fifth tiers of the wedding cake had toppled over and had rolled over as if they were wheels. They ended up on the other side of the room and it was quite a job finding them. Renato was now in the hall repairing and reassembling the cakes. A door had been left open and a cat had jumped up on the cake knocking those top tiers off. I believe the cat ran away and was never seen again. The poor thing had quite a shock.

My legs went like jelly. I was more concerned about the wedding cake than my own wedding and the ceremony that was going to take place in a couple of hours' time. I was feeling sorry for Caroline. Our magnificent wedding cake ruined! All I can remember was when Caroline joined me at the alter I turned to her and said that the cake had collapsed. I don't think she understood me, which was just as well, but I was quite preoccupied. However, Renato made a wonderful job of repairing it.

We had a most beautiful service conducted by Reverend Ian Miller. The church pews were packed. Afterwards, we celebrated that special day in our life with the most joyous atmosphere, a wonderful buffet and drinks amongst our dearest family and friends. Many people travelled a long way.

In the evening many friends and family continued the party at The Old Forge and finally Mr and Mrs Iacaruso spent their honeymoon night at the Welcombe Hotel in Stratford. The following morning we arrived back in Dunchurch as my mother-in-law had arranged a wonderful lunch for all the families. There were about twenty-five people present and it seemed that the celebrations went on for quite a few days.

Caroline and I had no plans for our future at all. We thought it would be lovely to take a long honeymoon and we were thinking eventually of heading for New York, where we thought we would make our fortunes!

So we travelled to London with my parents and brothers and, after a few days, saw them off at the airport. We had an open railway ticket between London and Rome and we set off for Paris. I loved Paris and we spent lovely days visiting all the famous galleries. I remember that we went to various delicatessens and bought pâté, a bottle of red wine and French bread to have a typical picnic by the Seine.

Our next stop was Switzerland – the beautiful and historical town of Lausanne where I had worked many years before at the Nyffeneger patisserie. Lausanne is built on a hill, with winding streets to reach the top of the town and the large busy main square, surrounded by many beautiful jewellery, clock and watch shops. The old Catholic church at the far end dominates the view of the square, and gives it its name – Place St François (Saint Francis' Square). I took Caroline to show her where I had spent my younger years and where I had learned my skill in the patisserie. I met an old friend of mine, Peppino, who still lived there, and I introduced him to Caroline.

Going on a tour of Lake Lausanne was wonderful. It was a glorious and sunny day. The boat was going slow, with calm waters while we were admiring the view of those pretty chalets amongst the hills and small picturesque villages so near the lake. It was so romantic!

The morning we left we had fresh croissants with apricot jam (my favourite jam) with fresh coffee.

Our next stop was Milan, Europe's fashion capital. The moment we stepped out from the Central Railway Station, all eyes were on Caroline. Do you remember those light casual long dresses that the young were wearing in the sixties and early seventies – almost in the hippy times? Caroline loved those long dresses that were not only cool but very comfortable. Well, in Milan, in July 1975, Caroline could not even walk the streets. It was totally the wrong dress to wear and not fashionable. I heard one girl saying that she was wearing an evening gown! Can you imagine? We were both feeling so out of place and so embarrassed that we went to a store to buy a knee-length dress in desperation. Then we went to the Galleria Vittorio Emanuele, in the most beautiful part of Milan, and we went to my favourite restaurant and indulged ourselves with the fabulous coffee and the ice cream. I lost count how many scoops we had.

The next stop was Rome, and there we met up with my father. We went to the navy *Mensa* where he worked. He was in complete charge and well respected. They catered for about 300 officers a day. We met all his navy staff, who worked in the kitchen with him – usually about fourteen at a time – and we were taken to his office. Then a wonderful lunch was brought to us, the same as the officers would be having. Over the years when we went to Rome to travel on to Rosello we would stop for a lunch with Papa, and I have many memories of this.

This first time, though, Papa was coming back to Rosello with us as I was presenting my bride to our family and friends, and my parents had sent out invitations for a huge party that was to be held in our house in Rosello.

When we arrived in Rosello the party was about to begin. About 160 people arrived, and Caroline and I greeted every one at the door. As the guests arrived most of them handed me and Caroline an envelope. We were wondering why, and then my mother came and told us that everyone wanted to buy us a wedding present but she had suggested that a gift of money would be very welcome as we would not be able to take all the presents back to England. Even so, we had four irons, three sets of coffee cups and a few sets of scales for the kitchen, which we had little room to take back with us. We had about three or four weeks in Rosello, enjoying my family and friends and lovely walks in the woods.

From Rosello we returned to Rome and then made our way to Florence. It was already the end of August and we spent about a week in Florence. We loved the city and went to visit all the galleries and saw all the sights to be seen. Everywhere we turned we saw beauty and we were very happy at our choice to see this wonderful city.

Towards the end of the week we went to see the Duomo (Santa Maria del Fiore) and climbed up into the first part. Both of us were waiting our turn to go up into the cupola, when an American tourist who was climbing down looked at Caroline and told her that she should not go up any further in her condition. We had no idea what she meant – maybe Caroline's face was red, but I went up on my own and thought nothing more.

We then made our way back to England, stopping off in Dunchurch to see my mother-in-law and also to open more presents that had arrived. Charlotte and Ed had invited us to stay at North Glen, their home in Scotland, and so we drove up there to continue this long holiday. We loved our time there. Kirkcudbrightshire is a lovely area. Char and Ed had moved to Scotland after they left America and settled down there with their son, Tom. They were living close to Hal and Julia Cheetham and my mother-in-law's dearest friend, Kath McGregor, who was

Julia's mother. They were great friends of the family going back many years.

Up to the time of our marriage, Caroline had been working at The Rutland Court Hotel in Chelsea for a wonderful gentleman called John Wilson. Over the past seven years Caroline had been working a lot at this hotel, but also doing a lot of travelling; and sadly she had also been in and out of hospital on several occasions. She had been advised at one point to give up hotel management, which had been a shock as that was her training, but her seventy hours a week was not doing her health any good. So I was lucky that when I first met her she was at the Royal Academy of Dancing. We were still in Scotland when John Wilson rang to say that his secretary had left him very suddenly and would Caroline please come and help him in the office and he would give us a room in the hotel. John Wilson was very ill at this time and without further ado we returned to London. We had no further idea when we were going to leave for America. We were in no hurry. We settled in the hotel, and during this time I helped out in the kitchen there.

One morning Caroline had been saying that somehow she felt something was not quite right so she took a sample to the chemist in Sloane Street. Charlotte was staying a few days with us in London and that evening we all met up at the hotel and Caroline rushed in with her news. We did not know whether to laugh or cry but we were so excited – in fact, more speechless than anything. Caroline was pregnant! A honeymoon baby! No wonder the lady told her to turn back from climbing up into the cupola at the Duomo in Florence. When I had married Caroline she had been told that she would not be able to have children. Caroline had a son, David Thomas, who was born in April 1967. His name was changed to Anthony and sadly he was adopted. Caroline's health suffered to such an extent that illness followed illness and finally the doctors told her that it was not possible for her to have any more children. It was her cross to bear. In those times it was very different from today.

As I was the eldest son, Caroline had told me to tell my parents there would be no grandchildren. I never told them and they and both families and friends were overjoyed at our news. Our doctor at this time was the well-known Dr Ronnie Williams of Sloane Street, who was known to bike all over his area to see his patients. In fact, one of the Sunday magazines wrote an article about him. He notified the consultant who had looked after Caroline for many years that Caroline was pregnant and the answer he got was to tell Caroline to "Call the baby Miracle." It meant that plans to go to America were firmly cancelled. Now we had to make our plans for our future to include a baby!

We were still living in the hotel and so we started to look for a flat. We scoured the papers and all of the advertisements were saying 'no pets, no children'. We eventually found a lovely first-floor flat on the Sheen Road in Richmond. It was September. Miss Thorne interviewed us and thirty-five other couples and she chose us. We moved in and I found a job soon after.

I remember our first Christmas was spent at The Old Forge in Dunchurch. It was a happy time, but Caroline would finish work in the spring and I would have to find a permanent position to take on my responsibilities.

THIS IS WHAT THE WORLD . . . THINKS OF ME

I first met Pino through our respective business's when he moved to Harbury with Caroline and Edilio. I soon discovered what a fantastic chef Pino is.

The Pino I know is a kind hardworking man who loves his work, and it shows. A happy family man, who has many talents including watercolour painting and gardening. He loves nature, and delights in welcoming all into his garden during the annual village open garden weekend. This is one occasion where his sense of humour shines through, with him adding lemons and peaches to his trees as if they had actually grown here!

His courage, positive attitude and openness with his cancer has been an inspiration to us all. I am indeed lucky to know and call Pino a true friend.

Mary Muglestone, Harbury

I have been fortunate in having Pino and Caroline as very good friends for the past 16 years. Pino is one of those people, who made a great success of his life despite serious obstacles. Initially, he did this simply by creating wonderful food, which has given great pleasure to a lot of people. Pino is an exceptional chef, who has won much acclaim. About 11 years ago, he had facial cancer and now part of his face has been rebuilt. Faced with that sort of adversity, most people would go into decline; but not so Pino. He has remained cheerful and gets on with life. In fact he has done more than that; he has raised a lot of money for charity and written two books.

A year last Christmas, we were unable to persuade him that his recovery from his latest operation was much more important than the food he was going to cook for us; so you can see what an unselfish perfectionist he is!

John Ormond, Santon, Isle of Man

POMODORI RIPIENI CON RISO E BASILICO
VINE TOMATOES WITH RICE AND BASIL

6 vine tomatoes
60g/2oz cooked risotto rice
1 small spring onion, finely chopped
1 clove garlic, finely chopped
6 large leaves sweet basil, shredded
1 tbsp olive oil
½ tsp salt
A few rounds black pepper
½ glass cold water
6 whole basil leaves
2 tbsp olive oil

Choose medium-sized, firm tomatoes and cut the tops off them all. Keep the tops to one side, so they can be replaced later. Gently remove the flesh over a kitchen bowl, with a melon baller or a small teaspoon to retain the shape of the tomatoes.

Meanwhile, boil the rice for 15 minutes in plenty of water. Then strain and cool under cold running water, and put into a bowl. Strain the water from the tomatoes, chop the flesh roughly and add to the cooked rice with the spring onion, the garlic, basil leaves, olive oil and salt and pepper. Mix all the ingredients well.

Fill the tomatoes using a tablespoon, replace the tops, add a little seasoning and bake in an earthenware dish with the water, sweet basil, and olive oil. Serve on individual plates with 2–3 tbsp stock and a basil leaf on the top.

Serves: 6
Preparation: 20 minutes
Cooking: 20–25 minutes
Oven: 200°C/400°F/Gas 6

Chef's note: Serve warm. If cooked before it is better to reheat it. This recipe is only enough to be an accompaniment to a main course. You can double this recipe to make twelve tomatoes or six large beef tomatoes, to serve as a starter.

ARROSTO DI CAPRIOLO CON SALSA DI CIOCCOLATO
ROAST VENISON WITH CHOCOLATE SAUCE

Shoulder, haunch and saddle of venison are large joints, which are suitable for roasting after marinating. For wild or farmed venison follow the same method.

1 haunch of venison weighing 2kg/4lb
4 slices of back bacon, to cover the meat
Salt and freshly ground black pepper
2 tbsp cooking oil
A few venison bones, for the stock

Marinade:
1 bottle of red wine
1 medium onion, chopped
1 carrot, peeled and diced
1 celery stalk, washed and diced
1 clove garlic, unpeeled and crushed
1 bay leaf
5 juniper berries, crushed
1 teaspoon black peppercorns, crushed

The sauce:
Wine from the marinade
4 tbsp cooking oil
Vegetable marinade
4 tbsp red wine vinegar
600ml/1 pint stock
100g/4oz bitter chocolate
2 tbsp whipping cream
A pinch of cinnamon
Salt and pepper

The roux: to thicken the sauce
60g/2oz butter at room temperature mixed with
60g/2oz plain flour

Order the haunch of venison. Ask the butcher to prepare the meat and the bones for you. The marinade must be made one day in advance. In a stainless steel basin put the venison meat, add the diced vegetables and the spices, pour over the wine, cover with cling film and refrigerate for 24 hours.

Lift the meat out from the basin and keep it on a dish in the fridge. Strain the marinade through a colander over a bowl and keep the vegetables.

Make the stock: Put the bones in a fairly large saucepan with 1½ litre/3 pints cold water. Add 1 small, chopped onion, ½ celery stick, 1 small, peeled and sliced carrot, a sprig of thyme, a few peppercorns and a little salt. Put the lid on the pan, and simmer the stock over a low heat for 40 minutes. Strain the stock through a fine sieve or muslin.

Make the sauce: Heat the oil in a saucepan, add the vegetables and cook over a low heat for 10 minutes to colour lightly. Add the red wine vinegar and reduce until it has almost completely evaporated. Add the strained marinade, bring to the boil and reduce by half. Add the stock, bring to the boil, skim and simmer for about 20 minutes. Thicken the sauce very lightly with the roux by using a small amount at a time. The sauce must coat the back of a spoon. Add the chocolate, the cream and the cinnamon. Adjust the seasoning and taste (it should already be tasty). Strain through a fine sieve into a large saucepan. The sauce can be made before roasting the meat.

To roast the meat: Preheat the oven. Pat dry the venison haunch and season with salt and pepper. In a medium-sized pan heat 2 tbsp of oil until hot and sear the haunch all over to colour lightly. Cover the meat with the bacon and roast for 1 hour rare, 1¼ hour medium, 1½ hour well done.

Remove, cover with silver foil and leave to rest for a further 10 minutes so the meat can relax before being carved.

Chef's note: To correct the sauce. Depending on the wine used and maturity of the venison the sauce may lack bite or be a little acid. If it is too acid, add some redcurrant jelly or a pinch of caster sugar, if it is too sweet, sharpen with a dash of red wine.

Serve: 6–8 or more
Preparation: 30 minutes
Cooking: 1 hour plus
Oven: 180°C/350°/Gas 5

PATATE GRATINATE
POTATO GRATIN DAUPHINOISE

700g/1½lb potato
300ml/½ pint milk
300ml/½ pint double cream
90g/3oz Gruyère
1 clove garlic
2 sprig of thyme
Salt
Freshly ground black pepper

Peel the potatoes. Slice them ½cm/¼in thick. Bring to the boil the milk and the double cream together with the garlic, thyme, and a little salt and pepper. Add the sliced potatoes and parboil for 7 minutes.

Lift the potatoes out onto an ovenproof dish, pour the liquid over and sprinkle with the Gruyère cheese and bake in a preheated oven for 40 minutes.

Serves: 6
Preparation: 20 minutes
Oven: 180C°/350F°/Gas 4

Chef's note: One of the best types of potato to use for this dish is the Maris Piper.

TERRINA DI FRUTTA D'ESTATE CON GELATINA DI MELONE
REFRESHING SUMMER FRUITS IN MELON JELLY

1 melon (over 500g/1lb 2oz in weight), preferably charentais or ogen
110g/4oz sugar
100ml/3fl oz hot water
2 lemon zests
6 leaves gelatine, soaked in cold water, drained or ½ oz (1 sachet) gelatine powder, soaked in lemon juice
1 small orange
250g/8oz raspberries
250g/8oz strawberries, hulled

Sugar syrup:
8 tbsp hot water
4 tbsp sugar

Cut the melon in half, scoop out the seeds and then cut into 12 boat-shaped pieces. Remove the skin and cut the flesh into small cubes, place in a bowl and add sugar and water. Leave overnight.

By the morning the melon will have had all its juice extracted. Strain the juice and reserve the melon cubes – you will need 500ml/15fl oz of juice, add water if necessary or white wine if you prefer.

Boil the melon juices for 2 minutes with the lemon zest. Add the gelatine leaves or the gelatine powder. Leave to cool until slightly thickened, but not set.

With a potato peeler, make orange zest and cut the orange peel into fine strips without the white pith and boil in plenty of water for 5 minutes. Drain and refresh under cold running water. In a small saucepan make the sugar syrup by boiling for 2 minutes, then add the orange zest and boil for a further 2 minutes. Cool, and then mix with the raspberries in a bowl.

Wet the inside of a terrine and line it with a large piece of cling film.

Place 6 tbsp of the melon jelly at the bottom of the terrine and leave to set. Add the raspberries, and then the melon pieces and strawberries (cut in half if they are large ones). Leave the remaining jelly to thicken a little more before pouring it over the fruit in the terrine. Leave to set overnight in the fridge.

To release the jelly, invert onto a flat board or platter. Peel off the cling film. Cut out with a serrated knife dipped in hot water. Serve with cream – a good way to serve this is to place a slice of the terrine on each plate and decorate with raspberries and a few mint leaves.

Makes: 1kg/2lb 2oz
Serves: 6 or more
Preparation: 45 minutes
Terrine: 1 litre/2 pints

Chef's note: I have chosen strawberries and raspberries for this terrine because I like their flavours and colour. However, you can substitute any fruit you prefer as long as they are not too wet which would prevent the jelly setting properly.

THE FINNISH EMBASSY

Ogni nuvola ha un filo d'argento
Every cloud has a silver lining

In the New Year of 1976 Caroline and I were settled in Richmond, Surrey. Caroline was still at the hotel and I was working near the British Museum for a family when one afternoon the Ambassadress of Finland, Madame Camilla Tötterman, telephoned me to ask me to attend an interview for the position of head chef on the recommendation of Domenico (Mimi). He is also from Rosello and, if you remember, had first brought me to England for the Italian Embassy. He was working at the time as the head chef at the Norwegian Embassy and the Töttermans were old friends of the Ambassador and Ambassadress of Norway.

The following day, Caroline and I went to see the Ambassador, Dr Richard Tötterman, and his wife, Madame Camilla Tötterman, at their residence in Kensington Palace Gardens. The interview turned into a discussion of places and people I had worked for, which seemed to impress them greatly. In turn, they talked about their way of life, their previous diplomatic postings and their Finnish customs. The Ambassador and Madame Tötterman could not have been more charming. I liked them very much from the beginning and I knew we could all work together very well. I was twenty-eight and eager to start work for them.

A few weeks later, on 1 May 1976, I began work at the embassy, feeling very much at home already. I had the run of the kitchen and was in charge of the shopping and organising the menus. I could cook whatever I felt was appropriate, according to the time and season of the year. I remembered wondering to myself years ago, when I was starting out, if one day I would be able to recreate the beautiful dishes that the chef was preparing at the Belgian Embassy in Rome. Now, at last, I was able to do so.

The Töttermans were both gourmets. They enjoyed their food, appreciating everything that was done well. They encouraged me to experiment with new recipes and flavours. During my eight years at the embassy, I catered for the most beautiful parties, cooking for Their Excellencies' friends, other ambassadors and ministers of many nationalities, including many of the Finnish Government and our own British Government, and many people from the arts and the media.

The menu for a party would be planned between Madame Tötterman and myself. We would meet weekly in the morning in her office on the first floor overlooking Kensington Palace Gardens with its residential embassies and private houses on both sides of the road.

Security men in top hats and tails with dark-green uniforms would guard both entrances from Kensington High Street at one end, and Bayswater at the other end. Old maple trees lined the avenue, with their massive floral crowns towards the sky, and the old-fashioned gas lamps gave a charming atmosphere to this avenue. The dense and soft green foliage from the long tree branches stretched out across the embassy entrance. This would shade the first-floor windows, and made the Ambassadress's office cool and slightly dark.

As she sat at her polished desk, with the chair half turned and looking towards me, we talked not only about food but also about books, art and paintings. Madame Tötterman is fluent in German and French and later on took lessons in Italian. She was an expert in paintings of Russian icons. She had a successful exhibition of her paintings in Helsinki.

On one of our usual meetings she told me, "Last night, Pino, the Ambassador and I went to have dinner with our Russian neighbour. What I did find very interesting was the way their chef served the main course of the fillet of beef Wellington. The fillet of beef had first been slightly pan-fried, then sliced with the duxelles between each slice and rolled up in puff pastry. It was beautifully decorated with pastry leaves and then baked, which made it so easy to serve and unusual."

I was truly impressed, and pleased that she was passing on a good tip to me. And from then on I took a leaf from the Russian chef's book.

Different courses would be decided on to balance the colours, sauces, vegetables and puddings and, of course, if we found that a particular guest had had a particular dish at a previous party, the menu had to be changed.

Even now, with experience, things could still go wrong at a party, but the best part of the day was at the end when, feeling tired, I was happy that everything had gone well and the meal had been a success.

Madame Tötterman introduced me to some Finnish dishes like coulibiac (salmon and rice in pastry); Karelian pastries with egg, butter and rice; baked puff-pastry stars with prunes; and *pulla* yeast coffee bread. These Finnish specialities were eaten at Christmas time. The famous punch, glögg, was made when the Ambassador and Madame organised the embassy staff party. I would also make some Russian dishes: the classic borscht, pirog, a Russian bread filled with a layer of vegetables, Blini, and braised cabbage with thinly sliced carrot.

As the autumn months approached and the days grew shorter, my thoughts turned toward the more warm and comforting food. These were meals that related well in the past years and which we would rarley cook nowadays.

I would ring my butcher, Mr Clutworthy at Smithfield Market, to request an oxtail, and the ears, tail and trotters from a pig. Mr Clutworthy curiously asked what I was making.

I replied, "A bollito misto." I would boil the meat slowly, with a large onion studded with cloves, and a bouqet garni. It would be served with boiled, mixed seasonal vegatables and a caper and parsley sauce. It was a lovely wholesome dish.

Another favourite of the Ambassador, was either a savoury or sweet soufflé – but especially a savoury with ham and watercress or just cheese. He would truly enjoy the soufflé and I delighted in seeing the dish empty.

René, the French onion seller, would often come and see me with strings of onions and garlic on his way to the French Embassy, which was just a few buildings away. One day, Caroline saw him outside on the road near our embassy pushing his bicycle. His forehead was covered in sweat, his red cheeks were glowing and he was gasping for breath. Long strings of shining brown onions hid the bicycle wheels and almost touched the pavement. Caroline invited him to come and meet me. On returning from my Italian holiday, my family gave me a couple of bottles of punch, a strong black syrupy drink that is produced in our area and drunk in the winter days. After our first meeting, René would often turn up in the morning, rubbing his cold hands and complaining to me about the cold. I used to make him sit at the kitchen table and would offer him a glass or two of punch to warm him up. He loved the stuff, and he was always welcomed in my kitchen.

Once a week the pools collector would come to pick up my coupons. Like everybody else I was hoping that one day I would strike lucky. The embassy back doorbell would ring exactly at six o'clock in the evening on a Friday, and I always knew who it was. I would ask him to follow me into the kitchen, where I kept the filled-in coupons and the money ready to hand over. The first time we met, I was confronted with a six-foot-tall man, well built, very pleasant and in his late fifties. He asked me if I had recently started working in the embassy, and where I was from. I replied that I was from Italy.

"I have been to Italy," he told me.

"When?" I asked him, thinking that he meant recently on holiday.

"I was there during the Second World War for nearly six years," he answered.

I was moved and saddened at the same time to have met this nice man who had given six years of his youth in my country.

"And which part of Italy were you in?" I enquired.

"I was posted to Salerno."

"Have you also been to Cassino?"

"No," came the reply. "I never went to the other side of Italy."

We started chatting and I told him the reason why I asked. I knew the town of Cassino, and another small town nearby called Venafro, which I go through on my way home. Around the outskirts, there is a big French military cemetery that can be seen from the main road. It is beautifully tended, with tall pointed deep-green cypress trees rising above the cemetery walls. A long flagpole is placed next to the entrance of the cemetery wrought-iron gate, and the French tricolour flaps in the wind.

This region is called La Regione Campania, or Il Mezzogiorno, which means the midday sun. It includes the Neapolitan area with its famous olive and citrus groves and the ever present plum tomatoes, buffalo mozzarella and other simple and good foods. It has a luscious green watercolour landscape of tree-covered hills, dotted with terracotta roofs and sun-drenched farmhouses with faded lime-painted walls. Fully cultivated strips of land are planted with vines, corn and sunflowers. Peaches, nectarines and apricots are picked from orchards and put in baskets early in the morning, whilst still fresh. The fruit is then sold to local and out-of-the-area shops or kept for the farmer's own family use.

Along the verge of the road under the shade of trees, lovely farming women would be waiting to sell their freshly picked home produce of red peppers, purple shiny aubergines, tomatoes and courgettes still with their yellow/orange flowers on. During the fig season, you can feast your eyes on the beautiful displays of wicker baskets layered with large fig leaves of ripened sweet and soft fruit, ready to eat. On our way to Rome to return to England, Caroline would ask one of my brothers to look out while he was driving and to stop and buy a kilo of figs. Their faces would light up in smiles. Caroline adores this aphrodisiac fruit.

I remember the day, two weeks after going to the embassy, when our baby was born. Caroline had gone into St George's Hospital at Hyde Park the night before and on 14 May I had my first luncheon party to prepare for the Ambassador. Needless to say, I was not in full control or concentrating on the meal that day, but all went well and as soon as I had finished I rushed to the hospital in time to be with Caroline for the birth of our son, Edilio – the most beautiful baby in the world. He was just the most perfect little baby and all was well with him. Caroline had had shingles on her face a few weeks before the birth, and after Edilio was born Caroline had meningitis.

At first it was undiagnosed or we were not told. Caroline had to lie flat on her back whilst in hospital, and the following week I decided I wanted them both to come home after eleven days in the hospital. Mark (Caroline's nephew) and I drove up to the main entrance of the hospital, then open onto Hyde Park Corner. Mark had just purchased a huge convertible American Cadillac, so my Caroline and our darling son were driven home to Richmond in style with the top down. Every time I go around Hyde Park Corner I recall that day!

At the end of May the Töttermans took their summer holidays, so I was able to look after Caroline and Edilio. It was the summer of 1976, the hottest in many years, and we were fortunate that our flat was large and airy. We had to keep the curtains drawn because Caroline could not bear the light. Edilio was christened in August that year and he was named Jonathan Edilio David. We had a wonderful party. The Töttermans were present and gave our son a beautiful silver loving cup.

A few months later we moved into a third-floor apartment within the embassy. Also working at the embassy was a lovely girl from Madeira called Manuela Henriques. We always thought she was quite young and were amazed later on to find she was quite a bit older than us. Her husband had died and she had a grown-up family of two daughters and a son and later on she had another son. She was a very smiley friendly person and all our friends and family warmed to her. Our neighbours were the Russian Embassy on the right and the Iraqis on the left. The windows on the back of our bedrooms and the kitchen had a view of Kensington Palace Gardens, and the beautiful manicured embassy lawn. The view extended to the Iraqi garden, an overgrown and uncared-for one, while the Russians had cleverly divided theirs with half lawn and half tennis court. This poor tennis court never had any peace or rest! From daylight we could hear the tennis ball hitting the rackets, and at night the floodlights were on so that they could play.

The diplomatic staff were in full force till dusk, exercising and sweating. Now and again a few balls would go astray and land on our lawn. Caroline would sometimes throw them back, or pretend to talk to them for fun, placing them near her mouth and saying, "Hello, hello, I wish to make contact and talk to you." She couldn't keep this little secret to herself and one day when the Töttermans were away in the summer the Finnish naval attaché threw a drinks party at the embassy. Caroline was walking with him in the garden and several tennis balls were on the grass, so Caroline told him what she did.

At the first opportunity he told the Russian second in command about it and when Caroline was going out from the embassy with our son, Edilio, he approached her and said, "You are the lady who talks to our balls!"

Caroline was asked by the Ambassadress to join the staff. She was offered the post of major-domo, having qualified in hotel management. This meant that she was the only lady butler in all the embassies in London at that time. She was ideally qualified and ran the household impeccably. Whatever problems arose, at whatever time, she was there with her calm efficiency and a smile. She was responsible for preparing and organising guests' arrivals and she would be there to receive them. When we had large functions Caroline would call Charles Candy, the head butler at Buckingham Palace, to discuss the events that were forthcoming. Over the following years we got to know Charles, Cyril, Tony, Christopher, Arthur and, last but not least, Ernest Bennett, who used to be the Queen's head page.

I always enjoyed it when Dr Tötterman decided to give a party for his fellow ambassadors and members of the British Government. Usually I would be given plenty of time to think calmly about a menu for the occasion, or I would ask the Ambassador myself if he liked me cooking one of his favourite dishes for his colleagues. I knew that his favourite dish was soufflé, but that would be difficult for a party of eighteen. Not many chefs have such a chance in their lifetimes and visions of so many ambassadors at the table would flash before my eyes!

On many such occasions, a luncheon was given for the Honourable William Whitelaw, at which the Ambassadors of Switzerland, Iceland, Denmark, Sweden and Norway were also present. One of these menus is reproduced below:

Prawns with Rocket Leaves

***

Noisette of Lamb
with Coriander Sauce

***

Roast Potatoes with Bay Leaves
Glazed Baby Carrots and Braised Vegetables

***

Chocolate Soufflé with Green Chartreuse

***

Café

This was a very good menu for luncheon, where the entire guest list was comprised of men; and when it came to dessert I could not go wrong. Fortunately, I had made enough to be served twice, as Mr Whitelaw said to Caroline, "I shouldn't, but I will!"

Caroline, as I said, used to get in touch with other butlers when we needed help to serve at table, and in this way I came to be introduced to Princess Michael of Kent through Ernest Bennett, formerly the Queen's head page, who used to come to the embassy to help out when we held dinner parties for VIP guests. We all liked him; he was very amenable and had the right sort of experience along with his impeccable manners.

The post of an ambassador normally lasts for four to five years, and then he moves on to another country or is recalled back home by his government. In the case of our ambassador, his posting was extended and he became the Doyen of the Court of St James, the highest and greatest honour that an ambassador could ever receive. This meant that he became the senior of all the ambassadors and the head of the Court of St James in London. His job was not only to look after his own embassy and its affairs, but his diary became busier and he had to attend many more functions.

The embassy at Kensington Palace became more of a focal point after this, where our ambassador would receive and welcome new colleagues at their new postings. The Ambassador and the Ambassadress gave the most beautiful and generous hospitality to their guests – an experience that I have never forgotten. I still look back on it with nostalgia. The Töttermans made a big difference to our lives. They gave us confidence, and in the second year at the embassy they encouraged us to buy our first home. Thank goodness we did! In the seventies it was possible for us, but nowadays that same house is worth well over half a million pounds!

During the time we were at the embassy we met their two children, Anna and Stefan, and whilst they were at school and later at university they would come and stay in London during their holidays, especially at Christmas. Stefan is now married with four children and Anna is a well-known and respected surgeon in Oslo, Norway.

We also met the Ambassador's brother, Christian, who had been the consul for Finland in Monaco. He and his wife, Diana, often came to the embassy and they eventually settled in England and made their home in Bath. They had three children, Claire, Nicky and Robin. Caroline got to know Claire quite well when she used to come to England and stay at the embassy. Claire lived in Switzerland and she later had two girls, Carlotta and Emma. Nicky is now married and living in America; and finally Robin is also married and has a business in Bath.

We spent our early married years at 14 Kensington Palace Gardens with our son, Edilio, and we really loved this time in our life. We were very sad when the Ambassador, Dr Richard Tötterman, and his wife, Madame Camilla, left for Switzerland to take another ambassadorial post in Basel and later at the Holy See in Rome. They are still very much in our hearts and we keep in touch with them.

GAMBERETTI CON FOGLIE DI RUCHETTA
PRAWNS WITH ROCKET LEAVES

An excellent summer first course, it is light and refreshing.

600g/1¼lb large cooked, peeled prawns
Juice of one lemon
2 tbsp olive oil
A good pinch of paprika
Salt
Freshly ground black pepper
6 handfuls rocket leaves, washed and dried, stalks removed
1 loaf brown bread, thinly sliced
Butter
1 fresh lime

Sauce Vinaigrette:
12 tbsp olive oil
2 tbsp good balsamic vinegar
Salt
Freshly ground black pepper

For the prawn dressing: In a large bowl, combine the lemon juice, olive oil, paprika, salt and pepper. Stir well to amalgamate all the ingredients. Toss the prawns in the dressing just before serving.

For the salad dressing: Combine the olive oil, balsamic vinegar, salt and pepper. Stir well to mix all the ingredients.

Arrange the rocket leaves on plates or on a large serving dish. Pour over the vinaigrette. Place the prawns in the centre of the dish. Garnish with lime wedges and serve with buttered brown bread.

Serves: 6
Preparation: 20 minutes

NOCETTE DI AGNELLO CON SALSA AL CORIANDOLO
NOISETTE OF LAMB WITH CORIANDER SAUCE

A noisette is a small, round and thick slice cut from the loin or best end. They are boned, trimmed of fat, shaped and tied into round fillets. The butcher can prepare them for you if notice is given, or they can easily be shaped and prepared at home.

18 noisettes of lamb, each weighing about 100g/4oz each
3 tbsp olive oil
100ml/3fl oz Noilly Prat or Dry Martini (vermouth)
100ml/3fl oz chicken or vegetable stock
200ml/6fl oz double cream
150g/5oz butter
1 tbsp of fresh coriander leaves, chopped
Salt
Freshly ground black pepper
12 round white crostini bread, fried in butter until golden and set aside on absorbent
  paper

Beurre Manié:
30g/1oz butter, softened and mixed with
30g/1oz butter

Season the noisettes both sides. Heat the oil in a frying pan and seal the lamb for 1 minute on both sides. Transfer the lamb to a baking tin and roast in the oven for about 5 minutes or longer until it is cooked to your liking. Remove the lamb from the oven, transfer to a dish and keep warm.

To prepare the sauce: Pour the fat off from the baking tin. Add the vermouth and the stock, bring the mixture to the boil and let it reduce a little. Pour in the cream and season with salt and pepper. Thicken the sauce lightly with the beurre manié (if necessary), and sieve into a clean saucepan. Adjust seasoning. Add the chopped coriander and keep warm. Warm up the crostini in the oven for a few minutes.

To serve: Place the crostini bread on warm plates or a large serving dish. Arrange the lamb noisettes on top pour over a little sauce and garnish with a few sprigs of watercress. Serve the remaining sauce in a sauceboat.

Serves: 6
Preparation: 30 minutes
Oven: 180°C/350°F/Gas 4

SOUFFLÉ AL CIOCCOLATO E LIQUORE
CHOCOLATE SOUFFLÉ WITH GREEN CHARTREUSE

This is a delicious soufflé. The combination of the chocolate and the liquor goes well together with a distinctive flavour. You can also use Cointreau or Drambuie.

300ml/9fl oz milk
60g/2oz butter
60g/2oz plain flour
80g/3oz caster sugar
3 tbsp cocoa powder
6 tbsp liqueur
3 egg yolks, size 4
5 egg whites
Icing sugar to dust

Butter a 1 litre/2 pint soufflé dish and sprinkle with sugar, shaking off the excess. Alternatively, use ramekins of about 7–8cm/2¾–3½ diameter by 4cm/2½in high. Baking time 10 minutes. Bring the milk to the boil. Add the sugar to dissolve. In another pan melt the butter, add the flour, mix, and cook for 1 minute. Add the milk and dissolved sugar, and stir with a wooden spoon to make a thick paste. Cook for 1 minute.

Off the heat, add the cocoa powder to the mixture along with the chosen liquor. Mix well. Add the egg yolks one at a time. Beat the egg whites firmly with a pinch of salt, but not so they become stiff. Fold one-third into the mixture and then stir well. Add the remainder of the egg white by folding gently and then pour the entire mixture into the soufflé dish.

Bake in a well preheated oven.

Before serving, dust with icing sugar, and serve with cream on the side.

Serves: 6
Preparation: 20 minutes
Cooking: 30–35 minutes
Oven: 200°C/400°F/Gas 6

PRINCESS MICHAEL OF KENT

L'odore del soufflé al Grand Marnier é divino
The smell of the soufflé with Grand Marnier is simply divine
(The butler bringing the soufflé into the dining room)

Mr Ernest Bennett was always impressed with the dinners I cooked at the embassy and he said that he would like to recommend me to Princess Michael, as he often went to help her butler. Soon, the lady-in-waiting – Jumbo, as she is known – came to discuss this, and after that I often went to the palace to cater for the Princess when she had dinner parties. I loved going there.

The first time I was asked to cater I was thrilled with excitement. I had discussed the menu and courses with Jumbo the previous week and everything was well organised for me to start. I also prepared some of the food in advance to give me more time and to familiarise myself with the equipment in the kitchen. We had decided on the following menu:

Seafood Gratin

***

Filet of Beef
Béarnaise Sauce

***

Roast Potatoes with Rosemary
Courgettes and Baby Carrots

***

Mango Ice Cream
Apricot Sauce

When I arrived at Kensington Palace with Caroline, I rang the well-polished brass front doorbell, and the butler in his smart uniform came to answer. The door opens into a tiny hall, with a chequered black and white tiled floor, and a rug and a sofa that take up most of the space. Beyond that was a soft lemon-coloured corridor leading to the dining room and kitchen on the left; and to the right was a stunning but comfortable drawing room. I was very impressed with the quiet and relaxed atmosphere. I was shown the kitchen and given a quick tour of the dining room by the butler. It was a rich and elegantly decorated dining room with a beautiful portrait of the Princess wearing a blue ultramarine satin dress with a tiara, hanging on the left wall. On each side of the portrait was an arrangement of antique china plates, in the shape of a diamond, hand-painted with exotic birds decorating them. Opposite was a high mantelpiece with carved dark wood, a coal-gas fire and antique porcelain jardinières resting on top. Facing the door was a large gold-framed mirror above a sideboard, and two large windows on either side. The table was beautifully laid with the finest linen, silver, crystal glasses, candlesticks and a printed menu in front of every guest.

What caught my eyes was a lovely pair of silver salt and pepper pots, in the shape of artichokes that looked so real. Another thing that struck me was the most unusual hand-painted, antique dinner service, with rare patterns and design – the most beautiful and delicate porcelain that I have ever seen.

Caroline and I started to unload the car and ferry food in trays back and forth very quietly, as we did not want to make a single noise. I went back into the kitchen to start sorting out my things and took a deep breath.

Later on, before the dinner party, the Princess came down to the kitchen to meet me. Dressed in a beautiful long silk gown, she introduced herself to Caroline and me. At the first meeting, I felt at ease and had confidence that I had a good rapport with her and that she placed her trust in my work. She has continued this trust towards me and I have a great respect for her family. I admire her immensely. She is a truly beautiful woman and she has great presence.

Just before I left the palace on that first occasion, the Prince and Princess came into the kitchen to thank me. They were so pleased that everything had gone well and had been just right. They said their guests, including Princess Alexandra and her husband, Sir Angus Ogilvy, had enjoyed the dinner and the lovely evening.

Later on, the Princess would come into the kitchen to see Caroline and me. She was always kind towards us and I always felt comfortable when attending the palace, whatever the occasion. The Prince would also come into the kitchen and very courteously ask what they would be having for dinner. The children, Freddie and Ella, would come down from the nursery, popping their heads round the side of the door, curious to see and to greet me, and to ask if there would be any dessert left after the dinner for the following day.

A dinner party at the palace was always a thrill for me. It was a pleasure to be involved with Their Royal Highnesses and their guests, and to ensure that the evening was going to be remembered for some time to come. The Prince and Princess, although they live in a very beautiful and elegant home, surrounded by beautiful old antique artwork, have a taste for simple dishes. The Princess fell in love with soufflé dishes: orange and Grand Marnier, chocolate and green chartreuse or passion fruit. The Prince adores chocolate desserts, and loves indulging in chocolate gateaux, mousses and truffles.

I recall one day in 1985, on the day of the Trooping of the Colour, when I went to the palace to cook lunch for the Princess, who had invited other members of the royal family, including the Duke and the Duchess of Kent, and other guests. On that day it was pouring with rain, and I was told that they were going to be late because the Duke had to go home to change his clothes as his uniform was soaking wet.

The Princess had requested asparagus with hollandaise sauce as a starter and cold poached salmon as a main course. She must have felt that if something went wrong at least the main course was not going to be spoilt. Normally I would cook the asparagus spears in advance and cool them under running water, ready to be reheated when all the guests arrived, so the late arrival would cause no problems for me.

The Princess's kitchen was well planned, and beautifully decorated – not too big, but long and bright with a glossy cork floor and a high ceiling. A watercolour depicting a corner of Buckingham Palace Garden hung on the wall. Antique old Victorian ceramic tiles were laid around the kitchen sink and on the wall above the wooden worktop. The varieties of these old-fashioned rare tiles in soft colours complemented the decor so beautifully.

The kitchen was comfortable and airy, with a big sash window open at the end that looked out over a small patch of garden by the driveway.

I took Teresa, a friend, with me to help on this occasion. I began to get impatient because of the long wait. Every time I heard a car arrive, I rushed to the window and put my head out to see the car. Then I would hurry to put the asparagus in the hot water, only to be told by the butler that the Duke had not arrived yet. The asparagus had to come out. This scene went on several times until the poor asparagus looked limp and exhausted, and it was a great relief when I could serve it at last.

I continued to go to the Palace until Caroline and I decided to leave London and head for the country to start a new life in the country.

Several years ago, I received a phone call from Jumbo, asking me if I could go to help the Princess in her country house. She needed someone to cook for two weeks whilst the family, their guests and the Princess's cousin were staying there before going on holiday abroad. I did not hesitate for one moment and I replied that I would be delighted to go to Gloucestershire to help her out with the cooking, whilst Caroline was left in charge and supervised our own business. Caroline and I drove there together. I had never been in their country home before, although I know Kensington Palace so well. Caroline and I were most impressed by the quietness and the surrounding gardens, the horses roaming in the fields and their lovely home.

The Prince was outside and welcomed me with the words, "How very kind of you to come," and he greeted Caroline as well. The Princess was very pleased to see us both and she must have felt a great relief that I was there at last and I was able to take over the kitchen. Caroline returned home and kept our catering business going with great efficiency. I was taken to my cottage on the estate a walking distance from the manor house, and shown around by the housekeeper, Jean. The cottage was small, with its own front door, self-contained and very beautifully decorated.

Opposite my cottage there was a small patch of green with bantam hens pecking grass blades. Next to it there were several horseboxes and horse heads looking out over the stable doors – the perfect country picture! The horses were well looked after by the lady grooms, who lived in a flat opposite the stables. The Prince and Princess love their animals and a few portraits of their favourites horses hang in the country house. Pat, the stable manageress, took great care of them. From the cottage to the kitchen was a short walk, but I enjoyed getting a little fresh air, and I would walk around the estate to enjoy the view and the smell of the fresh blue lavender plants which filled the borders. The Princess's kitchen was hot, with an Aga on all the time. It was beautifully designed, with walls painted in yellow.

Four veneer cracked antique plates, blue-rimmed, depicting wild mushrooms were arranged on the right, above the Aga. The cabinet doors were painted in rural green. Wide shelves were crammed with cookery books and old terracotta pots filled with every imaginable kitchen utensil. There were two upright fridges, in which I could never find space to store food; and a heavy wooden farmhouse table, uncovered in the centre of the kitchen, had to be always kept supplied with a bowl of fresh fruit for the family. Here the staff ate, and sometimes the children and their friends too. The floor was laid with old-fashioned polished flagstones. It was a wonderful old country kitchen.

Two large deep freezers were in the basement room next to the wine cellar, with a few wooden cases of champagne and Bordeaux wine on the floor, with the top of the boxes opened and other bottles on wine racks. It was not the cellar one would imagine. There were not rows of old vintage wines with the correct temperature storage. The Prince and Princess enjoyed a small glass of wine. The freezer was packed with frozen food and kept in reserve just in case. I had to go downstairs to take whatever I was short of out of the freezer.

Two flights of stairs were connected to the main staircase, not far from the beautiful decorated entrance of the manor, which was full of paintings and family photographs. These staircases led down to the basement. A dim light would show you the way. The room was also filled with old and unwanted house contents – framed pictures, furniture, lampshades and so on. I would look around the room as if there might be someone standing there in a corner looking at me. It was cold and smelt musty like damp. I could feel a chill and my skin turning into pimples. I opened the freezer door to take out what I wanted, whilst turning my head and constantly looking over my shoulder as if a ghost could be watching me. I used to slam the freezer door and run upstairs back into the kitchen.

A few days after I had arrived in Nether Lypiatt, the staff informed me that the manor house was haunted, and there was the ghost of a blacksmith who made his appearance whenever he felt like it. At first I dismissed it and I thought they were trying to frighten me, as I was a lot on my own in the house when all the staff had gone home.

The cause of the alleged curse and the haunting happened when the manor was built in the 18th century. The owner was a Judge Coxe, who asked for the name of the finest blacksmith to build the most beautiful and ornate pair of gates for the house. However, when the Judge tried to summon the blacksmith, he was told, "Mr Warren is due to hang on Monday, Your Honour." The history does not relate for what crime.

Determined to have Warren's expertise available to him, the Judge granted the blacksmith a reprieve, and he was hired to build the lovely gates – the very same gates that are there today. After the completion, the legend continues, the reprieve turned out to be only temporary, and the Judge had the death sentence carried out. Seeking revenge for this injustice, the blacksmith returned from the grave to roam the manor.

At one time the rooms had been blessed by a priest, supposedly freeing the manor from the spirits imprisoned there. I recall one evening when just the Princess and I were in the house. I cooked the dinner for the Princess and took it upstairs to the drawing room on a tray, where she was going to eat it on a low table. Later I went to fetch the tray and cleared the kitchen. Before I left I went to wish her goodnight and asked if she wanted something else. She replied, "No thank you, Pino, I am all right. And on your way out please lock me in." I could hardly believe that the Princess was not frightened all on her own until next morning when the staff would be there.

Haunted or not, the Princess loved being there and she transformed the manor into a loving home – a place which gave her and her family a lot of pleasure.

A large oriental cage was placed in a recess next to the Aga with several birds inside. There were also two Siamese cats that were the Princess's 'babies', and they kept me company in the kitchen.

Next to the kitchen a door led into the dining room, where there was an exquisite pale-yellow decoration on the walls. A fine collection of old hand-painted plates, with different exotic flowers decorating each one, was hung on the walls in a beautiful display. A huge, intricately decorated rug covered the entire floor. There was a long mahogany table, always covered with a white tablecloth, in the middle of which was a large silver bowl full of silky red roses, picked by the Princess herself in her rose maze garden. They would give a lovely scent all around. The dining table was always beautifully laid by the butler with very old pieces of fine china and silver cutlery for the family and their guests' meals.

During those two weeks I felt very much like I had gone back to my old days and I felt free with planning, shopping, cooking, and organising my work the way I wanted; the Princess has always given me carte blanche. The house was full of a happy atmosphere. The entire staff, including the gardener, was always coming to see me as they liked the kitchen atmosphere, and they were always asking me what they were going to have to eat. The gardener's first morning stop was to see me and ask if I needed anything from the vegetable garden. I would ask if there were some rocket leaves, carrots or fresh courgettes, or if there were any courgette flowers I could serve for lunch. Courgette flowers are delicious when coated in batter and deep-fried in oil. I cooked some lovely meals whilst I was there: prawns in rocket leaves, artichoke in vinaigrette, and timbale of spinach and mushrooms with tomato sauce. That gave me a lot of satisfaction, and everyone was pleased. I would also serve fresh raspberries and redcurrants with a rich strawberry mousse. Sometimes I would pick fresh wild strawberries in the garden myself.

At the end of every meal her children, Freddie and Ella, their cousins, and their friends were sent to the kitchen to thank me. In the afternoons I would go to have a rest in the cottage, as I had another busy evening ahead of me.

Every morning at daybreak I could hear a bantam cockerel crow in the green. At first I was not paying much attention, but eventually I noticed how beautiful it was to hear the cockerel singing. Then, as the days passed, I realised that I didn't need my alarm clock any more. I started to double lock the windows, but that was not enough. I put my head under the duvet – not good either – then under one pillow, then under two pillows, but the cockerel never seemed to stop crowing. I often thought, 'If only I could wring his neck for spoiling my sleep!' But I suppose you do not wring a royal cockerel's neck!

On my last day, I was very sad to leave this beautiful house, full of life with guests and children. Caroline came to fetch me and we went to say goodbye to the Princess. While they were talking she took Caroline to her rose garden and cut some roses to make a large bouquet to give to Caroline. We returned home and I felt I had had the best working holiday ever – a break and a change of scenery. The Princess had as a token of gratitude also given me two beautiful scented yellow rose bushes for my garden, which were named after her.

THIS IS WHAT THE WORLD ... THINKS OF ME

I am Pino's accordion teacher of several years now. Pino is my only pupil. I gave up having regular pupils when my other music commitments got too hectic. So why do I keep Pino on?

It might be because I can't resist the lovely cakes and other nice foods he gives me every time I visit. Or may be it's because of the guided tours around the garden. Or perhaps it's that I get to see his latest watercolour. Or it could be because he just LOVES to play the accordion and he even practises! He has a special feel for it and enough enthusiasm for the world. Or may be it's because he's an awfully nice person and I think he's great!

Anna Ryder of Rowdy Music, Warwick

Pino creates so much love and beauty for us all with his boundless energy in his kitchen, art studio and garden.

Janie Wingfield-Stratford and Annabel, Oxford

UOVA IN TARTALETTE CON GRANOTURCO E SALSA OLANDESE
POACHED EGGS IN PASTRY WITH SWEETCORN AND HOLLANDAISE SAUCE

This is a lovely light starter that I served many times at Kensington Palace, as it is one of Princess Michael of Kent's favourite dishes.

6 tartlets:
250g/8oz bought puff pastry
6 free-range eggs, size 1
250g/8oz canned sweetcorn

Hollandaise sauce (see recipe opposite)
18 leaves of watercress

Roll out the pastry to 2 mm/¼in thick and cut 6 circles large enough to cover the tartlet moulds (slightly larger than the poached eggs). Place the pastry in the tartlet moulds; trim the edges, place over an oven tray. Cut six round greaseproof paper disks a little larger than the tartlet, put them over the pastry in the moulds and fill with rice or dried beans and bake. Remove the rice or dried beans.

Poach the eggs in boiling water with a little salt and a few drops of vinegar, for 2 minutes. With a slotted kitchen spoon lift the eggs out of the water, trim off some of the egg white with a small knife.

Make the hollandaise sauce and keep warm. Warm the sweetcorn in a small saucepan and keep warm to one side.

Warm the tartlets in a low oven and then place some sweetcorn and a little sauce in the bottom of the tartlets. Place the egg in the tartlet over the sauce and the sweetcorn. Pour over just enough sauce to coat the eggs and decorate with three watercress leaves over each tartlet. Serve on individual plates.

Serves: 6
Preparation: 30 minutes
Cooking: 10–15 minutes
Oven: 200C/400°F/Gas 6

Chef's note: The eggs can be poached in advance and reheated in warm water (if you do this, cool them quickly in cold water after cooking). This dish can also be served as a main course with a green mixed salad.

SALSA OLANDESE
HOLLANDAISE SAUCE

250g/8oz butter – unsalted
4 egg yolks
Juice of half a lemon

Melt the butter in a pan, and allow to cool a little.

Beat the egg yolks with the lemon juice in a medium Pyrex bowl. Whisk for 30 seconds until light. Put the Pyrex bowl over a large pan half-filled with hot water (bain-marie). Whisk constantly until the mixture is creamy and thick. Do not let the water boil. Whisk in the tepid butter a little at a time. Do not add the butter too fast or the sauce will curdle.

When the sauce has started to thicken, the butter can be added a little faster. Taste the hollandaise – if you prefer it a little sharper then add a few drops of hot vinegar. Season to taste and serve warm.

Makes: 300g/10oz
Preparation: 5 minutes
Cooking: 15 minutes

Variations: For a delicious minty Hollandaise sauce, add 2 tbsp of finely chopped mint at the end and keep warm. This is an ideal accompaniment for lamb.

COULIBIAC DI SALMONE
SALMON IN PASTRY WITH DILL BUTTER

This was the most requested dish of Prince and Princess Michael of Kent at Kensington Palace. The Princess loved to have it served for her guests at their dinner parties.

2 kg/4lb 4oz fresh salmon, filleted
1 piece of silver foil
2 tbsp olive oil
Juice of half a lemon
1 tbsp chopped fresh dill
A few rounds of sea salt
Freshly ground black pepper

For the filling:
6 hard-boiled eggs
180g/6oz cooked rice
1 egg, beaten
60g/2oz butter, melted
1 small onion, finely chopped
1 tbsp chopped parsley
1 good cupful of fresh dill, cut with scissors
1 beaten egg to glaze
250g/8oz good quality puff pastry

For the dill sauce:
250g/8oz clarified butter (see recipe on page 132)
2 tbsp chopped fresh dill

Pour the olive oil over the silver foil, roll the salmon in the oil and then leave the salmon skin side down. Add the lemon juice, dill, salt and pepper. Fold the head and tail sides of the foil into the centre first then make a parcel by closing the longer sides. Place it on an oven tray and bake for ten minutes. Remove from the oven; unfold the silver foil and leave to cool off. The salmon at this stage is barely cooked, but don't worry.

Boil the eggs for 8 minutes, cool under running water, shell and keep to one side.

Cook the rice in plenty of salted water for 15 minutes, drain and cool under running water. Put the rice into a small bowl and then add the butter, onion, parsley, salt, pepper and the beaten egg. Mix well. Keep on the side.

Lightly butter an oven tray. Roll out the pastry 2mm/⅛in thick and 45cm/18in long by 40cm/16in wide. Place it over the tray. Cut a little pastry from the sides to use to decorate the coulibiac.

Brush a little of the beaten egg on the pastry to a measurement 10cm/4in square. Spoon one third of the rice onto the pastry. Cut the salmon in half lengthways and remove the skin and the black formed on the back without breaking it too much. Place half the salmon over the rice. Add a few rounds of black pepper, and sprinkle with some more dill and line two eggs (sliced with an egg slicer) one next to another. Repeat the same again, spoon the remaining rice over the eggs and press down lightly to hold the shape. Brush the rest of the pastry with the egg wash. Fold over the two shorter sides first then make a parcel by closing the longer sides. Make small light incisions (about 2½cm/1in apart) with a knife to let the steam escape. Brush with more egg wash; decorate with pastry motifs and bake for 20–25 minutes and make sure it is lovely and light golden in colour.

For the sauce: Heat the butter gently until it melts and all the bubbling stops. Remove the pan from the heat and let it stand until the salt has sunk to the bottom. Carefully pour the fat through a sieve into a clean pan, add the chopped dill and keep warm.

To serve: Lift the salmon from the baking tray and leave to stand for a few minutes before slicing it to serve on individual plates. It can also be placed on a serving dish and served at the table.

Serves: 6 to 8
Preparation: 1 hour
Baking: 10 plus 20–25 minutes
Oven: 200°G/400°F/Gas 6

SOUFFLÉ ALL 'ARANCIA GRAND MARNIER
ORANGE SOUFFLÉ WITH GRAND MARNIER

This is a delicious soufflé for a dinner party, served with segmented oranges, or you can serve it at teatime for a special occasion with friends. It is very simple to make – have a go at it.

300ml/9fl oz milk
80g/3oz caster sugar
60g/2fl oz butter
60g/2oz plain flour
1 large orange
3 large oranges, for segments
6 tbsp Grand Marnier
3 egg yolks, size 4
7 egg whites
Icing sugar to dust

Butter a 1 litre/2 pint soufflé dish and sprinkle with caster sugar, shaking off the excess, or use ramekins of about 7–8cm/2¾–3½in diameter, 4cm/2½in high. Baking time 10 minutes.

Bring the milk to the boil and add the sugar to dissolve. Melt the butter, add the flour, mix and cook for 1 minute. Add the milk, and stir with a wooden spoon to make a thick paste. Cook for 1 minute.

Off the heat, grate the rind of the orange and add it to the mixture along with the Grand Marnier. Mix well. Add the egg yolks one at a time. Beat the egg whites firmly with a pinch of salt, but not so they become stiff. Fold one-third into the mixture and then stir well. Add the remainder of the egg white by folding gently and then pour the entire mixture into the soufflé dish.

Bake in a well preheated oven.

Before serving, dust with icing sugar, arrange the orange segments on a dish and serve with cream on the side.

Serves: 6
Preparation: 20 minutes
Cooking: 30–35 minutes
Oven: 200°C/400°F/Gas 6

THE IVORY COAST EMBASSY

Se il paradiso esiste veramente,
il primo posto sarà per i cuochi
If heaven really exists,
the first place would be for the cooks

We saw the post for a chef at one of the African embassies in London advertised in the evening paper, and as I was unable to attend the interview Caroline went along. She was interviewed by the second in command, as the Ambassador was awaiting his posting to London. I was accepted for the job on the basis of Caroline's interview. At first I was cooking just for the Ambassador's children as the family were going to be altogether when the posting was finished in Belgium.

My day in the kitchen started after I had done my daily morning shopping around the open market in Hammersmith, buying fresh groceries – meat from the butcher, fish from the fishmonger and so on – without knowing what was going to happen. The embassy was situated in one of the most fashionable squares in London, but was not one of the most grandiose houses, as one would expect to find. The Ambassadress never kept an appointments diary, and so we never knew who was going to come for lunch or dinner. At the last minute she would call me and ask to have her meal put aside to keep warm in the hotplate rather than dine at the usual time, or return home with a group of friends expecting a meal immediately. So sometimes I was completely thrown as I would have very little in stock. Although you do not need much to make a splendid meal, sometimes I would not even have the basic ingredients to prepare something that made me feel good and pleased with my work as a chef.

One of the funniest things that has ever happened to me happened here at this embassy, and I don't think I will forget it for the rest of my life. The occasion was a state dinner party at the embassy for members of the Foreign Office and other guests. On the menu, duck *à l'orange* was the main course, and hazelnut meringue with raspberry sauce was the dessert.

The starter had been served and I was finishing the decoration of the duck to be sent upstairs for serving. The housekeeper, who was helping me, then placed the dish in the food lift and closed the doors. The next thing I knew was the sound of the whole thing falling down the lift shaft with a clatter of tumbling silver. Not knowing what to do, and panicking, I ran upstairs and asked an assistant butler from an agency, smartly dressed and wearing a few gold medals pinned on his lapel, to go into the dining room, as I wanted to see the Ambassadress immediately. Through the side of the door, I saw the Ambassadress getting up and the guests looking at one another and raising their eyebrows.

I told her what had happened and asked her to go back into the dining room and make an excuse to the guests about the missing main course. "Tell them the chef has fallen down, broken his leg and has had to go to hospital," I suggested.

Her answer was that I should go in and tell them!

"But I should be in hospital," I said.

Obviously, I had to think of something else. I rushed back downstairs to where our Filipino butler was at the lift shaft with a hammer and chisel trying to release the duck and the dish, which he eventually managed. I grabbed hold of the duck portions, washed the lot, put them back on the dish, hastily redecorated them and took them upstairs myself to be served to the guests.

There was far worse to come, though! I always follow the same recipe when I make my meringue, and cook it always to the right crispness, but this time I do not know what happened. After the first disaster and my panicking, I sent the hazelnut meringue to the dining room, but later found that the guests couldn't put a knife through it, and that it had split in half by raising two butterfly wings as if it was going to take off, the cream squirting out onto the serving dish.

It was the most disastrous dinner party I have ever cooked for. Everything from the start, with the pancakes and walnuts, to the finish went completely wrong, and it was no use blaming the cooker or the kitchen utensils. It was simply one of those days, and I felt really bad and sorry for the Ambassador and the Ambassadress. With great shame and embarrassment I give you the menu:

Herb and Walnut Crêpes
Cream Sauce

***

Duck à l'Orange

***

Potato Croquette
Mangetout and Carrots Vichy

***

Hazelnut Meringue
Raspberry Coulis

The Ambassador and his family were charming people and were always very polite towards me; he told me once he regarded me as a brother. I liked them too but something was not quite right. The menus were never discussed or planned between the Ambassadress and me, and I also felt there was inadequate communication, which is very important, so after several months I left. The Ambassadress was very upset indeed and made a long telephone call to Caroline to persuade her to convince me to return, but I had made up my mind not to go back. It was not an easy place to work as everything seemed out of place, and I could never be sure what sort of day it was going to be. It was very much a time for me to change direction.

One afternoon, whilst I was still at the embassy I decided to visit a dear friend for a chat. Leonardo Gagliardi is also a chef and he is retired now in Italy. He worked at a house in a lovely cobblestone mews off Eaton Place with a very wealthy family, not very far from my job. Before I rang the doorbell, I noticed to my left a window box full of freshly grown sweet basil plants, which reminded me of our part of the world.

'Typical of Leonardo and his basil plants! He uses it for the tomato sauce,' I thought.

The other window boxes on both sides of the mews were a blaze of colour with beautiful hanging geraniums in wonderful colours from bright red to pink. He was very pleased to see me and invited me inside for a coffee. While we were chatting I found out that his brother Emidio had worked at the same embassy as me years before. Emidio had had a few problems, as I had, so I did not feel so bad when I left.

We were neighbours once when we lived in Italy and I had stayed in touch with Leonardo, Emidio and his elder brother, Peppino, ever since. When I was a little boy I had become very close to their sisters, Maria and Lucia, and their two younger brothers, Cosimo and Pierluigi. Pierluigi is sadly not with us any more. We shared happy days and played in front of our highly polished stone doorsteps.

Below the church, on the steep stony hill (known as *Il Colle*, as I have already mentioned) stood the ruins of the old Convent of the Clarisse, in Rua delle Monache (Nunnery Way), a quiet, narrow, dark street with a row of four houses. The first was where I played with my friends. Then there were two more houses with forever locked front doors. The occupiers had emigrated to Argentina, never to return. In the last house lived a husband and wife, Concettina and Mercurio. On the left side of their front door a small hand-finished rush chair and a low wooden table always leaned against the wall. It reminded us that someone lived there. The sun shone on the narrow street only in the afternoon and during the sunset. It brightened the street corner up and gave a warm feel to it. Concettina would sit at the table with a scarf tied under her chin to peel the potatoes and shell fresh beans for supper. This was like a painting by the Impressionist Camille Pissarro.

On the opposite side of the street, the convent was not very far from us and in our sight at all times. Weeds growing in profusion between the stony steps, and cracks on the walls, showed how neglected the building was. The convent was not very big, and had probably held around thirty nuns, who lived and prayed there. The precise date when the convent was built is not known, but it probably dated from circa the 12th century. My friends and I were always curious to see the inside of the empty shell of this building. I remember the remains of the front door were still standing. The doorway was built in large rectangular stone blocks, arched on top with a pediment in the centre, and a maxim written in Latin, like many religious buildings. Planks of knotted unshaven wood were nailed together and tied around the door frame with wire to stop us getting through.

Another way to sneak inside was to climb the dilapidated stone walls from the back of the convent. It felt like a small adventure and excited us to look around for traces of something like a relic or pieces of broken pottery to keep. Instead there was only earth and stones scattered all over the place; it was a great disappointment.

On a corner of the street, in front of a stone wall that used to be a house, stood a round cast-iron fountain, painted in a dark-green colour and embossed with a long pointed-leaf motif which encircled the top of the fountain and the water basin below. Its gentle running water at all times had many uses. How lovely it was to see the neighbours standing patiently and chatting next to it with one hand resting over the fountain, while the pan was filling up with water!

There was also Rosina, our old donkey, with long ears and a light-chestnut-coloured coat. She would also drink the water collected from a steel bucket. My father would often comment, "This donkey is treated like a lady!" (*Questo asino e trattato come una signora*) Our grandmother, Concettina, loved Rosina very much. She loved brushing her coat and caring for her. She saddled her up and rode into the countryside, where she loved to cultivate our lands. She would set out in the morning and come back in the evening with Rosina loaded with whatever she had harvested. This could be a sack of fresh corn still wrapped up in their own leaves, a sack of new potatoes, or fresh beans to be shelled and dried out for the winter. Rosina was a working donkey and she lived in the stable with the green-painted door. When Rosina was finally made redundant she was sold. My grandmother was so upset, but she had become too old to take Rosina out to work, and so we waved goodbye to her. *Addio, bella Rosina!*

At times I used go riding with my grandmother to keep her company. She would tell me where the boundary of our land and woods started and finished, pointing in all directions and telling me to remember it. A small stone wall in one corner or an overgrown blackthorn would be pointed out as a sign for the future. My mother very rarely went to see our land being cultivated, and I never remember her working with her mother. I imagine that before she got married she must have helped her; but when she got married and started having children she spent her time at home and looked after us.

I saw my mother then as a modern woman together with her other friends, with no time or energy for digging and sowing the land. The husbands of many women in the same area either joined the navy or ran kitchens throughout Italy; some even went abroad and all sent money to their families regularly. There was no need for them to go into the countryside, so the job was left to the older generation, who were so used to working in the fields. Eventually they retired and then they all died. The third generation have all left and now there are very few orchards being cultivated. The fields are mowed because there is only one young farmer left and all the terrain that at one time was the pride of Rosello lies abandoned.

The fountain was the meeting point, our little corner, and we had to collect the water for our houses in copper basins (*la conca di rame*) – and we children got soaked at the same time!

Back to the Gagliardi: in this family all the males became chefs and worked in many wealthy homes all over Italy and England. Peppino at a young age worked in Cuba during the Fidel Castro revolution. His poor mother was very sad. I remember her saying, "My poor Peppino is in Cuba, and they won't let him out." But many years later he came back to Europe and married a Spanish lady.

While I was still working at the Finnish Embassy, Caroline and I were invited to go out for dinner with a friend of ours. Before the meal had even started, our friend introduced me to the owner of the restaurant, whom he happened to know, and disclosed to him that I was a chef from the Abruzzo region. The owner, on hearing this information, replied, "Our head chef here is also from the Abruzzo region, and I know that all of his brothers are also chefs, but I don't know the name of the village that he comes from. If you wish to visit him, please feel free to go into the kitchen and say hello." On entering the kitchen, to my great surprise, I found a face I instantly recognised; and I was overjoyed as I greeted Peppino once again.

THIS IS WHAT THE WORLD ... THINKS OF ME

My husband Renato and Pino come from the same village in Italy, Rosello. I first met Pino when he came as a young sous-chef to work with my husband who was head chef at Kensington Palace. When Pino introduced us to Caroline, his wonderful wife to be, we just all clicked and have remained friends, good and true, ever since. They are a fantastic couple. We were so proud to be asked to be God parents to their baby son, Edilio who has grown up to be a credit to them both.

Pino is so talented, we wish him well in knowing that he will excel in everything he turns his hand too.

Daphne Percario, Rosello

Pino is an inspiration to us all having had the honour of accompanying him through the darkest moments of his life I was amazed by his courage in meeting extreme adversity head on and true to form his tenacity of will continues to carry him forward to achieve success in all that he does.

Anne Thomas, Cornwall

CRESPELLE CON ERBE AROMATICHE E SALSA ALLA PANNA
HERB AND WALNUT CRÊPES WITH CREAM SAUCE

This is a fairly easy recipe to cook that can be prepared in advance and cooked while you have a drink with your guests. It is good as either a light starter or a main course.

20 prepared pancakes (see recipe opposite)
250g/8oz spinach, blanched
250g/8oz frisée lettuce, blanched
110g/4oz watercress, blanched
30g/1oz walnut, roughly chopped
200g/7oz soft cream cheese
¼ tsp salt
1 egg yolk
Freshly ground black pepper
2 tbsp Parmesan cheese
Pinch of nutmeg

To seal the pancakes, use a mixture of:
1 egg yolk
½ tsp plain flour
2 tbsp milk

For the sauce:
60g/2oz butter
400ml/12fl oz double cream
Freshly ground black pepper

Drain, cool and squeeze the spinach, lettuce and watercress. Chop very finely and mix with the other ingredients. Leave to stand for a while. Lay each pancake on a flat surface and put about 1 tbsp of the prepared herb and walnut mixture on it. Brush the edges of the pancake with the egg yolk mixture and fold in half to seal. Put the crêpes in a buttered ovenproof dish, big enough to arrange them all flat next to each other.

To prepare the sauce: Melt the butter, add the cream, and bring to the boil. Season with the black pepper and pour the sauce over the pancakes. Cook for about 20 minutes, being careful not to overcook.

Serves: 6

Preparation: 1 hour
Cooking: 20 minutes
Oven: 180°C/350°F/Gas 4

Chef's note: I like to serve this dish as a main course too with minted new potatoes, baby carrots and mangetout.

CRESPELLINE
CRÊPES

180g/6oz plain flour
2 eggs, size 4
2 tbsp melted butter
½ tsp salt
12 tbsp milk
100ml/3fl oz water
Oil to cook the pancakes

Add the flour to the eggs and mix with a whisk. Add the butter, salt and milk, and mix well. Add the water gradually so as not to make any lumps (sieve if necessary) and leave to stand for 15 minutes.

Put a little oil on a kitchen towel and use to grease the frying pan. Cook on a medium heat one at a time. Flip the pancake over with a palette knife or toss by flicking the wrist and lifting the pan away from the body. Each side of the pancake should take about one minute. Set aside and leave to cool.

Makes about: 18–20 pancakes
Preparation: 15 minutes plus standing

Chef's note: These pancakes could be used with either a sweet or a savoury filling. For example, for a sweet pancake you could use lemon and sugar or a fruit filling. For a savoury pancake you could use a cream sauce with smoked salmon, prawns. or mushrooms etc.

ANATRA ALL 'ARANCIA
ROAST DUCK IN ORANGE SAUCE

A duck dish with orange sauce that is simple and different, with orange zest and orange juice. Served with segments of fresh oranges. The sauce is light and exquisite.

2 Gressingham ducks, weighing about 1½kg/3lb each
4 tbsp cooking oil
Salt
Freshly ground black pepper

Sauce:
568ml/1 pint duck stock
3 large oranges
8 tbsp caster sugar
4 tbsp water
1 tbsp wine vinegar
3–4 tbsp cornflour

Garnish:
3 oranges, segmented
Small bunch of watercress

Make the duck stock with 750ml/1½ pints of cold water, the giblets, a good pinch of mixed dried herbs and a little salt. Simmer for 20 minutes and strain.

Pour the oil and rub into the ducks, and sprinkle them with salt and pepper. Place the ducks in a roasting tin and roast for 30 minutes at a high temperature to give them a good start. Remove from the oven and drain the fat off. Reduce the heat and cook for a further 1½ hour, turning and basting occasionally. When cooked, lift from the pan and set aside. Meanwhile, carefully remove the zest from two oranges using a potato peeler. Slice the zest into thin strips and blanch them in boiling water for 5 minutes. Run under cold water and drain.

With a sharp knife, remove all the skin and white pith from the oranges, first by slicing off the two poles as close to the segments as possible, and then by removing the remaining skin and pith, following the shape of the fruit. Carefully segment the fruit over a bowl and reserve any juice for the sauce.

Squeeze the juice from 3 oranges and reserve for the sauce.

To prepare the sauce: Put the sugar and water into a fairly large saucepan and cook very gently until it is a light golden colour. Add the wine vinegar away from the heat carefully, stir and add the orange juice and duck stock. Simmer gently for a few minutes. Thicken the sauce with cornflour that has been thinned with a little orange juice. Adjust the seasoning, strain into a saucepan add the orange zest and keep warm.

Pour some of the sauce into the oven pan. Cut each duck into 4 pieces then the legs and the breasts into halves and place it over the sauce.

Keep warm in the oven at 140°C/275°F/Gas 1.

Before serving place the duck pieces under a very hot grill to crisp the skin.

To serve: Arrange the duck pieces on warm plates or on a large serving dish and coat with some of the hot sauce. Garnish with the segmented oranges and a few sprigs of watercress.

Serve the remaining sauce separately.

Serves: 8
Preparation: 1 hour
Cooking: 2 hours
Oven: 200°C/400°F/Gas 6 – then 170°C/325°F/Gas 3

CROCHETTE DI PATATE
POTATO CROQUETTES

500g/1lb 2oz potatoes
30g/1oz butter
Salt
Freshly ground black pepper
Pinch nutmeg
1 whole egg and 1 yolk

To coat:
2 eggs, beaten
Pinch of salt
A little flour
Fresh or dried breadcrumbs
1 potato, peeled and cut into matchsticks
Oil to fry

Peel, wash and quarter the potatoes. Cover with cold salted water and bring to the boil until cooked.

Drain well. Place the hot potatoes in a fine sieve and push them through with a pestle. Put into a pan and stir with a wooden spatula over a high heat to evaporate all the moisture. Remove from the heat and add the butter, salt, pepper and nutmeg. Adjust the seasoning and while stirring vigorously, add the whole egg and egg yolk. Put the mixture into an icing bag with a plain nozzle.

Dust a baking tray lightly with flour and pipe little mounds about 2cm/1in diameter and 3cm/1¼in high, to form a rough pear shape. Insert a potato matchstick. Dust each croquette with a little flour and leave in the fridge to set for a while.

Beat the eggs for the coating with the salt and dip the croquettes into this and then the breadcrumbs, adjusting the shape as necessary with a small palette knife.

Plunge the croquettes into very hot oil and as soon as they are crisp and golden, drain on a paper towel and sprinkle with a dash of salt.

Serves: 6 or more
Preparation: 30 minutes
Cooking: 20–25 minutes

MANGETOUT

500g/1lb 2oz fresh mangetout
60g/2oz of butter
Salt

Top and tail the pods. Refresh them in cold water and drain. Bring to the boil a pan of salted water. Add the mangetout, cover the pan and bring it back to boiling point. Cook for three minutes, drain and place in a vegetable dish. Add the butter and serve at once.

Serves: 6
Preparation: 10 minutes
Cooking: 3 minutes

Chef's note: It is important never to let the mangetout overcook, they should be crunchy and they should be well drained of water. This vegetable can also be cooked ahead. To do this, cook for 1 minute, drain and cool under running water. Transfer into an ovenproof dish and reheat in the oven with a knob of butter and a little seasoning.

CAROTE VICHY
CARROTS VICHY

700g/1½lb medium to small size carrots
1 small glass of water
1 piece of butter, walnut size
Salt
Freshly ground black pepper
1 tbsp finely chopped parsley

Peel the carrots and slice them thinly. Rinse under cold water. Place the carrots in a fairly small saucepan. Add the water, butter, a little salt and a few rounds of pepper. Cover and cook them on a moderate heat until all the liquid has evaporated. Do not overcook.

The mixture of the butter, the juices from the vegetables and the reduced liquid produce a thick syrupy sauce. Sauté the carrots in this mixture until covered with a shiny coating. Adjust seasoning.

Place the carrots in a vegetable dish and sprinkle with fresh, chopped parsley to serve.

Serves: 6
Preparation: 15 minutes
Cooking: 8–10 minutes

Chef's note: For carrots with cream, follow the cooking method for the carrots above. When the sauce is reduced, moisten them again with 100ml/3fl oz double cream. Shake the pan to mix the sauce and place in a vegetable dish.

MERINGA ALLA NOCCIOLA CON SALSA DI LAMPONI
HAZELNUT MERINGUE WITH RASPBERRY SAUCE

A meringue is a light mixture of a sugary nature that may form the base or the topping for a dessert. For a very light meringue and the best result, an electric mixer works faster and produces a closer-textured meringue.

4 egg whites, size 4
250g/8oz caster sugar
A few drops of vanilla essence
30g/1oz toasted hazelnut, not too finely crushed
2 sheets parchment paper

For the filling:
400ml/12fl oz whipping cream
2 tbsp caster sugar
A few drops of vanilla essence
Icing sugar to dust
Raspberry sauce (see recipe over)

Dot two baking trays, measuring 31cm/12in square, with a little butter and line with the parchment paper. With a pencil draw a 23cm/9in diameter circle by using a plate or something similar.

Whisk the egg whites, sugar and the vanilla essence with an electric whisk until the mixture becomes white, very stiff and glossy. This will take approximately 20 minutes but is dependent on the machine you are using.

Spoon the meringue into two mounds, and then with a palette knife spread on the prepared baking sheets trying to keep inside the line you have drawn. Spread the mixture gently for lightness. Alternatively, for a better look, you could use a piping bag with a large plain nozzle and pipe from the outside rotating inwards towards the centre of the circle. Pipe a few rosettes to decorate around the top. This, I am afraid, requires some practise. Sprinkle over the hazelnuts, dust with icing sugar and bake. Leave to cool completely.

Whip the cream until soft peaks form. Place one meringue half on a dish, spread half the whipped cream evenly over the top and then place the other half meringue on top with the hazelnuts facing upwards. Press down lightly and spread more cream, dust with icing sugar. Serve whole. At the table, cut into slices and serve with the raspberry sauce.

Serves: 6 or more

Preparation: 10 minutes
Cooking: 55 minutes
Oven:120°C/250°F/Gas ½

Chef's note: This type of meringue can also be used for pavlova, meringue shells and meringue nests, which can be filled with whipped cream and topped with fresh fruit.

SALSA DI LAMPONI
RASPBERRY SAUCE

450g/1lb fresh or frozen raspberries
150g/5oz icing sugar
2 tablespoons kirsch (optional)
Juice of half lemon

Put the raspberries and icing sugar into a liquidiser. Purée and sieve, add the lemon juice and kirsch. If you prefer a sharper sauce, add more lemon juice.

Makes: 450g/1 pint
Preparation: 15 minutes

Chef's note: This colourful sauce has a refreshing and tangy taste and accompanies many sweets. It is especially good with rich desserts, where it will be a refreshing contrast to flavours.

THE BARON HEINI VON THYSSEN'S FIFTH WEDDING TO CARMEN

Vino rosso per il Barone e champagne per la Baronessa
Claret for the Baron and champagne for the Baroness

We came back from our summer holiday in Italy after leaving the Ivory Coast Embassy. The telephone rang and Caroline answered. It was Anne Franchescelli, a friend of ours. She asked if I could go to help a colleague in a couple of weeks' time, along with Anne's husband, Benito.

It turned out to be Antonio de Lucia, a well-built man with dark hair and nice manners, from Roio del Sangro, a small village next door to Rosello. He needed help for the Baron Thyssen's fifth wedding to Carmen 'Tita' Cervera. The papers described him as 'the richest groom in the world'.

I had known Antonio's brother, Bruno, for a very long time – ever since I worked at Kensington Palace with Princess Margaret, when Bruno had been working at the Dutch Embassy as head chef. Bruno was a great colleague with a very long career in private houses and embassies, and now he worked for the Baron. Bruno was away at the time so his brother, Antonio, organised the wedding breakfast. My wife did the arrangements with Anne, as her husband, Benito, also from Roio del Sangro, who worked at the Spanish Embassy as head chef, was coming too.

Benito was picked up from work soon after he finished serving the dinner, but they had to wait until midnight before I could finish my work. We soon left London. Antonio was driving and Benito and I had not got a clue where he was taking us. I did not know the Cotswolds very well, but I knew it was one of the nicest parts of England, with the most beautiful villages, rolling fields and green landscapes. On the way we kept chatting and reminiscing over old stories and funny events of our past jobs, trying not to fall asleep. We drove along country roads and passed through pretty villages and finally we arrived at the estate and drove along a winding road with trees on both sides, which led from the gatehouse to Daylesford House. I could only imagine the beautiful view from the manor looking towards the countryside in the moonlight. The long drive felt almost the same distance as from London to Moreton-in-Marsh! I suppose I was tired of travelling. We arrived at 3 a.m., had a drink in the kitchen and went to bed. By 7 a.m. we were up and in the kitchen.

We had lots of work to do and food to prepare, starting with the breakfast and then lunch. The guests were beginning to arrive from Europe and the United States. The butlers were busy welcoming them and seeing that they were comfortable. Meanwhile we were getting on with preparation for their lunch and the evening dinner for forty guests and then for the big wedding breakfast the day after. Their guests could not have been luckier when they arrived at one of the most magnificent country manors in England. Everything was ready and prepared for them.

The Baron was the proud owner of one of the most fascinating and exquisite collections of paintings in the world. Many of them were scattered around the world, where he had other homes. Some of his large collection hung in the manor house. The paintings were by old and contemporary masters. A very famous painting by the Impressionist Cézanne, 'The Card Players', hung on the dining-room wall, facing the kitchen door. The door swung open and shut one hundred times a day, and I could not help but stop and admire the painting.

Rare and priceless works of art were displayed around the living room in glass cabinets, and the rooms contained the most valuable pieces of French furniture I have ever seen in a home. I am a lover of art myself and although I worked very hard for the wedding breakfast, I felt very lucky to have had the opportunity to be shown around the house by the butler to admire the art collection.

While we were at work, the kitchen door suddenly opened and the Baron appeared. He was a tall, slim, smartly dressed figure with his hair swept back. He looked very distinguished and broke the silence with the words *"Antonio, buongiorno."*

Antonio looked surprised to see the Baron at that hour, and, turning to me and Benito, he said, "This is il Signor Barone," and we greeted him like a couple of children.

"Buongiorno, Signor Barone," we said, bowing our heads at the same time.

He was looking for his butler to be served his breakfast. "Where is everybody? I am waiting for my breakfast."

We had been so busy we had neglected the most important person in the house! Benito's remark was, "With the house so well staffed is this poor man going to starve?"

Oh, didn't we have a good laugh!

Antonio, an old maestro himself, had the menu all beautifully written down and ready for us to see, and he explained what we had to prepare for the long day ahead of us. He had worked in many grand private houses throughout Europe and in various embassies in Italy and Great Britain. He was a truly professional chef, and I felt very privileged to have worked with him.

The walk-in fridge and the larder were full to the door with the freshest and the very best – a great house. As we say amongst ourselves, this truly was a baron with one hand on the heart and another in the pocket!

I asked Antonio why he had so much food in stock, and he replied, "I must always be prepared as it is not as easy as being in London to find the ingredients I need. The number of guests might also change, so it is best to be prepared for the worst."

The preparation for the wedding went on all day. Slicing, chopping and cooking was a never-ending process while a Spanish TV channel prepared to film the wedding ceremony. A man entered the kitchen to record some footage while we were preparing the meal. He wanted to see and film something interesting, and the only thing that came to mind was to open the oven door to baste the roasting ducks. The lovely smell of the crispy skin hit his face and he asked if they were for the wedding feast. I said, "No," and laughed. "They are going to be for the staff lunch today."

A few years ago Bruno came to our home with his wife, Maria, as well as Benito and Anne Francheshelli, and Maria brought me the tape of the wedding.

On the morning of their wedding day, Friday, 16 August 1985, it was pouring with rain and the musicians were already playing melodies in the grand salon, including 'I'm Getting Married in the Morning' and the Baron tried to dance a step or two to keep up with the tune. The Baron, a tall and distinguished man with a great presence was smartly dressed in black morning dress with a white rose in his buttonhole. The bride, Tita, the soon-to-be new Baroness wore a beautiful two-piece suit (by Paris couturier Jacqueline de Ribes) in a cream silk with a matching ribbon tied at the back of her head. She also wore the huge pear-shaped diamond ring which was an engagement present from the groom. She looked stunning. The bride's mother, Senora Cervera, wore a light-coloured dress, and a large designer hat, which was half in black and the other half in white. The men in suits and the ladies in stunning clothes and covered in diamonds were all drinking cups of coffee and fresh orange juice, while the wife of motor magnate Henry Ford II was snapping pictures of the happy couple and their guests.

The party then left for the register office, where no expense was spared when the sixty-four-year-old tycoon married for the fifth time in the sleepy Cotswolds town of Moreton-in-Marsh. He spent £1,500 filling the register office with white chrysanthemums, pink carnations and white gladioli.

They were welcomed back with glasses filled with the finest Crystal champagne, vintage 1975, and dishes of canapés. The Baron made a small speech and thanked everybody for attending their wedding day. The butler, Vittorio, was pouring the champagne endlessly while everybody was enjoying the drinks and dancing.

The happy couple and the sixty guests sat down in a beautiful marquee decorated with masses of flowers, at tables laid with the finest silver cutlery and crystal glasses. They started the wedding breakfast with a *tasse* of warm strong beef consommé served with a fine julienne of vegetables cut into very thin matchstick shapes. Russian beluga caviar followed this, served inside two castle-shaped moulds that were made out of ice, complete with turrets, and then placed on a serviette over silver dishes. It all looked very impressive and unusual with its gleaming wet look. Thinly sliced buttered brown bread and chopped hard-boiled eggs with lemon wedges accompanied this dish.

As a main course, we served roast stuffed quails on potato nests. The potatoes were sliced into fine matchsticks placed between two wire nest shapes and fried in oil until crisp. The quails were boned and stuffed with a light stuffing and then lightly roasted, and placed over hard-boiled, shelled quails eggs in the nest. (As an alternative to the potato nest a bread crouton can be used instead, or use the recipe for *Quail on a Bed of Straw* (see page 191). For dessert we prepared a simple dish of *crêpes Suzette flambées* with a Grand Marnier and orange sauce. Throughout the entire wedding breakfast the food was accompanied by vintage wines.

A string quartet of jolly men had been flown in especially from Vienna in order to accompany the meal with beautiful classical and romantic music. This produced a lovely and joyful atmosphere for the happy couple and their guests. The violinist, tall and handsome with a thick crop of hair swept back surprised everybody. He put his left hand in his jacket pocket and pulled out a tiny violin perhaps 15cm long complete with strings, which he tucked in under his chin and started to serenade the bride and groom while the musician accompanied him to a perfect melody. I can always remember the faces of these lovely and happy men all the way from Vienna walking inside the kitchen door. "Hello!" they would say, wobbling towards me; and turning my head away from the stove there they were again! Smiling and ready for the next meal! 'But by golly, these musicians are always hungry!' I would murmur to myself.

The most impressive part of the meal, the pièce de résistance, was the wedding cake, of course. Three tiers of continental sponge cakes were filled with pastry cream, liqueurs, and strawberries, and each layer was coated with icing and beautifully decorated by Antonio. Below the bottom tier was a wooden square box of the same size. It was a few inches high with several holes in the back to let the air through and a little birdcage door to one side. Two small white doves were put inside the box and the wedding cake was wheeled into the dining room. The guests were not aware of the hidden surprise. The bride opened the cage door and took the doves out, to the amazement of the guests. She held them in her hands for a few minutes and smiled amidst congratulations, toasts and best wishes. The doves were released into the air to the sound of rapturous applause. At the end of the wedding breakfast, the Baron and his new wife, Baroness Carmen, got up from the table and cut up the wedding cake for their friends.

This event has always been in my memory, not to be forgotten. As a token of appreciation and a thank you, the Baron gave me two bottles of Crystal champagne, vintage 1975, and a jar of beluga caviar. I have kept the champagne but the beluga caviar was eaten long ago.

QUAGLIE SULLA PAGLIA
QUAIL ON A BED OF STRAW

A simple dish, with a beautiful presentation.

6 quails, ready for cooking
60g/2oz butter
4 tbsp olive oil
6 sprigs of thyme
1 small onion, finely chopped
3 large potatoes
Oil to fry potatoes
Salt
Freshly ground black pepper

For the sauce:
568ml/1 pint quail stock or chicken stock
300ml/9fl oz red wine
Salt
Freshly ground black pepper

Beurre Manié:
30g/1oz butter, softened and mixed with
30g/1oz flour

Garnish:
12 quail eggs

Season and truss the quails. Melt the butter and oil in an oven pan and fry the quails with the thyme for about 5 minutes over a gentle heat, browning all over. Transfer the pan to the oven and cook for 25 minutes, turning and basting the birds at least twice. When cooked, remove from the pan and keep warm.

Meanwhile, peel the potatoes and slice them thinly lengthways and then sideways to make matchsticks. Wash and pat dry. Fry a few at a time to soften them. Keep in a colander until all are cooked, then refry in hot oil to brown and crisp. Drain the potato matchsticks on kitchen paper, sprinkle with a little salt and keep warm. (They can be cooked in advance and warmed up in the oven.)

Boil the eggs for 3 minutes, cool under running water, shell very carefully and keep to one side.

To prepare the sauce: Put the onion in the pan that the quails were in and sweat until soft. Pour in the wine and reduce by half on high heat for five minutes, then add the warm stock and reduce also by half for another five minutes. Thicken the sauce with the beurre manié. Adjust seasoning and sieve.

To serve: Arrange the potato matchsticks on warm plates or on a large serving dish and place the quails, with the string removed, on the straw bed. Garnish with the quail eggs. Pour a little hot sauce over each bird. Serve the remaining sauce separately.

Serves: 6
Preparation: 30 minutes
Cooking: 25–30 minutes
Oven: 200°C/400°F/Gas 6

Chef's note: If you prefer to stuff the quails. Make a light stuffing with 2 slices of white bread made into breadcrumbs and soaked in 6 tbsp milk. Add 150g/5oz chicken livers chopped, 2 finely chopped rashers of bacon, 2 beaten small eggs, 1 tbsp chopped parsley, 1 tbsp thyme leaves, 2 crushed cloves of garlic, salt and pepper. Mix all the ingredients to make a smooth, soft mixture. Spoon a little stuffing into each quail and close. Cook as above.

Braised globe artichokes.

Poached eggs with sweetcorn and Hollandaise sauce.

Roast lamb with mint.

Scallops and asparagus in a pastry shell.

Chicken fricassée with peppers and tomatoes.

Roast duck in orange sauce.

Sole fillets in white wine sauce.

Raspberry flan.

Fillet of red mullet with grapefruit and curry sauce.

Strawberry gateau.

Roasted vegetables Mediterrannean style.

Asparagus salad with Parma ham.

Cutting our wedding cake.

My nephew Tom, sister-in-law, Charlotte, brother-in-law, John, my mother and father, (behind) my American brother-in-law, Edward. My mother-in-law, Blodwen, me and Caroline, my younger brother, Mario, Nuna and Uncle Tom.

Edilio at five years old at the Finnish Embassy.

Edilio and Caroline in Venice.

Caroline and Pino.

The croquembouche, the classic French wedding cake.

CONCHIGLIA SAN GIACOMO IN CROSTA
SCALLOPS AND ASPARAGUS IN A PASTRY SHELL

This is a pretty way of presenting scallops and asparagus spears in an unusual pastry shell that took me some time to create. However, it really is worth the effort.

750g/1½lb puff pastry
18 large scallops, halved
1 bunch of asparagus
1 egg yolk mixed with
2 tbsp double cream to glaze
1 small shallot, finely chopped
6 tbsp butter
150ml/5fl oz dry, white wine
300ml/½ pint double cream
Salt
Freshly ground black pepper
Chopped chives

Garnish:
A good handful, of rocket or watercress leaves

Tie the asparagus and cook in boiling salted water until just tender (about 8 minutes). Cool the spears under cool running water and drain. Trim to about 3½cm/1½in long. Keep warm in the oven.

Roll out 3 pieces of puff pastry each to a 40cm/16in square and approximately 2mm/⅛inch thick. Place the cardboard shell shape over the pastry, and with a knife cut around it, leaving an extra 1½cm/¾in border. Fold the edges of the pastry over the cardboard, transfer to a baking tray and remove the cardboard. Dampen the edges with a little water, cut another piece exactly the same size and place over it. Glaze and score the stripes to give it a shell look (see diagram and photograph over). Repeat five times.

Bake for about 15 minutes. Leave to cool, cut the tops off very carefully and tidy the insides with a small knife, taking care not to damage the shells. Set aside (the pastry shells can be made well in advance). Keep warm.

Halve the scallops lengthways coat them with a little flour and season with salt and pepper. Melt down the butter in a frying pan until very hot but not burning. Add the scallops and cook for 1 minute on each side. Place on a plate, cover and keep warm. In the same pan, sweat the shallots very quickly, then add the wine, and boil to reduce by half. Add the double cream, bring to boil and leave to reduce until the sauce coats the back of a spoon. Adjust the seasoning. Return the scallops into the sauce and stir. Place a pastry case in the middle of each plate. Fill the pastry cases with equal amounts of asparagus and scallops. Sprinkle with the chopped chives. Replace the pastry lids. Arrange the garnish leaves on one side of the plate, and serve.

Serves: 6
Preparation: 45 minutes
Cooking: 15 minutes
Oven: 200°C/400°F/Gas 6

Chef's note: The effort for this recipe is a long one. I recommend serving it as a main course, with fresh, boiled baby carrots, french beans or spinach.

CRESPELLE FLAMBÉ
CRÊPES FLAMBÉES

500ml/16fl oz milk
30g/1oz caster sugar
A pinch of salt
150g/5oz plain flour
Grated rinds of ½ orange
2 whole eggs, size 4
30/1oz warm melted butter
110g/4oz butter
10 tbsp Grand Marnier

Pour two-thirds of the milk into a bowl, add the sugar, salt, flour, the grated orange rinds and the eggs. Beat hard to mix. Work in the rest of the milk, add the warm melted butter and 3 tbsp of Grand Marnier.

Melt the butter in a small saucepan. Grease a small frying pan with the butter. Cook each pancake on a medium heat on both sides, sprinkle with a little sugar and fold into four. Put the pancakes, overlapping, on a well-buttered dish and keep warm. Put the remainder of the Grand Marnier into a small saucepan to warm up. Pour over the pancakes, set alight and serve.

Serves: 6
Preparation: 30 minutes

Chef's note: This is an easy recipe to prepare.

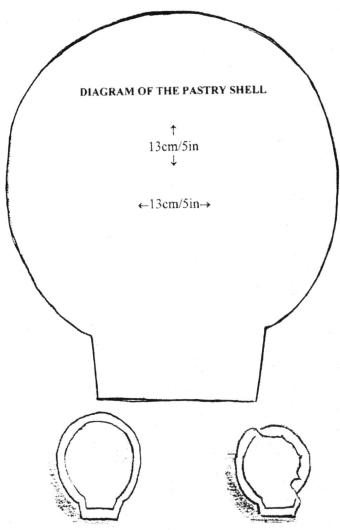

DIAGRAM OF THE PASTRY SHELL

↑
13cm/5in
↓

←13cm/5in→

1. Place the card over the pastry and cut around it.

2. Fold the pastry over the card shell. Remove it from one corner carefully

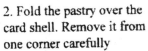

3. Cut out the pastry to the same size. Place it over the pastry shell base.

4. Brush with the egg mixture. Score stripes with the back of a knife. Bake.

THE ROYAL TRAFALGAR THISTLE HOTEL

Prima della cucina novella, i cuochi erano come apprendisti di bottega che mischiavano colori per i pittori. Dopo questa sono diventati tutti grandi artisti
Before the nouvelle cuisine, cooks were like apprentices in a workshop mixing colour for the painters. After that they all became great artists

For some time I had wanted to return to the hotel life. I had at the back of my mind the happy days from my youth and my colleagues at the Michelangelo Hotel in Rome. I needed a complete change. I liked the new trend towards the nouvelle cuisine. I wanted a new job, to be able to get up in the morning, have a warm drink and go to work free from the shopping bags in each hand and housekeeping bills in my wallet. I felt a great relief when I started at the Royal Trafalgar Thistle Hotel kitchen. The overflowing boxes of fresh vegetables, meat and fresh fish already delivered in the larder section were a lovely sight. They were waiting to be sorted out and used accordingly at the station you were assigned to.

The day shift would start at 8 a.m. and continue until 4 p.m., and 4 p.m. until midnight was the night shift. Here I could end my shift, brief my colleagues on whatever needed doing, pass on the station, remove my apron and walk out of the kitchen. On my days off, I knew that there were other chefs to cover for me, and for once I could forget my work and leave behind the kitchen scene.

To have free time was very different to working in the private houses. There I had to leave the meals ready cooked, plated or to be warmed up by whoever was on duty. I was in charge, and trusted. I had to look after my employers as they came first. I couldn't just take time off because I would have nobody to cover for me and I would have a responsibility towards the household. I saw this job at one of the top London hotels advertised in the evening paper and applied for it. Over the years I have kept a record of menus and taken photographs of the finished dishes I prepared for parties, always thinking that one day later in life I could look back through the albums and appreciate the memories of the people and places I had worked.

I was interviewed by Alan, the head chef, who looked at the photos, browsing through the pages several times. Then I went to meet the general manager, David Thompson, and the post was mine.

I was absolutely determined to return to a way of life I had been used to and so from the first day I worked well with the staff at the hotel. Soon I was thrown back, so to speak, into the frying pan I enjoyed. The hotel boasted a beautiful brasserie, one of the many open during the eighties. They were very fashionable at the time. It was newly refurbished with lovely soft decor, and a fresco on the ceiling of a large and exaggerated nude of a woman, which I found very interesting! I couldn't take my eyes off it every time I went inside the restaurant area. Next to the main entrance, on the right, was a well-furnished bar and opposite, in the dining area, was a table display covered with a white tablecloth on which a big bouquet of fresh flowers and wicker baskets of fruit and fresh vegetables were displayed with a cheese selection on a board. Freshly baked baguettes were brought in by one of the chefs.

We used to take it in turns to go into the dining area as we were curious to see what was going on. The smell of the warm bread filled the restaurant and whetted the appetites of our customers. French windows overlooked a small patio with table and chairs, and the customers ate alfresco, giving the Continental touch. The brasserie had seats for about seventy people. The atmosphere was relaxing and comfortable, with a genteel clientele. There were lots of lovely young people serving at tables, all smartly dressed with white shirts, black waistcoats, bow ties and long white aprons, very like a French brasserie.

After a few days, I noticed that some of these youngsters had already left. I could hardly remember their names! I couldn't believe that they were already gone! Then someone explained to me that they were on a tour!

"What sort of a tour?" I asked.

"Well, they come from as far as Australia, Canada, USA and South America and they work anywhere for a short time to earn some money, after which they move on to visit another country on the Continent."

"How nice!" I said. I never thought of a tour like that, let alone doing it! I have always worked and I couldn't imagine going around the world, as much as I would have liked to!

Between the hotplate and the serving area, I met the most wonderful and interesting young people I have met in my life. I loved it! I got on extremely well with my colleagues and Alan, the head chef. We had a good working rapport and understanding in the running of the kitchen. Alan had a lot of respect for me and my cooking, and an infinite trust in me. He eventually said I could have my weekends off.

I was very close to a colleague, Hassan, from Madagascar. He was a good chef with a great talent. He had worked in Paris in renowned restaurants before arriving in England. We shared a lot of ideas and thought alike about how food should be. I liked to introduce something new and unusual – a quick selection of special dishes on the brasserie blackboard were changed every day.

Carol Finney was another dear colleague of mine. She joined our kitchen team after I had been there a while and we got on straight away. I loved to work with her. She was a good cook with great talent and a sense of duty. She had been at college and worked in various catering outlets. She was a very sweet young lady, petite with red hair and always in pristine whites. She was creative and loved making desserts for the sweet trolley. When she left the hotel to get married to her fiancé, Guy, we remained in touch for several years and exchanged letters and news in the catering world. Then they moved away with their children and I received a Christmas card without her address; the following year I received another, but I couldn't answer her as I had no forwarding address. We lost contact, but I still wonder what happened to Carol.

The daily menu had already been planned and printed earlier, and though it was nice, it was not too difficult and was without many complicated dishes. I wanted to give an outlook towards the French and the Italian cuisines, and to give a Continental taste. The foods had to be plated and presented with certain flair, with a clean rim and with the nouvelle-cuisine look. I found it interesting and exciting, and enjoyed the novelty of creating a new dish. The fashion has not died down, though, and probably never will. There is too much competition between chefs to introduce a beautiful new dish full of warm colours and interest. I doubt if it will go back to the old ways.

The difference between the nouvelle cuisine and the old method is very simple to explain. The old meals were heavier, with several courses, and richer with big joints of roast meat served on silver platters. The meat was nicely carved and beautifully arranged with vegetables and potatoes next to it. Then the chef would dip a large ladle into a saucepan filled with a thick brown gravy and meticulously pour it all over the work that he had just finished, to cover it all up!

Then a new generation of chefs with new and bright ideas changed all that. Take a clean plate, spoon over your favourite sauce (just enough) and then place over some soft vegetable, like spinach, and make a little mound in the middle. The meat is carved, placed on the mound, garnished with your favourite vegetables cut and cooked in small sizes, and finally glazed with warm melted butter with the help of a brush. It is then served immediately.

It is still very hard to beat a lovely home-cooked meal, though, especially when all the family and friends sit around a big dining-room table. The starter of smoked salmon might be eaten, and the favourite family dish is brought to the table to be sliced. The crispiest roast potatoes and steaming vegetables are also placed on the table. Long arms are stretched out from all directions to serve. The gravy boat and the sauces are passed around. Glasses are filled up with wine to make a toast and to celebrate, before the end of the meal, a delicious bread-and-butter pudding. The word 'perfect' is as absurd as saying the 'perfect' party. A good meal and fine wines alone does not make a happy occasion. A table needs food lovers and an empty stomach with a jolly crowd.

Some of the dishes at the brasserie were soup *à l'onion*, soup *de moules*, *salade Niçoise*, *côtolettes d'agneau grillées* and *filet de porc aux pommes*. Two of my favourite courses, though, were toasted croissant filled with scrambled eggs and strips of smoked salmon and asparagus, and sirloin steak, coated with peppercorns, flamed with brandy and finished with cream. During the evening shift, one was entitled to one drink. I preferred a pint of lager. At this time the kitchen was not hot, but boiling! There wasn't a great deal of space and it was difficult to manoeuvre. I had the kitchen sink and the man responsible for washing-up behind me. With its low ceiling, the charcoal grill on, the gas salamander grill on and the cast-iron gas stove full on from 7 a.m. to midnight, it was like Dante's *Inferno*. So a cool glass of beer was most welcome as soon as I had a little time, and I often cooked my favourite steak *au poivre*, with a handful of fine potato fries, a grilled tomato and just a few leaves of lettuce. I would savour the steak with half a French baguette, finish my meal properly by mopping up the sauce and then sip the beer to make it last longer. They were moments that I will never forget. I would go back home feeling full and happy, and my Caroline would pat my tummy and say, "What did we have for dinner?"

Now, having had a tumour, I find it difficult to eat steak. Even when I cut it into small pieces it causes a lot of stress to my gums. The hot pepper sauce is also out of the question, as it would burn my tongue and gums after the radiotherapy. The fries and the bread crust are too hard to chew. A few years after the operation I do enjoy now and again a small can of beer, but I am frightened of abusing it and damaging myself. I had to give up a small pleasure, but there are so many other nicer ones.

As a senior sous-chef I was in charge of the main courses and also introduced fresh *patisserie* to give the restaurant a new image. I was probably the only chef in the company who used to make gateaux and pastry on the premises. It all started by chance. After the lunch service I was sorting out my workstation in peace and quiet, when I went into the walk-in fridge to get a sauce. I noticed a pound of sweet pastry lying on a shelf and I proceeded to make a French apple flan. In less than an hour the flan was out of the oven. The next day I glazed it and it was on the brasserie trolley. The hotel management were delighted that at last we could make our own desserts. Prior to that, even the profiteroles were bought in.

Every kitchen has its ups and downs and this one was more colourful than others. There were two male dishwashers to look after the sink. Tony worked during the daytime and he and I became such good friends that we could have a chat about almost anything. He had been a monk for over ten years and he left the monastery for some unknown reason – maybe he had some sort of disagreement with the church that he did not like to talk about, but nobody knew the actual reason. We thought it was quite strange; he had great knowledge in theological study and church matters. At times it was difficult to follow his way of thinking. He was a very nice and kind person with a very different background to everyone else in the kitchen. What I remember of Tony was that when I gave him a meal he was so grateful that he thanked me in Latin with the words '*Deo gratias*'.

The evening dishwasher sometimes didn't turn up, and we would watch the saucepans and frying pans piling up high in the sink. We knew that he was late by looking at the kitchen clock, knowing he should have been already at the sink by six o'clock. Fifi was from Morocco and had been with the Trafalgar for many years as a trustworthy employee. He was of average height, with a lean body. He was very fit. He was friendly and had a good sense of humour, and from time to time we would speak in French. Sometimes we had to look for a part-time dishwasher for the evening service, as the pans and the brasserie plates used to get out of hand. Leicester Square, being not very far from the hotel, was the answer. A group of elderly homeless men would be stationed near the Swiss centre under the clock, forming a circle while they were chatting amongst themselves. A few with familiar nicknames were Jimmy the Pipe, Alex the Pint and Bob the Job. A chef in white jacket would walk towards this group of men and after raising his hand and calling "The Royal Trafalgar", one of them would leave his friends and walk back to the kitchen with the chef.

On one occasion Jimmy walked back to the hotel with me. When Jimmy removed his jacket I noticed that his shirt wasn't as it should be – it was incredibly dirty. I went near to him, and in a soft voice I said, "Why don't you wash your shirt, Jimmy?"

He looked at me in astonishment. "But where, Giuseppe?" he said. "It won't dry in time for me to put it back on!"

"Go into the changing room, give it a quick wash and hang it up in the boiler room. There is a door next to the preparation room that leads to it."

By the end of the evening, Jimmy was pleased and smiled at my suggestion. They were good people – humble, but dignified. I liked them for their modesty and treated them well.

After so many years in London the hectic way of life was beginning to take its toll on us, and sometime it had to come to an end. Caroline and I had often discussed leaving London for a quiet country life, a cottage with roses round the door, a beautiful garden and afternoon tea on the patio.

We both had good jobs and by now we had our own beautiful home in Hammersmith, which we loved and where we could entertain our family and friends. It was a special time for us – after all, we had spent so many years of our lives resident in hotels, embassies and other people's houses. Edilio was growing up and was unable to get into our choice of school nearby. The alternatives were not what we wanted for him.

Alan knew of my hopes to leave London and move to the country. I gave my one month's notice. I continued to work as normal, like my very first morning. The days went by one by one and I was beginning to feel empty and sad at the thought of leaving behind the kitchen camaraderie.

"It won't be very long now," said Alan.

I felt a lump in my throat.

I left, and missed them.

Whilst I was working in London, I always kept in touch with colleagues who often asked me to help out at large receptions and banquets. I remember Benito Franchescelli at the Spanish Embassy who would ask me to help prepare banquets during the state visits of the King and Queen of Spain. Benito was very excited and concentrated very hard on his job. Being in charge of the embassy kitchen and preparing meals for the royal family of Spain, all the responsibility fell on his shoulders no matter how many people he had working for him. It was a great honour for him at the peak of his career. And we were all there in support of our friend. At the end of the visit, Benito was presented with a gold medal by the King and Queen.

Benito is not only a dear friend, but also an amiable and kind person. He has a good sense of humour and is great fun to be with; and, to say the least, he is a very good chef too, with many years in service.

Besides myself there were another four chefs – in fact, three were brothers, Emilio, Nicolino, and Michele Perella, also from Roio. Later in the evening Bruno joined us in the kitchen to help out at one of those banquets. The day before the banquet, we were mostly involved in preparation, and Nicolino and I spent most of the day at the sink cleaning and filleting the fish for the starter. Later in the day before the banquet, the embassy also held a cocktail party for a huge number of people. Before the banquet Benito assigned to each one of us what we had to do in order not to create confusion.

In the evening as all the cars drove into Belgravia Square, Benito made us stop cooking. We all left the kitchen at a hasty pace to stand outside with all our white jackets and aprons in line on the pavement not very far from the embassy front door so that we could see the guests arriving. The Queen Mother was the first to step out, and then was the turn of Queen Elizabeth and Prince Philip, followed by Prince Charles and Princess Diana, and the Duke and Duchess of Kent. Princess Alexandra and her husband, Sir Angus Ogilvy, were also among the total number of ninety guests.

Before the dinner we went to see the dining table – it was breathtaking. There was such a large amount of cutlery, glasses and flower arrangements that there was hardly any space left to see the table.

We were all ready in the kitchen, and an army of butlers in long tailcoats stood by to take an array of dishes through to the splendid dining room, starting with giant vol-au-vents with a seafood filling.

After five minutes, one of the Spanish royal aides who was supervising the banquet came rushing down to the kitchen shouting, "Benito, Benito, Queen Sophia is a vegan."

We all looked at each other, incredulous that nobody had bothered telling us.

"What could we make right away without making the Queen wait?"

"A soup! *Si, si*, a soup."

We got hold of a liquidiser and threw in a handful of mixed vegetables with some vegetarian stock. Quickly, we whizzed it, sieved it, and tasted it – it tasted yuck, horrible! Strangely enough, nobody asked the royal aide if Queen Sophia ate the soup.

The kitchen was far too busy with the next course, of several dishes of stuffed capons surrounded with the same vegetables as we had used to make the soup for the Queen. Then we needed to prepare the dessert, which was a mango ice cream which contained eggs and cream. I don't really know how much the Queen of Spain ate, but it was a memorable evening, full of excitement and high spirits, and I was proud to have been asked to share the evening with my friends.

It was always nice when a colleague would ask me to give him a hand when he was busy with his work, and also it was a nice change of scenery and good to have a chat about things in general. One evening I was called by my friend Domenico (Mimi), who was working at the Norwegian Embassy. He said he had a large official dinner party for which he needed some help. I went along to the kitchen where another friend of ours, Pietro (an embassy butler), was already there. He was having a chat with Mimi. After a coffee I was told the menu and I was asked if I could tie up the saddles of lamb to make sure the meat kept its shape while cooking.

Off went Mimi to one of the side kitchen doors to find some string, and when he returned he handed it over to me. I made a good job of preparing the meat, neatly and professionally tied with the string, which we then placed in roasting tins in the hot oven to give a good start. After thirty minutes we opened the oven doors to check the meat, but to our horror and disbelief we found that the string had completely gone; it had melted away, leaving not a trace. We looked at each other's faces in horror, thinking of what could happen to all the guests. What could we do but laugh in a nervous sort of way! We were worried about the effect this might have on the guests, but served the meat nevertheless. Fortunately no one seemed to suffer any ill effects. We told no one of this disaster, and it was not very long before we realised that we must have used nylon string – not very practical in a hot oven.

Other colleagues whom I had left behind included Mark at the French Embassy, my friend Renato who had left Princess Margaret and was now in a private house, Mimi at the Norwegian Embassy, Bruno at the Dutch Embassy and Filippo at the Italian Embassy, and all of them called on me for help at many functions.

It wasn't that I was just helping out my friends, I also enjoyed the excitement and preparation that went into serving a meal, and I was always proud to be part of it, as if the event were for myself and for my friends. I was always happy to share in functions with my colleagues. For my part, I never asked them back, but they never asked why. I used to prefer the company of Caroline's girlfriends for help. They all loved to come and help out, knowing that they would get a lovely meal at the end as well as a free cookery lesson: thanks to Janie, Joanna, Teresa, Margaret and Rhylva to mention just a few.

CORNETTO CON UOVA STRAPAZZATE E SALMONE AFFUMICATO
CROISSANT WITH SCRAMBLED EGGS AND SMOKED SALMON

For a quick snack or unexpected guests, this is a delicious and tasty dish. It is easy to prepare, and makes an excellent starter.

400g/12oz smoked salmon
6 croissants, medium size
12 eggs
2 tbsp fresh milk
2 walnut sizes of butter
Salt
Freshly ground black pepper
1 tbsp chopped chives
3 or 4 tbsp double cream (if desired)

Cut the smoked salmon into two-inch strips, put on a plate and keep aside.
Slice the croissants in half lengthways and put them under a low grill to brown them lightly, first the outside, then the inside.
In a bowl, beat the eggs with the milk, salt and pepper. Melt a walnut of butter in a small, heavy saucepan over a gentle heat, making sure that you swirl the melted butter around to coat the pan thoroughly. Pour in the beaten eggs and with a wooden spoon (preferably one with a flat end), stir well, getting the spoon right into the corner and the base of the pan to prevent sticking. Quickly remove the pan from the heat while the eggs are still soft and runny. Add the other walnut of butter, which will melt into the eggs while still warm. Finish off with a touch of class by adding 3–4 tablespoons of double cream. Spoon equal portions of scrambled egg over the flat sides of half the halved croissants. Place the strips of smoked salmon over the scrambled eggs, sprinkle with chives and place the other half of the croissant over the top.
Serve with a handful of mixed salad leaves with olive oil and a dash of balsamic vinegar.

Serves: 6
Preparation: 20 minutes

Chef's note: If you wish, you can substitute the smoked salmon with prawns or mixed herbs.

BISTECCA AL PEPE
STEAK WITH PEPPERCORNS

This steak has a hot, peppery taste, and is fried and then flambéed. The sauce is glazed with brandy and cream, and is slightly reduced before being poured over the steak.

6 entrecôte (sirloin) steaks weighing about 180–200g/6–8oz each
6 tbsp mignonette or spicy pepper, coarsely ground
60g/2oz unsalted butter, melted
4 tbsp cooking oil
6 tbsp brandy
300ml/9fl oz double cream
1 bunch of fresh watercress

Lay the steaks on a large dish and sprinkle with the pepper. Press gently into the pepper on both sides of the steak so that the pepper clings to the meat.

Heat half the butter and the oil in a sauté pan, copper or stainless steel if possible, and cook the steaks quickly over a high heat to sear the steaks on both sides. Turn down the heat and finish cooking them according to how you like them (a rare steak will take 4 minutes, medium rare 6 minutes and 8 minutes for well done). The steak should be turned a few times during cooking. When the entrecôte are done, remove them from the pan, transfer to a dish and keep warm on a very low heat while finishing off any other steaks. Return the already cooked steaks to the sauté pan. Pour over the brandy and set it alight.

When the flame has died away, remove all the steaks and keep warm. Add the double cream to the sauté pan, stirring continuously with a wooden spoon over a low heat to reduce and thicken the sauce.

To serve: Place the steaks on individual plates. Strain the sauce over a small saucepan and pour over the steaks. Garnish with a few sprigs of watercress and serve.

Serves: 6
Preparation: 20 minutes

SPUMA DI FRAGOLE
STRAWBERRY MOUSSE

A refreshing and a smooth dessert. Serve in a large glass bowl or in small ramekins. Garnish with extra strawberries

500g/1lb 4oz fresh strawberries
1 tbsp caster sugar
4 eggs, free-range, separated
150/5oz caster sugar
1 packet gelatine
juice, of half lemon
4 tbsp kirsch liquor (optional)
250ml/6fl oz double cream lightly whipped

Decoration:
250/8oz fresh strawberries hulled
60g/2oz caster sugar
A little lemon juice

Prepare the strawberry purée by whizzing the hulled strawberries with a tablespoon of sugar in a food processor for 2–3 minutes. Pass through a sieve, add the liquor if used and set aside.

Beat the egg yolks and the sugar with an electric mixer until they are pale straw in colour and thick. This will take at least 5 minutes. Heat 125ml/4fl oz of water until lukewarm, add the gelatine and stir until it has dissolved. Add the lemon juice. The gelatine must not be over-heated or boiled as it could burn. If necessary, place the jug in a bowl of hot water to ensure it has dissolved completely.

Gradually, add the gelatine to the egg mixture. Fold in the strawberry purée and the whipped cream very gently and pour into a glass bowl. Leave to set for 4–6 hours.

For the decoration, whiz the strawberries with the caster sugar in a food processor and sieve. Add the lemon juice and taste to correct the flavour. Serve on the side.

Serves: 6 or more
Preparation: 30 minutes

Chef's note: Other fruit such as raspberries, blackcurrants or apricots can also be used.

LEAVING FOR THE COUNTRYSIDE

Da Londra con amore
From London with love

Our thoughts now turned to moving into the country. In the mid-eighties it was a trend amongst our friends to leave the noisy and polluted city behind, and to find a dream cottage with a well-established English rose garden as in a pretty village postcard; also a good school for Edilio was top of our list. We had no trouble selling our home in London and the idea was to move to Warwickshire. We knew that area better than others and, of course, Caroline's mother lived there; and, really, it was not too far from London. We couldn't wait to move out of the hectic city life but oh, how we missed all our friends and colleagues! – people whom we had known for a very long time. We really missed everyone and everything, especially me. Edilio missed his school and his friends even though they came to stay most weekends. We never knew it would take so long to settle and at this time we were renting a house in Leamington Spa.

Then we found just the house we wanted. It was very, very old and had many rooms that were huge and we really felt that this was it – in spite of the fact that a tree was growing out of the chimney and the whole house needed an enormous amount of restoration. The day before we were going to sign for this house we decided to have just one more look at all the estate agents to see what else they had in our chosen village, Harbury. Edilio and I went running to the car. There was one more house to see in Harbury; the agent had telephoned the owners and we could go straight away. So off we went. I was telling Caroline and Edilio what the house was like.

It had five small bedrooms, two bathrooms and a small kitchen, but we really wanted a large kitchen so that we could sit in it – in fact, it really did not sound like what we wanted at all. Anyway, we got there and Anne greeted us at the door. She showed us into the sitting room. Caroline just walked into the sitting room and straight away asked how soon the property would be vacant. Then John arrived (Anne's partner) and showed us around the rest of the house. It certainly was big, with five bedrooms, two bathrooms and a sitting room that was similar to the one we had in London. But this also had a recess at the back, which was used as a sort of sun lounge. We eventually turned it into a dining area. The kitchen was not quite what we wanted but there was a gorgeous playroom-cum-study for Edilio, with a loo downstairs too. Then came the garden. It certainly was big for us and quiet and private too. We backed onto the burial grounds and so no building work would be carried out! and there were lovely trees planted there.

It was ours within six weeks and we named our new home Rosello as we had also named our home in London. One of the first actions we took when we arrived at our new home was to make another addition to our family: Holly, a beautiful miniature long-haired dachshund soon became a much loved member of our home and a source of comfort to all of us over the years whenever we were not well. She loved all the attention and gourmet meals. We used to joke with our friends that we were leaving London so that we could have a dog. Edilio had always wanted to have a pet and he had gone through the fishes, the budgies and then the hamster stage. It was definitely time for a dog, but our friends were expecting a huge hound!

Caroline took time to create our new home and the first summer was wonderful. There were lots of family parties, and friends came to stay. On special occasions, like my fortieth birthday, all the family came, and most of our friends from London. By this time we had acquired a piano as we were keen for Edilio to have lessons, so Caroline's mother played all our old favourites – classical music and modern songs! Charlotte brought a fantastic cake with a picture of me on the front of the cake, winking, and all around a mass of ladies' legs with garters and lace. Such fun! We must have had at least fifty people there, including our new friends in Harbury. They are lovely days to remember.

That first summer we went to Italy to stay with my mother in Rosello. We saw Papa too and they were, as ever, so pleased to see us – especially Edilio, their grandson. We had a gorgeous time, eating wonderful meals, meeting with all my family and friends, walking through the piazza and the woods and, as always, we spent a few days in Rome, just the three of us. As is our custom, we visited the *Fontana di Trevi* to throw coins in and we vowed to return again soon. We never realised that once we changed direction we would take very few holidays together for several years.

I had been offered a position in a large bakery business, Elisabeth the Chef, and David Owen (the owner) had asked me to help set up an outside catering company called Gourmet Catering. When we first came to Warwickshire it was still in the planning stages, so my first few months were spent in the actual bakery. I found that I was not really doing what I wanted, although, in retrospect, I gained valuable experience, so that when we started our own patisserie I managed it well. When the catering business was finally started, another partner took over and I realised that I could no longer continue with the company. However, I had great respect for the Owen family, who owned Elisabeth the Chef, and many years later, when I became ill, I was very fortunate to know them as friends as it was through their contacts that I was finally introduced to John Watkinson. . . . But that is another story.

We decided to go into business on our own. As a first step, Caroline put an advertisement in one of our local newspapers advertising freezer filling like casseroles and pasta dishes. In fact, it was a service for anything from weddings to dinner parties etc. The day after, our first customer called for an order, and then there were four more. Then came the first wedding buffet for over fifty people. Fortunately, we have a spacious kitchen and we were well equipped to be able to prepare and cook the food.

The order book was filling very quickly, and so I decided that I could leave

215

my work and become self-employed full-time. We had to transform one room of our house into a working kitchen with the help and guidance of Nick Ellison, the health inspector for our area.

We called ourselves Take Two Cooks, but we needed more than two. We had to recruit some staff, who were trained to help me. It would have been physically impossible to do all the work on our own. The Continental *patisserie*, which was our main line of business, is a very skilled and refined work. It requires a lot of patience and perseverance to achieve a good product. Some people are better and more natural than others, and we have been very lucky with our staff.

The first helper was Angela, and we were very fond of her. The first week that she came-we had several orders to fill and Caroline had come into the kitchen after delivering an order to see Angela facing the window and shaking. She thought she was laughing, but on looking closer realised she was crying. Oh dear, what was the matter? It turned out that Angela had made two quiches and forgotten to put the eggs in and she was so worried as we were just trying to get on our feet. We quickly assured her that we all make mistakes and really not to worry.

Not long after this Caroline became quite ill and was not able to work in the kitchen any more, and to add to our problems she was also unable to drive for several months so Angela took on that job as well because Edilio had now started as a day pupil at Princethorpe College; the Moore family, who became good friends of ours through their son, James, also helped with the trip to school. So during the term time Janet would pick Edilio up in the morning, and in the afternoon Angela would collect the two boys. One day Angela told us she was leaving as she had fallen madly in love with Rodney. He travelled all over Europe and she said she was going to travel with him. Eventually they married and now they are living in Denmark with their son, Christopher.

Then came Katey, who came to see me for the job after she had left school, despite the fact that she had no cooking qualifications or experience whatsoever. But she loved cooking.

"Pino," she said, "could I work for just one week with you? I haven't made up my mind yet what I want to do. I might go to university, or I could work a little longer to help with your business! I am not sure yet."

I replied, "One week is better than nothing; at least I can have an extra pair of hands."

The first week turned out to be three years. Katey loved to work with us and we loved her. We became very fond of each other. Petite and quick on her feet, she would move around like a butterfly with a natural touch for pastry work and a good eye for *patisserie*. Katey became almost one of the family – so much so that we forgot she was working with us, and we involved her with everything.

I once asked her jokingly, "How can you work in a house like this?"

"You don't know my house," came the reply, with a smile on her lips.

Katey lived at the Manor House in Harbury, and when her parents moved she went too. They moved to Rons Lench Court and Katey set up her own catering business.

After Katey, a bright, fun loving, happy girl arrived to help us – Helen Cooper

– whose parents ran the mushroom farm at Bishops Itchington. Helen was a competent cook – she was eager to learn and had natural flair. She finally left to get married to Andy – thus becoming Mrs Willougby.

Now Helen has three lovely boys, Josh, Ben and Jordon, and she has set up her own catering outlet. She adores cooking and still has her lovely chuckle along with a warm personality.

The main part of our business was supplying *patisserie* to many outlets in the Warwickshire area. The Hilton Hotel was the main outlet for us and we supplied them six days a week, sometimes seven, for almost sixteen years. Paul Hedges was the head chef at the Hilton, and still is to this day. He had come from the Bristol Hilton and eventually his wife, Linda, and their two children, Jason and Leanne, settled in Warwick. New house, new baby – the following year their youngest son was born, and he was christened Ashley Thomas. Caroline and I were asked to be godparents and we were delighted to be asked. Over the years the Hedges have become very close to us; whilst I was ill Paul and Lin made sure that Caroline was all right and that our business continued.

Caroline noticed a young chef at the Hilton, Matthew Whyles, who was in the kitchen on day release from Stratford-upon-Avon College. Caroline decided to ask him if he would like to give us a hand when we were busy, and in the meantime he could learn about *patisserie*. He turned out to be the most honest, reliable and trustworthy person in the world. He used to arrive first thing in the morning on his motorbike dressed up with all the paraphernalia!

On his first day at work, when he saw the sink piled up with mixing bowls, he had a good look at it and said, "I am not going to do the washing-up, Pino."

"Don't worry, Matthew; I will wash up," I replied.

Then suddenly he changed his mind. "I will help too, Pino," he said.

He must have thought that not only was he helping me, but also was learning a second job, after all. One of the Hilton general managers, Chris Allcott, once told Caroline that somebody like myself should teach this dying art, as too much mass-produced frozen desserts are brought in. He wanted the real thing and I certainly seemed to fill the bill.

Many hotel kitchens have shut down the pastry section due to the high running costs. The strict health regulations made it even more difficult, and I entirely sympathise with anyone who struggles to make *patisserie*, for these reasons. This section of the kitchen requires the highest standards of hygiene and cleanliness. When I was in Switzerland, liquid soap was not even allowed, and the utensils were washed with very hot water. This was to eliminate any risk of contamination.

At least seventeen years have passed since the day when Matthew first came. I feel that at least I have passed some of my skill to a younger colleague, which gives me great satisfaction, especially knowing that he will continue in *patisserie* and make good use of what I have taught him. He is a very dear friend to Caroline and myself. We have been able to leave Matthew in charge of our business and our home. Whilst I was ill and in the hospital over certain periods, Caroline stayed with me all of the time, and Matthew carried on our business with the help of only one assistant, a friend of Edilio's called Steve. Even when

I came home to recuperate he continued to help. I am for ever in his debt.

One of the sons of our neighbour, a virtuoso pianist called Richard Cox, came to see if we had a job for him. He was just seventeen and had been taught at home by his mother, Alison. He wanted to take a year off his studies before going to the University of Nottingham to read music. Caroline interviewed him and explained all that was going on in the laboratory! He looked very enthusiastic, and I was very pleased and looked forward to having him work with me. The only thing that I had to add to the interview was that the washing-up was compulsory! Richard had been coming over many times before he started work, to help us with various things for the autumn fairs, and he was familiar with the place. Richard turned out to be an inspiration, an intelligent bright young man, with a natural and creative flair for his work.

He was very interested in the *art culinaire*. At one point, he was considering giving up university to become a chef! We would talk about many things and keep up a good working spirit. He never ceased to amaze me. After work, in the afternoons his diary was always a busy one: driving lessons, giving piano tuition, directing a choir, playing the piano at his church on Sundays and cooking for his family and friends. I wouldn't be at all surprised one day to see Richard playing Beethoven's Fifth Symphony with one hand, and glazing an apple flan with the other!

Now, years later, our small catering business is thriving and we have a good reputation. We organise wedding parties, dinner parties and buffets. But my recognition goes also to Caroline, who organises my daily work, takes the orders and discusses with the customers what they require. Caroline also does the most difficult part of the business, the shopping, which is another job on its own! I could never do the work on my own; it would be impossible. We run the business together. We have acquired lots of customers by word of mouth, through publicity and country fairs. Customers recognise our products.

The most bizarre order that I was ever asked to make was to supply a pub in the area a few years back. The telephone rang, and the general manageress wanted to talk to me. She asked if I could make unusual-shaped bread.

"What sort of bread?" I enquired.

"Well, Pino," she said, "we have a private dinner party of all ladies and they want bread rolls shaped like penises to dunk in the hot soup as a starter."

"And how many do you want?" I asked.

"We need ninety penises for next week. Can you make them?"

I could have fallen off the chair; I didn't know what to say. Like a flash in my mind, I was thinking about the rolling out and what size they should be. I have never made anything like that before, and it was certainly not the time to practise. At the time young Katey was working with us and it would have been most embarrassing. This is not to mention Caroline delivering two brown cardboard bakery trays in the back of our car, full of penises! To put your mind at rest, they found a bakery that made them, and we were freed of the responsibility.

Not long after this I received another call, this time from Paul, the Hilton's head chef, a man that doesn't mince his words, so to speak. He came straight to the point: "Pino, I need 120 pairs of tits for Wednesday, the size of golf balls, made out of choux pastry."

"The size of golf balls when piped or baked?" I asked.

"Just the size of golf balls. I have to fill them up with mascarpone cheese, and arrange them on plates with some sauce so they look like tits."

I am not keen on the cheese filling. I am more a Grand Marnier cream filling man, but the order was done and turned out fine.

One morning I got up feeling tired and confused. I had not slept well and I had had an incredible dream. The dream was: I was lying in bed, and I saw a figure walking slowly from the door into our bedroom wearing a long white cotton nightdress. Her long light-brown hair was shoulder-length and uncombed. I pulled the duvet cover off and I got up. I walked to the end of the bed and I embraced this figure very tightly with both hands around her waist just for a few seconds. But it was if I was embracing the air; there was nothing there to hold or to feel. Then the figure walked away through our bathroom door.

I started my morning work, and I couldn't put a face to this figure, no matter how hard I tried. At twelve o'clock exactly, the telephone rang. It was my brother Lucio from Italy. I answered. He told me that our mother had died that morning at seven o'clock. My dream had been broken. Then I suddenly remembered the nightdress our mother used to wear and the colour of her hair. We were devastated, and felt a great sense of sadness and loss. She had been suffering with diabetes and other complications for a very long time, and at last she was at peace. I was at peace too. I had seen my mother two months earlier when I had visited home with Edilio. We both knew she was ill and now when I look back I am sure she was determined to stay alive till we had seen her. I recounted my dream to dear family friends, the Barclays, on a visit to London. Maisie told me that my mother must have been thinking of me at that time and she had come into my dream.

Life is no less hectic now; we have many friends locally and we formed a consortium with other small independent food producers in the area. We were called Warwickshire Fine Foods. The first year we had three stands to supply through the group at the Royal Show: the National Farmers' Union marquee, The Rural District Council and the Food from Britain stand. We made so many friends in the group and we had a lot of fun but none of us could give the time we would have liked to have given as we were all small producers. The small group that we were is now a much bigger concern, and has an excellent back-up of organisers. We had some very happy times. Dick Hammond was our chairman. Meg Rivers, a tall and a slender woman proud of her own product, made the most wonderful rich fruit cakes. She looked like an English rose, but in fact she was Australian. And Morris Burton bred quails. I went to see his farm several times and I remember that he showed me around his farm, where he kept and bred these beautiful little birds. These three have now sadly died and we miss them.

Dick and Judy Hammond ran Holly Bush Farm, where they had row upon row of fruit trees of plums, greengages and damsons, bushes of gooseberries, raspberries and redcurrants and fields of pick-your-own strawberries. Fresh vegetables were sold in the farm shop alongside home-made bread and meat from the butcher's shop. Many people visited this farm with their children to see all the animals and to see how a farm was run. They had a huge project going there. Sadly Dick and Judy parted, but Dick continued as chairman. He was an energetic man with great enthusiasm and drive to supply the public with the best. His cheeks were red from his outdoor life. He was very supportive to me and Caroline, often visiting us with wonderful baskets full of fresh strawberries, raspberries, loganberries, tayberries and other lovely summer fruits.

We really had such great support from one another and we purchased a lot of our raw ingredients from fellow members. We are always pleased to hear from these old friends.

Anne and Malcolm Thomas are close friends whom we are still very much in touch with. Anne ran Serendipity and supplied her fruits in alcohol and many unusual sauces all over England.

We still get our honey for use in our bakery from John Home, turkeys from Rod Adlington and cheese from Pat and David Fowler. We got our cheese for cheesecakes from Ram Hall run by Sheila Fletcher and her son, Stephen. Other members included Andrew Hamilton from Wellesbourne Mill, who created tea rooms to run alongside his organic flour business. We enjoyed the fairs held at the mill and other locations for Andrew's mother, Lady Hamilton, in support of the church at Walton. Other members we cannot forget and so they must be mentioned: Sheila and Brian Dalby with their home-made ice cream, Ann and Peter Turner from Lighthorne Herbs, Terry and Valerie Osbourne also making ice cream, Peter and Jennifer Woolliscroft from whom we got our cream delivered every week from their farm in Nuneaton and Richard Hobbs with his Gressingham ducks. David and Sue Eglin had a farm and trout fishing, Mike and Jane Exton had a wonderful food shop in Coventry, and I must also mention Margaret Titcomb and Jackie Keen. They were such precious days and they give me many happy memories.

Through a colleague we became members of the Midland Association of Chefs. We elected our chairman and president and an executive committee. When time allows, we attend meetings that are held monthly in various hotels in the Midlands, followed by a lovely lunch. Sometimes there are up to 300 people sitting in one room as one big family, which we both enjoy. It makes us feel proud to be part of the catering business.

Through this association, Caroline and I have met some lovely people. One great friend of Caroline's is John Heller, who is really the most jolly man imaginable, a true bon viveur, and a very well-respected master chef. As a full-time member I would like to have taken part in so many more events through the years, but, sadly, it seems that I never have time to be involved and to make myself seen the way I would have liked to. We did not realise that we would work just as hard at running our own business as working for other people in London, but we wouldn't change our way of life now.

THIS IS WHAT THE WORLD ... THINKS OF ME

I have known Car most of my life. We romped through boarding school together learning little other than how to laugh at life in general and ourselves in particular. She was never destined to marry a suit and a tie and thankfully met her swan, dear Pino, with whom she has paddled her merry way, deflecting life's slings and arrows ever since.

Consequently, I have the good fortune to consider Pino as one of my dearest friends, who sadly owing to work commitments we rarely see, but non-the less is always there at the end of a phone with genuine warmth and interest in all the family.

The things I love about this exceptional man are his unfailing kindness, his generosity of spirit, his tenacity and the many talents he has developed in the face of misfortune, which all add up to a multi faceted gem refusing to be dimmed by adversity.

Pino has that rare gift of accepting people for what they are and enhancing all that he touches with good humour and honesty.

Good luck with your new book and keep working your magic in and out of the kitchen.

Jackie Wade, Ely

MELANZANE ALLA PARMIGIANA
AUBERGINE WITH TOMATO SAUCE AND MOZZARELLA

This is one of our favourite ways to enjoy this vegetable dish. It is a delicious starter, or serve as a main course with a salad.

Tomato sauce (see recipe opposite)
4 large aubergines
Olive oil
A small bunch sweet basil
Salt
Freshly ground black pepper
2 fresh mozzarella cut into small cubes
200g/7oz mascarpone cheese

Make the tomato sauce and at the end of cooking thicken the sauce with 1–2 tbsp of cornflour mixed with enough water so the sauce is not too runny.
   Remove the green stalks and cut the aubergine in half widthways, then into slices ½cm/¼in thick (you should have 48 slices). Grease the baking trays with the olive oil. Lay the aubergines over it, season with salt and pepper, drizzle with a little oil and bake them for 20–25 minutes. Take them out of the oven, turn them over, and bake a little longer if necessary. The aubergines must be soft to the touch but not dry. Remove them from the baking tray, transfer to a dish, and keep them to one side.
   To assemble the dish: Grease an ovenproof dish. Arrange some of the aubergines at the base of the dish. Spread over some tomato sauce, sprinkle some mozzarella cubes, and with a teaspoon dipped in hot water add a few dollops of mascarpone and some sweet basil leaves. Repeat till you have four layers of aubergines, tomato sauce, cheeses and basil. Bake in a preheated oven for 30–35 minutes or until hot. Leave to stand for a few minutes, and serve

Serves: 6
Preparation: 30 minutes
Cooking: 20–25 minutes
Oven: 200°C/400°F/Gas 6
then at 180°C/350°/Gas 5

Chef's note: Another way is to enjoy grilled aubergines on the griddle: Remove the green stalks. Cut in half widthways, then lengthways to ½cm/¼in thick. Place in a dish and soak in olive oil. Place the aubergines over the hot griddle. Leave to brown on one side first before turning over. When done, season with salt and pepper, drizzle with olive oil and sprinkle them with chopped chives, and serve.

SALSA AL POMODORO
TOMATO SAUCE

This is an ideal sauce for all types of pasta.

800g/1lb 12oz Italian plum peeled tomatoes
6 tbsp olive oil
1 small onion, finely chopped
1 clove of garlic, crushed
1 tbsp tomato purée
1 good pinch of fresh, parsley, thyme and marjoram
10 leaves of sweet basil
1 good pinch sugar
Salt
Freshly ground black pepper

Pour the oil into a saucepan, add the onion and garlic, and fry over a low heat until the onion is soft but not brown. Add the tomato juice and chop the canned tomatoes to a pulp with a knife, before adding them to the pan, then add the tomato purée and the mixed herbs.

Bring to the boil, then simmer, stirring occasionally to prevent sticking. Add the sweet basil at the end of cooking. Adjust seasoning and the sauce is ready to serve.

Makes: 600g/1lb 5oz
Preparation: 10 minutes
Cooking: 20 minutes

Chef's note: One of our favourite and tastier tomatoes sauces I like to make is with baby cherry tomatoes. It really captures the taste of the fresh fruit. Simply substitute the peeled tomatoes. Cook in a fairly large frying pan so as not to squash them. And follow the recipe as above. Delicious!

BRANZINO ALLE ERBE
FILLET OF SEA BASS WITH HERBS

6 fresh sea bass fillets, each weighing 180g/6oz
6 slices fresh brioche bread, made into breadcrumbs
90g/3oz melted butter
6 tbsp parsley, very finely chopped
2 sprigs of thyme
A few leaves of coriander, chopped
2 tbsp olive oil
Salt
Freshly ground black pepper

With the oil, grease the inside of an ovenproof dish or oven tray. Wash the sea bass fillets, pat dry and place skin side down in the dish. Season with salt and pepper and add a squeeze of lemon juice.

Thoroughly mix together the breadcrumbs, the finely chopped parsley, the leaves off the sprigs of thyme and the chopped coriander. Spoon the breadcrumbs evenly over the fish fillets and pat gently with a palette knife to cover the top of each fillet completely. Pour the butter over the breadcrumbs and bake for 25 minutes.

To finish: Brown under a very hot grill, taking care not to let the breadcrumbs burn, and serve.

Serves: 6
Preparation: 15 minutes
Cooking: 25 minutes
Oven: 180°C/350°F/Gas 4

Chef's note: Serve this fish dish with minted, small new potatoes, mangetout and buttered baby carrots.

CROSTATA DI LAMPONI
RASPBERRY FLAN

This is a lovely fruit flan to serve during the summer days.

Sweet orange pastry (see recipe on page 226)

For the filling:
250g/8oz mascarpone cheese
60g/2oz caster sugar
400g/7oz fresh raspberries
200g/7oz raspberry or strawberry jam
With 2 tbsp of kirsch (optional)

Make the pastry in advance and leave to rest. Preheat the oven.
　　With a pastry brush, grease the inside of the tart tin and dust with a little flour. Roll out the pastry to about ½cm/¼in thick, and line the 23cm/9in loose-based tin, ensuring that the pastry is even. Trim off any surplus and press the edges of the flan dish with your fingers to raise the pastry a little higher than the edge. Pierce with a fork a few times. Cut a piece of round greaseproof paper slightly larger and place at the bottom of the tin, fill half way with rice or beans and bake for 20 minutes. Leave to cool. Remove the greaseproof paper.
　　Beat the mascarpone cheese with the sugar to a light consistency, and spread over the pastry. Arrange the raspberries over it.
　　Melt the raspberry jam with 2 tablespoon of water or kirsch and sieve. With a kitchen brush, glaze the flan evenly to finish it off.

Serves: 6 or more
Preparation: 30 minutes
Baking: 20 minutes
Oven: 180°C/350°/Gas 4

Chef's note: If you wish, you can make this lovely raspberry flan in a round ovenproof dish. It looks good too. You can also try other fruit such as figs, nectarines (but glaze with apricot jam), strawberries, redcurrants or others.

PASTA A LL 'ARANCIA
ORANGE PASTRY

250g/8oz plain flour
150g/5oz unsalted butter, at room temperature
60g/2oz icing sugar
Finely grated rind and juice of one small orange

Sift the flour and sugar into a bowl. Add the butter and the finely grated orange rind. Rub with your fingertips until the mixture resembles sand. Stir in the orange juice until the dough just begins to stick together. Gather up the dough and pat it into a ball, wrap it in cling film and refrigerated for 30 minutes before using.

Preparation: 15 minutes plus resting time

MARIA AND THE COCKEREL (Il Gallo)

"Angiolina, Angiolina!" A voice echoed in the air coming from nowhere. Angiolina turned her head, having just reached the corner of the piazza while walking back home with heavy bags, one in each hand – the groceries she had been to get from our general food store.

Maria, on the other side of the road, was lifting her right arm up and waving with her hand to stop. She wanted to ask something. Maria had come back to the village on holiday with her family from Rome, where they had been living for many years. She had somehow lost our local accent and could not help but communicate in fine Italian.

"What is it, Maria?" said Angiolina in our familiar dialect and looking as if she was in a bit of a hurry.

"I must ask you a great favour. I know you have a beautiful cockerel –" said Maria.

"Yes," Angiolina replied.

"Well, I would like to buy it," Maria said.

"You can't buy it," said Angiolina.

"You see," said Maria "it is not for me, but it is as a present for someone, and I thought a cockerel would be a special gift."

"I know it makes a special gift," replied Angiolina, "but my little hens need the cockerel,"

"So you cannot sell it to me?" Maria asked.

"No, I am very sorry," said Angiolina with a faint smile on her lips, "how can I take their husband away from my poor dear little hens?"

Maria looked disappointed at Angiolina's reply and realised why she couldn't part with the cockerel.

POLLO RIPIENO CON PREZZEMOLO, SALVIA. ROSMARINO E TIMO
ROAST CHICKEN SCARBOROUGH FAIR –
WITH PARSLEY, SAGE, ROSEMARY AND THYME

1 large chicken, 2kg/4lb in weight
110g/4oz fresh breadcrumbs
30g/1oz butter, melted
1 small onion, chopped fine
1 tbsp finely chopped herbs – 2 parts parsley, 1 part sage, 1 part thyme,
2–3 sprigs rosemary
1 egg, size 4
Salt
Freshly ground black pepper
1 litre/2 pints vegetable (carrot, leek) water

Put the breadcrumbs into a bowl, stir in the melted butter and the onion, and add the chopped herbs and season. Beat the egg lightly and mix with the breadcrumbs.

Using a small spoon, fill the neck end cavity of the bird with this stuffing. Place the chicken in a roasting tin; brush the top with melted butter or oil and sprinkle with salt and freshly ground black pepper. Lay 2–3 sprigs of rosemary over the chicken and roast in the centre of the oven for 30 minutes to give it a good start. Reduce the heat and continue to roast, basting occasionally until the skin is brown. Leave to stand for a few minutes before carving.

To prepare the gravy: Lift the chicken out and place on a dish. Skim most of the fat off the cooking juices. Add 4–5 level tbsp of flour to the roasting tin and stir to make the roux. Add the warm vegetable stock, not all at once, stir and bring to the boil to thicken the sauce. Adjust the seasoning and strain into a saucepan. Keep warm.

To serve: Carve the chicken and arrange on warm plates or on a serving dish. Pour a little sauce over and serve with warm game chips. Decorate with fresh watercress. Serve the remaining sauce separately.

Serves: 6
Preparation: 15 minutes
Cooking: 1½ hour
Oven: 200°C/400°F/Gas 6
lower: 180°C/350°F/Gas 4

Chef's note: Once stuffed, the bird should be trussed so as to keep it in shape during cooking, and to hold its shape when carving. If a trussing needle is not available, use poultry skewers and string to secure the bird.

TORTA DI FORMAGGIO CON FRUTTO DELLA PASSIONE
PASSION FRUIT CHEESECAKE

Biscuit base:
250g/8oz digestive biscuits
125g/4½oz unsalted butter

Cream cheese:
200ml/7oz cream cheese
200ml/6fl oz whipping cream
100g/3½oz icing sugar
2 tbsp milk
Rind of 1 lemon

Passion fruit jelly:
8 good passion fruit, puréed to 200g/7oz
100g/3½oz sugar syrup
2 tsp lemon juice
3 leaves gelatine or ¼oz gelatine powder

An electric beater is ideal for this recipe.

Crumble the biscuits, melt the butter and mix them together. Form a base by pressing the mixture down into a 21cm/8in loose-bottom sponge tin with spring. Line the sides of the tin with a strip of greaseproof paper. Place in the fridge to set.

Lightly beat the cream cheese with the icing sugar, lemon rind and milk until it becomes smooth and light. Add the cream and continue beating until it is lightly whipped. Spread over the chilled base and smooth out.

Cut the passion fruit in half, scoop out the insides and force through a sieve. Check the weight and add a little water to bring the quantity to 200g/7oz.

Make the sugar syrup with 5 tablespoons each of caster sugar and hot water. Mix thoroughly. Soak the gelatine in cold water until soft.

Put the passion fruit purée, lemon juice, and sugar syrup into a saucepan. Bring to the boil over a low heat and simmer for 1–2 minutes or until the liquid is clear. Drain and add the gelatine, (powder gelatine poured into the liquid) stir and leave to cool almost to setting point. Pour this over the cheesecake mixture, and leave to set in the fridge for several hours.

Before serving, place the cheesecake over a dish, realise the side spring. Dip a small knife in hot water and loosen the sides. Peel the paper off and serve.

Serves: 6 or more
Preparation: 50 minutes, plus setting time

THE CANCER

Prendi un giorno alla volta, e domani fai lo stesso
Take one day at a time, and do the same tomorrow

A friend of ours from London, Hilary, was visiting her mother in Rugby with her husband, Karim, and they called to say that they would like to see us that afternoon. We said that they could join us for dinner. It was lovely to see them and to get together as old friends, talking and reminiscing about things of the past, and enjoying laughter and a lovely meal. Karim and I talked a lot about French food as he had spent some time in France when he was younger.

When we had enjoyed the meal and it was time for our friends to leave, Caroline went with our car to escort our friends to the nearby motorway for London. While she was out, I cleared the kitchen, and then poured myself a glass of brandy. I sat down and thought about enjoying it. I used to drink a glass of brandy or a liqueur occasionally, sometimes after dinner with friends. In my family, the cabinet was not complete without a bottle or two of something strong, especially during the winter months!

That evening, as I started sipping the brandy, I felt a burning sensation on my lower lip – a hot and unpleasant feeling that I have never experienced before. 'Unusual!' I thought. Then, I placed the tip of the glass more inside my mouth, trying to sip the alcohol and cover my lip so as to avoid the pain. I could still feel the burning sensation, though. I felt my lower lip, and realised that there was a small lesion there. I thought at first that it was a cold sore and I was sure that by applying some lip cream it would heal in days. It didn't go away after that, though, and all sorts of strange thoughts went through my mind.

At the age of seventeen, I had fallen ill with a skin disorder called scleroderma, an illness that affects the tissue and muscles of the skin. It makes it difficult to close the fingers, and the skin on the face becomes tight. I was lucky enough to have caught it in time and the disease was stopped by strong drugs, but nevertheless I need to be checked regularly. For years I have been seen and checked by a dermatologist wherever I have lived. My specialist, Dr Charles Holmes, has looked after me since we moved to the Midlands, and has taken great care of my health.

I went to see him for the usual check-up a few years back. (By then I had had an attack of rheumatoid arthritis and was treated by Dr Weinstein, who put me on a course of strong drugs.) I had pointed out to him a small cut on my lower lip that was giving me a little discomfort. Dr Charles Holmes prescribed me an ointment and in days it cleared. In the meantime, I kept taking the drugs for my arthritis.

Now it was different; I could feel a very small hard lump, but I never thought that it was the start of cancer. I went along to my GP to ask him to prescribe me the same ointment as had been given to me by Dr Charles Holmes. I had written the name on the last page of my address book just in case one day I might need it again. The name of the ointment came in very handy, but this time it did not seem to have much effect.

I had my usual appointment booked to see my dermatologist at our local hospital, but this time he wasn't there, and another doctor saw me instead. Sitting at his desk opposite him, I mentioned the cut on my lip. The doctor looked across at me and, hardly moving his body from the chair, he told me that if it got any worse, I should come back and see him again. I left the hospital and the doctor did not even touch my lip.

The next appointment I had was to see my consultant, Dr Weinstein, for a complete check-up. All was well regarding the arthritis, but he said that he didn't like the look of the lip. He suggested making sure I actually got to see Dr Charles Holmes at the hospital.

Caroline always accompanied me, and she made another appointment for me after I had seen Dr Weinstein.

For some reason Dr Charles Holmes could not be at the hospital for my appointment again, but instead a younger female doctor saw me and took a small tissue sample from my lip for a biopsy.

We had to wait one week for the results. We came back home. I went straight to bed with a couple of stitches, a numb mouth and no worries whatsoever. It was our son Edilio who was not very happy about my condition, although we tried hard to reassure him that there were no big problems. Caroline had asked the doctor what it might be, and she had replied that it could be cancer, but I hadn't heard that. In fact, I do not think either of us had. In any case, it had not registered or we had tried to put that word to the back of our minds.

We went back for the result a week later. A nurse I knew invited me to enter a room, but it was not the one that I was familiar with.

"Sit down, Mr Iacaruso; Dr Charles Holmes will see you very soon," she said.

Caroline was standing near the door and Dr Charles Holmes walked in from a side door holding the sheet of paper with the test results in his hands.

"I am afraid it is skin cancer – a carcinoma – Mr Iacaruso," he said.

Instantly I felt a chill going down my spine and a lack of oxygen around me. I am sure that if I hadn't been sitting on the chair, I would have fallen on the floor like a deadweight. Caroline started to cry and took a handkerchief out of her handbag to wipe the tears away. We both looked at each other in shock. I had never thought for one moment that I might be next!

Suddenly, the nurses and the doctor were very kindly trying to reassure us and were telling us not to panic. They told us that it was a very common type of cancer called carcinoma, which lots of people get, and which is treatable. We were comforted and reassured by these comments and by the knowledge that we could see a plastic surgeon, who could operate and reconstruct my lower lip after the cancer was removed. We had a choice: we could be helped by Mr

Anthony Groves, either through the NHS or through a private clinic. We left the hospital in a daze and we decided to go out to lunch; Caroline took me out as a treat. She was trying very hard to keep the conversation going between us. Although I was half listening, I couldn't stop thinking about my cancer. It was like a nail stuck in the back of my head. On returning home, Caroline started ringing various clinics so that she could make an appointment as soon as possible with Mr Groves, but she could not get hold of him. We wanted to have this thing removed quickly to stop the cancer growing, but a wedding breakfast had been booked for the following month, and we could not let our friends down.

Through her patience and savoir faire Caroline made our first appointment with Mr Groves and the following week, in April 1995, I had the cancer removed. It was a very small operation, although a serious one, and I was sent back home the same day. The surgeon had beautifully reconstructed my lip; we were very happy and we breathed a sigh of relief. My check-up at the private clinic went by with an all-clear from the doctor.

The summer after that affair was a beautiful warm summer, full of activities. In my spare time I enjoy gardening, although I had been advised to wear a hat to protect my face from the sun. We took a week's holiday to Jersey together with our son, Edilio, and his godmother, Maureen, who was visiting us from New York. We had a nice rest, but I had hoped for better weather.

Our garden summerhouse had been delivered, and so I spent time wallpapering it to make it good and cosy. In September, Caroline and I took our son, Edilio, to Caerleon, where he was to study for a BA in film and video. Before leaving, I promised that I would visit him as often as I could.

About the same time as we took Edilio back, the well-known author and broadcaster, Henrietta Green, published a new book: *The Food Lover's Guide to Great Britain*, in which our business is featured amongst those of many other producers. At the end of November, Henrietta, in order to promote the book, invited a dozen of the best suppliers to exhibit their own produce at St Christopher's Place in London. We felt very privileged to be asked. I went full speed on baking to have a good stock ready for the fair, while Caroline wrote and sent invitations to all our London friends so that they could come along and visit our stall. Just about everyone we knew turned up, either the first evening or over the next few days while we were there.

It was a lovely evening, meeting everyone who came to our stall and impressing them with our beautiful display of goods. Amongst our friends there was Dorothy Everard, Lord Snowdon's ex-secretary. We had known Dorothy since the days I worked at Kensington Palace and we have always kept in touch. Dorothy looked at us both; we were so pleased to see her again after such a long time. She drew Caroline aside and said that she was concerned for my health: "Keep an eye on him, Caroline," she said.

The evening progressed and another friend of ours arrived – Malcolm Thomas, whose wife, Anne, was already helping Caroline at the fair along with our nephew, Mark. Malcolm was driving me home to Warwickshire that evening and we left as soon as we could. I enjoyed that evening very much but was very glad to be going home because I was beginning to feel very tired.

Caroline must have thought that I was tired because I had put all my energy into the fair and the business.

Two weeks after the end of the fair, on 13 December, I got up to start my usual working day. I began to feel unwell. I was dizzy, and I could not concentrate on my morning's work to finish the order that I had. I have not forgotten that morning yet. A stabbing, nasty pain on the right side of the mouth came from nowhere. Quite uncomfortable! I felt a sore with my tongue. I began wondering if I had had something similar to this before, or whether it could be just an infection that in a matter of days might be gone. I knew, though; somehow I could feel inside me that the cancer had returned – a secondary one. I was sweating and felt cold.

I tried not to think about it and to work with a free mind. The *homo sapienti* tells us when something is seriously wrong with ourselves. We feel it inside no matter how hard we try to hide our worry. Half of me was saying that it could not be another cancer, and the other was saying that it must be cancer because of these stabbing pains on the side of my mouth. I was hoping the former would be right. I kept it all to myself that day and I did not say a word to Caroline of how anxious I was until the next day. My soul was shivering in fear.

An appointment was arranged straight away for Mr Groves to examine me. Another biopsy was taken, and the surgeon confirmed that the tumour had spread to the corner of my mouth. He called our home and spoke to Caroline, suggesting that he could remove the tumour within days, before he went away on holiday.

A year before, David Owen had telephoned Caroline to ask if we would donate canapés for a charity event that he was supporting in which Rory Bremner would perform at one of Stratford-upon-Avon's theatres. Of course we agreed and it came to the time that this function was being held. In fact, it was the very week my cancer was diagnosed. That week we had a call from them to say that the number was for 250 people and we duly made a beautiful selection of just over 1,000 canapés and took them over to the Owen's home. On entering their kitchen, Caroline told them that it would appear that I had a secondary facial cancer.

They looked astonished to say the least and they both said, "Do you know who these canapés are for?"

We didn't have a clue.

"They are going to be served at the party to raise money for the Get A-Head Charity Appeal," said Mrs Owen. "Mr John Watkinson, a surgeon, is a specialist in cancers of the ear, nose and throat at Queen Elizabeth Hospital in Birmingham and he is a personal friend of David's. He has asked us to help with this event, which is raising funds to help people who have cancer at the Queen Elizabeth Hospital."

On leaving, I said that we made these canapés with all our hearts, and hoped it would help to raise a lot of money. News came back to us that they were very much enjoyed by everyone, and that Mr Owen had told the surgeon that the chef who had made the canapés had facial cancer. Mr John Watkinson immediately said that I was to go and see him. Mr Owen very kindly made an appointment on my behalf to see the surgeon the following week, on 25 January 1996.

A dear friend of ours, Anne Thomas, drove us to the private clinic in Birmingham for the first consultation, which was where an end and a new beginning in my life took hold of me. We introduced ourselves to Mr Watkinson. He told us to sit down. We handed over a letter from my GP, John Hancock. He read it and asked us a series of questions while he filled in another sheet of paper: age, date and place of birth, all my past illnesses, and so on. I was looking at his writing and thinking, 'More paper on my medical notes!'

"Remove your jacket and tie, sir!" the surgeon said. "Open your mouth wide; I have to feel the tumour."

He then looked inside my nose and my ears and down my throat. It was a truly horrifying experience! Returning to his desk, he wrote down in front of us that I had cancer – carcinoma of the right cheek, buccal mucosa, extending just to the anterior commissure of the mouth. He then added, "If there is something that I cannot do, I will tell you straight away, Mr and Mrs Iacaruso."

My blood turned stone cold. As a great specialist, we had gone to him privately to seek the best treatment available, and of course he put his cards on the table and told the two of us the truth. Fair enough! He looked concerned and preoccupied with my scleroderma, which indicated a high risk. His concern was that if the radiotherapy did not eradicate the tumour, I might need radical surgery on my cheek. A new skin graft would then have to be taken from the inside of my arm, which might not take on my face! Also, the operation per se did not look very nice. I did not hear or understand a word of what he said. My mind must have been absent. I learned about all this later.

Mr Watkinson told us to go home and said that he would put together a team of specialists and then contact us. Meanwhile, I had to shave off my beard and return to the hospital two days later for dental clearance (to have all my teeth extracted). We reached home and we got a message left by Mr Watkinson saying that we had to return to Birmingham immediately. He wanted the oncologist, Dr John Glaholm, to see me. Off we drove straight away, with Anne still at the steering wheel.

Dr Glaholm examined the tumour and the neck, and they both came to the conclusion that the radiotherapy would blast the tumour off. There was a great chance to eradicate it completely without surgery.

Prior to the radiotherapy, I arrived on Thursday morning, 1 February 1996 at the Queen Elizabeth Hospital. Tests had to be carried out for the next morning's surgery of dental clearance. Before the operation, Dr Scot Russell, the anaesthetist, sat next to my bed to explain the procedure and how the maxillofacial unit carried out the operation.

Two days later, I left the hospital without a tooth in my head, and I got rid of my toothbrush and toothpaste. Even without my beard and teeth, though, we felt we were at the right place, and that we had one another. Caroline, Edilio and I were a formidable team, and very strong to face whatever was going to happen. I was faced with a new way of eating, not a diet. All the food had to be soft, puréed, boiled or poached. My gums were extremely sore for weeks. I had to give up a lot of my favourite food dishes, like a humble plate of pasta or a slice of meat, but I never dramatised about it; I had to accept it if I was to get through my illness. I didn't have any other choice. I suppose being a chef helped me to choose a varied menu without getting bored.

Meanwhile, more check-ups followed to examine my gums and to see how well they were healing.

I received a letter from the hospital asking me to attend an appointment at the oncology department, where a plastic cast of my face had to be made before the radiotherapy began. A cold wet plaster was spread all over my face and an uncomfortable feeling took over. I wondered how long it would be before it was finished. The plaster was left to set for a while and then eventually it was removed. A technician then made a mask of rigid transparent plastic. After the mask was made, I had to wait for my next appointment to try it on, as the mask must fit accurately. During the radiotherapy the mask is placed on your face, and clipped onto both sides of the radiotherapy bench to keep the head still on a padded metal plate.

Another visit to Dr John Glaholm followed, and I was given a date to start the radiotherapy. Our dear friends, Anne and Malcolm Thomas, had told us that they would take me to Birmingham on alternate days to Caroline, which was indeed a great help.

At 12.30 p.m. every day, Caroline or Anne and I would set out for Birmingham for a two-o'clock appointment after I had finished my morning work. We would enter the vast radiology department with its many rooms, all of which were numbered to deal with different types of cancer. I would announce my arrival at the reception desk. They would thank me and tell me to walk towards suite number 2 where we sat in a small but long corridor-like waiting room, which was already filled with other patients sharing the same problem of cancer. In front of us a low table was covered with outdated magazines, and I would flip through the problem pages (I was curious to read about other people's problems) while Caroline or Anne would get a coffee from the department kiosk, usually staffed by female volunteers. Sometimes, I would make a batch of home-made shortbread biscuits and give them to the kiosk to sell, or I might give some to the radiologist's girls, which always delighted them.

A radiologist would call my name, and I had to walk into a room with an irradiating machine in the middle of it.

There were three young female radiologists, and one of the three would offer a cheery smile and say, "How are you today, Giuseppe?"

"I am fine," I would reply. "The cheek is more painful, but we've got to go through with it."

I had to strip down to my waist, and I managed to surprise them because I remained the same weight throughout the radiotherapy. I had been warned that during the therapy one loses weight, but I had kept eating as much as I could, especially puddings, because they were soft to eat and they could keep up my strength.

The nurse that was weighing me used to remark with a laugh, "Giuseppe, you are the only patient that I know who has not lost weight!"

I then lay down on the machine's bench, and, by turning my head to the left, I could see the radiographer picking up my labelled mask from amongst three shelves full of clear, empty plastic masks. She would clamp my mask over my face, and press the back of my head onto a padded metal plate. The radiographer aligned me under the green laser beam set into the ceiling and then a button would be pressed. I counted the warning beeper's thirty beeps while the machine irradiated away. The warning beeps are to give the radiologists time to get out of the room and behind the lead screen.

My sessions did not last very long as the tumour was only small – about 1cm in diameter. I could feel it, and see it in the mirror and we all thought that the cancer would be cured easily. Halfway through the treatment the tumour was becoming softer and misshapen and the oncologist, Dr John Glaholm, (as well as us!) was thrilled that the radiotherapy was working well. My cheek was becoming redder, though, and the skin burnt with pain. The beard roots had burnt out and some of the hair on my neck too. It became impossible to have a good night's sleep. I would wake several times in the night with my mouth and tongue dried up due to the salivary glands being affected by the therapy. We had a night light that Caroline would tap, and it would stay light for at least a minute, which was time enough for me to dab my mouth with a cotton bud drenched in olive oil so I could go back to sleep.

Since the operation, I have to use vaseline to keep my gums and nostrils moist through the night. At first, it was not very pleasant, but then I became used to it. Now I couldn't leave home without it.

I was prescribed morphine to ease the pain. One evening before going to bed Caroline filled up the spoon a little too much. What an ache! The following morning I felt as if the floor was moving under my feet, and the ceiling was spinning around my head.

Every weekday for twenty days we travelled to Birmingham. As a landscape painter I would observe and admire the countryside in silence. While the car was going through the winding roads I would look at the wonderful open fields in more depth: the trees, the flying birds, the beautiful hills, a tractor ploughing the earth, and the land cultivated for the next harvest. I would make a frame with my eyes like a print in my mind, and I used to ask myself if I would see this beautiful scenery full of life and activities the year after. You are told that everything is going to be all right, but I also had an inner fear inside me. The oncology department in any circumstance is not a happy place to be.

Many patients are unaccompanied, and one day we asked why this was. Was it because their partners were unable to take time off work? We were quickly told that sadly a lot of people cannot cope with their partners' illness and stress, and they stay away. During my therapy I kept my spirit and humour high. I didn't want to frighten my family by moaning about my ordeal, or how my appearance had changed. We used to go out to places; I never wanted to become a recluse because my face was not as I wanted it to be.

One day we went out shopping. While I was waiting in the car our friends, Janet and her daughter, Lucy, came by to say hello. They couldn't believe the state I was in and hardly recognised me. We had a chat about how I was getting on and I never remember saying anything about the cancer. Then I heard from Caroline that Janet had been so upset she had cried all the way while driving back home.

On the last day of my therapy, I was with Anne and the radiologist asked us to follow her to Dr Glaholm's office. On entering I was presented with the largest bouquet of flowers I had ever seen. I was speechless and amazed. I couldn't understand why I was given the flowers. Then they told me that they were for being a good patient, for waiting and never asking when I was going to be called, not even when the machine was serviced and the radiotherapy sessions were running late. They said they were very touched by my kindness in bringing some pastries to help raise money for the coffee shop.

Six weeks after the radiotherapy the tumour had not responded. The tumour was getting larger and more painful. It was easily irritated when it was in contact with food. We both became worried and had to ask, "Why is the cancer not cured?"

Caroline made a personal phone call to Mr John Watkinson at his home on Sunday, 30 April explaining our concern. On 10 May we went back to the Queen Elizabeth Hospital and both Dr Glaholm and Mr Watkinson saw me at the outpatient clinic. The registrar took the last biopsy in the surgical room next door. Outside, a Macmillan liaison sister was comforting Caroline, who was in tears.

"Why do you cry, honey?" I asked as I was coming out of the room. "I am the one who should cry, not you!"

I approached Mr Watkinson's desk. "Well, Mr Iacaruso, are you right-handed or left-handed?"

"I am left-handed like any genius!" I swiftly replied, thinking it was a good humorous answer. But it didn't provoke any smiles – he had other things on his mind, and looked pensive.

"You have to come into the hospital next week on 16 May," he said.

The day before I had to go, I was gathering a few things to take with me: a pair of pyjamas, a washbag, a few tapes and a book on Pavarotti. In the afternoon I sat on my bed at home, next to my bedside table, which has three drawers. I pulled the middle one open, where I keep my very first black leather wallet – the same one I had when I left home at the age of fourteen. In there in various small compartments I kept the same photos of my parents, my brothers and sisters, and the saints' figures which the village celebrates on 7, 8, and 9 September – St Nicholas, Madonna of the Grace and St Bartholomew. I was going to take the Madonna of the Grace with me, but I could not find it. I don't know how long I sat on the bed for – I had searched everywhere for the picture without finding it.

Caroline walked into the room and asked me what I was doing there.

I replied that I was doing nothing, just looking.

"But what are you looking for?" she asked.

"Ah, just something."

"Well, what is it?"

I didn't want to tell her that I was looking for the Madonna of the Grace. I felt stupid and silly that at my age I wanted to take the picture to help me to get through. In the end I confessed. The next thing I knew, Caroline had phoned our friend Daphne, the wife of Renato, who comes from the same village as myself. She told her what had happened with my picture, and Renato, who happened to have the image of the Madonna of the Grace in his wallet, sent it to me at the Queen Elizabeth Hospital. I received it the day after the operation, and pinned it on the cork board amongst other get-well cards.

As I sat on my bed that afternoon, I had the opportunity to think about the operation. What my mind went through was not a dream but a vision: I would place the image on the hospital bed headboard to help me through. How? I don't know, perhaps with a piece of string or Sellotape. But a nurse would then tell me, "Giuseppe, the image cannot be left like that. It needs to be put in a sterilised plastic bag." On the morning of the operation I would be wheeled into the theatre room on the same bed – my bed, the bed I spent the night in – still with the image pinned on the headboard looking down on me to protect me. The surgeons and the theatre staff would be dressed in their clean and crisp green uniforms, busy getting ready. There would be all the silver equipment laid at hand. The lights would be fully on, and I would be asleep. Then, just at the last millesimo of a second, before the surgeon used the scalpel and as he felt for the tumour for the last time, he wouldn't be able to find it. No matter how much he would search, it had gone! Disappeared! The Madonna had given me the grace. The surgeons and staff would shout in jubilation, "This is a miracle, miracle!" My lovely face would be spared. . . .

But, as an Italian saying goes, the reality is another pair of hands.

On the morning I was due to leave for the hospital I delayed the departure for as long as possible. I don't know what I was thinking of. I went on tidying the garden, and emptying old earth from the flower boxes and refilling them with new earth. I wanted to have them ready to plant geraniums on my return home from the hospital. Caroline later told me that she had rung the ward and explained that I would be a little late and, as ever, the lovely staff on East 5 realised that I was anxious. They told Caroline not to worry, but I would have to have a few more tests done before the operation so three o'clock would be a good time to be there. I am a very orderly man, cautious and optimistic. I could sense no need to rush, and I knew that I would not be able to lie in the hospital bed thinking that I had left behind an untidy garden. In charge of the business were my chef, Matthew, and my assistant, Steve.

Caroline and I drove to Birmingham.

I was booked for eleven, but we didn't arrive until well after two o'clock. The room I was to be in had two beds; another patient, called Keith, occupied one of the beds – he had been operated on the week before for cancer of the nose. My bed was made up, with my name, Giuseppe, written on a card and placed on the headboard.

Soon, with Caroline in tow, I was sent to different departments in order to run the standard tests of my blood, my heart and my general condition, all of which felt very good.

We had a lovely room in the head-and-neck unit, which is on the fifth floor, and which looked like a private room with its bright walls and airy feeling. Glass doors opened onto a balcony, overlooking a part of the back of the hospital. The

238

balcony, which ran along the whole of one side of the ward, was very appealing to me, but it was not usable. I unpacked my few things and placed on my bedside table a small bouquet of freesias. I also pinned the first get-well card on the board; our friend, Janet Moore, had given it to me. As the afternoon moved on, nurses and junior doctors came to examine me and take more details.

A Catholic priest by the name of Father Francis soon paid me his first visit, and he promised to come and see me again to give me Communion after the operation. Later in the day Mr John Watkinson brought along a new surgeon, Mr Steve Dover, a man I had not yet met but who was to become part of the operation team. Later on, when I had check-ups in the maxillofacial unit to look at my cancer and to check my strength and the inside of my arm, it was this man who carried out the tests. Mr John Watkinson, after my operation, remarked that if the operation had not been carried out, I would have been a dead duck. A few months after the operation, I invited him over for lunch, and I gave roast duck as a main course!

I soon settled down in the hospital. Caroline and Keith's family were chatting away like old friends, and we are still friends to this day. I had all the confidence in the world that I was in good hands and that all would be all right in the end. Caroline, for the duration of my stay, booked a room at the nurse's home, which was just across from the main building, and this meant that we could be together.

Soon the day turned into night, and then the night into morning, and by seven o'clock Caroline was at my bedside, all beautifully made-up. A nurse handed me some tablets to take one hour before the operation in order to make me drowsy. I had to be in the operating theatre by 8.15 exactly.

Dr Scot Russell, the anaesthetist, who was a gentle and kind person, came in and sat next to me to take me through the operation again. At the allotted hour, an elderly Indian man and a theatre nurse came into my room to wheel my bed to the anaesthetic room next to the operating theatre, where Dr Russell would give me the anaesthetic. Caroline and more nurses followed me in procession. At the door Caroline gave me a kiss and waved goodbye.

I was transferred onto the operating bed. Dr Russell gave me an injection accompanied with a few words while the Indian male nurse placed the gas mask over my mouth and in a soft voice said, "A little gas, sir." All the while this was going on my right hand was holding tightly to the hand of one of the nurses, and then I went out like a candle.

A team of five surgeons worked on my face for nearly ten hours. My right cheek and part of my lips had to be dissected to remove the tumour, and then reconstructed with a flap of skin taken from the inside of my right forearm. My forearm was given a skin graft from my leg. Caroline spent most of the day in the hospital chapel, and Keith's wife, Jenny, and their daughter comforted her. Mr Watkinson came out from the theatre to reassure her that the operation was going fine, and she also kept in touch with my family in Italy by telephone, giving news as the day progressed. Caroline has been a wonderful wife, homemaker and mother all through my illness, and she has been a pillar of strength that I couldn't have done without.

At 7.30 in the evening I was waking up in the ward. Caroline was sitting there and then Dr Marcel Macnamara came to see me and said that the operation had gone extremely well. I had no pain but a lot of discomfort, and was mainly just relieved that it was over and that at last the cancer had been removed. I remember winking at Dr Marcel and she and Caroline smiled back at me. Soon after that, I started to roll my eyes several times and to look at Caroline on my left side. I was trying to make signs for her to look up at the clock that was hanging above her head, but she couldn't understand what I wanted. I began to get frustrated – frustrated that my wife couldn't understand her own husband after so many years of being married. She thought they had done something to my brain. She rang for the nurse, and told her that she couldn't understand what it was that I wanted. The nurse replied, "He wants to know the time!"

I nodded off, I awoke, I nodded off, and I awoke. Anne and Malcolm came to see me and stayed with Caroline awhile. My eyelids were heavy and my body was sedated with morphine. In fact, I had never realised that I would not be able to communicate orally after the operation, and I had to write notes now rather than talk. I now understand that this was because I had a temporary tracheotomy in order to maintain a safe airway during my recovery from this type of surgery.

The tracheotomy was most irritating and I hated it, especially during the suction and the cleaning of it. My neighbour, Keith, agreed. When the tracheotomy tube was first removed the site would not heal, in spite of the stitches and, on eating, the food would leak out and make a mess. I was pinned to the bed by a dozen tubes and a heavy plaster on my right arm, from where they had taken the skin flap to reconstruct my cheek. A thin layer of skin had been taken from my left leg to graft onto my forearm, and this also restricted my movement. It seemed that tubes were all over me. There were two inserted on one side of my neck to assist fluid drainage. There was an intravenous drip inserted into my left hand to which more tubes were connected to give antibiotics, glucose and morphine through the vein. There was also a tube connected to a catheter that had been shoved up my little brother to carry away my urine. Finally I had a line connected at the end of me, to a plastic ring around my toe, to monitor my oxygen level and pulse. There was also an inflatable plastic cushion around my left arm that would inflate automatically through the night to check my blood pressure, and a beeping machine that monitored some of my cardiovascular attributes.

Well-wisher cards kept arriving by the dozen, including a telegram from Prince and Princess Michael of Kent. The board on the wall was completely covered. I never thought I had so many friends who cared. On the first Sunday after my operation prayers were said for me in three churches simultaneously.

Caroline bought a draw-and-erase board to make it easier for us to communicate with each other. She stayed with me and hardly left my bedside, which pleased Mr Watkinson. My sister-in-law, Charlotte, came down from Scotland for what was meant to be a short visit, but instead remained for nearly a week. She visited me on the second day and Caroline and I were pleased to see her. She was staying with a friend in Birmingham and was coming the next day again. That evening Caroline called her and asked her why she was staying with a friend when she should be with us – so the next day she came with a little bag and stayed the rest of the week. Keith and I were entertained by her long conversations and she kept all our spirits up.

For a short time I was bed-bound and uncomfortable. The heavy plaster on my right arm was in the way, there were yards of bandage on my leg, my right arm was tied with tubes, and I just couldn't move properly. It was as if I weighed a ton. The nurses kept coming, though, and gave me all the attention I needed; and Mr Watkinson was very pleased with the way I was responding to the treatment after the operation. At around eight o'clock every morning he would come into the room to see if I was feeling well, and if there were any problems with the new skin.

A few days after the operation I was allowed to see my face for the first time. A nurse brought a mirror into the room while Mr Watkinson was there. "What do you think of your new look, Pino?" he asked.

I hesitated at first, smiled and then replied, "I look a little different."

What could I have said when this wonderful man had saved my life? Could I say how terrible I looked? Could I say that I was not happy like that? I had to accept it, though, and have now accepted it. After nearly five years I must be the most known patient around Warwickshire, and the ENT department are very proud of me.

When the first tubes began to be pulled out, I began to feel more cheerful. A few days later our son, Edilio, came to see me, and the three of us spent a long weekend together. It must have been an awful shock for Edilio to see me like this. He was at university and I am thankful he had not come the first weekend after surgery. When he came the main part was over and the three of us treasured the quiet and peace around us; and we all had to adjust to what was really a kind of different life ahead of us. The main difference was that when the three of us were together, at home or abroad, I would be quite unconcerned by people staring; but I knew Caroline and Edilio noticed and they were most protective and I think a little bit angry. Several years on, the three of us have got used to me. After all, I am still the same husband and father and I value our love and friendship.

Keith had left his bed by then and gone home. I began shuffling round the long corridors to exercise my leg now that the bandages had been removed, and Caroline would support me past the other wards. Everyone was either recovering from recent surgery, or was waiting in some relapsed state which called for intensive care. In one bed was an Italian woman who had had major surgery and couldn't talk any more, and in another was an elderly Indian man who was very ill. All his family and relations were visiting at the same time, when all the poor man needed was his peace and quiet. Others were recovering silently, unvisited, just looking around and staring at things. I said to Caroline, "Aren't these patients so very ill!" forgetting that I was one of them.

One afternoon, Father Francis came to see me, and, as I remember, I was on my own and not feeling too well. The tracheotomy was worrying me. He had been several times and said to me, "The first time I came you were being operated on, the second you were asleep, and the third I was told you couldn't talk. Now I want to give you Communion."

He handed me a card and told me that we should recite The Lord's Prayer. I nodded my head in agreement, and sat on my neighbour's bed with my back against the balcony door. Father Francis stood in front of me.

"Our Father, which art in Heaven, Hallowed be thy name. Thy Kingdom come, thy will be done . . . "

Then suddenly I burst into tears, still holding The Lord's Prayer card in my right hand. I was sobbing like a child, and I couldn't stop. The tears were streaming down my face. One hundred things were going through my head: the condition I was in, my father, my dead mother, my brothers and sisters far away from me in Italy, and my darling family, Edilio and Caroline, and what they were going through. Father Francis placed his right hand over my forehead to comfort and reassure me. He recited the prayer all on his own. That was the first time I had cried since the cancer took hold of me. That day, I felt the lowest that I had ever been.

Two weeks later, on a Friday morning, I was sent back home, and was kept in bed for the entire weekend by order of Caroline. She said to me that the doctors had said so, but I never believed that they had! On Monday morning, I went downstairs to see the chefs. I wanted to know how they were getting on, and to inspect the work they had done.

My first trip out was to Sainsbury's (for a change!). This was the moment of truth for me, going out and facing the world in my changed state. I ended up just looking ahead and pretending that people weren't looking at me, but I knew they were. I could detect them out of the corner of my eye, their faces and their reactions to what they saw. I would pretend that I hadn't noticed. You don't see somebody with a face like mine walking around often, and our eyes are there for us to see things that are different. At the checkout, a nice elderly lady very politely asked what I had done. I replied that at the weekend I had had a fight with Frank Bruno, but she didn't hear me. My voice was muffled and my cheek was swollen, so I was going to have to try harder to make myself understood, but Caroline quickly put the record straight.

Some friends came to see me one afternoon and they remarked how well I looked and what a good job the surgeons had done on my face. Caroline remarked that there was also the risk that the new skin might not have taken due to my skin disorder. She has also said so many times how lucky she is that she still has her darling man and that Edilio still has his father.

At one point when the illness first started we had been told it could be just a matter of time before something happened to me, and all I can say now for both of us is how fortunate we have been. We have the utmost faith in our doctors and now, a few years later, they have become very dear friends along with their partners and children. May I say, we have been truly blessed.

My days soon returned to being as normal as they could be. I would go outside into the garden to try to do some work for half an hour. This was the most I could manage, as I didn't have the strength for any more; the operation had taken it away from me. My meals had to be different from that of everyone else who was at home. Before I could start to eat, I had to place a standing mirror on the table so that I could spoon the food towards where the mouth hole was, for I had lost the direction! Every sort of vegetable I had was boiled and reduced to a purée, boiled fish was mashed, mince was also mashed and whatever gravy was around was delicious. It was a pity that it wasn't until much later that I discovered couscous, which I found filling, soft and nourishing. At times, I could have killed for eggs and bacon or a proper meal. But given time and patience I knew that everything would be all right. My intention was never to make an illness out of it and to cause anxiety to my wonderful family over here and in Italy.

I have learnt so much since the cancer, especially the virtues of being patient and more tolerant. Why had this happened to me? I have never taken it out on anybody or got angry. Certainly I would have preferred to have my face as it had been. In the September of the same year that I came out of hospital, I received a phone call from Carlton Television, and a young woman asked me if they could film me for a food programme. When I enquired who gave her my name she answered that I had been highly recommended by a friend of hers. Caroline took over the negotiation and phone calls were exchanged. Although Caroline mentioned to this young lady about my facial cancer, she still wanted to meet me. I would have liked to appear on television like so many other chefs, but I don't know if I would have been good or bad. I felt that for once I might have had the chance to show my skill on television, but sadly the cancer took that away from me. I was in the right place, but at the wrong time! Never mind.

Since then two other companies got in touch and one suggested that they would not show my face, just my hands making whatever. The second company came to film one day and when they had first come I impressed them with many different kinds of *patisserie*. Their next request was that when they came to film nothing was to be prepared. We would have to start from scratch. The day duly arrived and four films were made. We have them still. It was a disaster because they wanted me to make a French wedding cake, the croquembouche. You need to make preparations, and to be told on the day was a mistake. If there should ever be another chance, I really would have to know in advance what I was doing. You cannot make an omelette without any eggs.

The cancer has changed me and, although I am still busy with my cooking for our business, I have learnt to slow down. I bless the sunrise each day. My life has become more precious then ever, and I look forward to having a good working day, and to reaching the peak of the mountain at the end of it.

The year after the operation, in June, we were asked to cater for a buffet for over 150 people to raise money for the Get A-Head charity. This was for the ENT department and the Macmillan nurses. I decided that I would also donate two watercolours of mine to be auctioned, and that I would also be auctioned to cook a dinner for eight at someone's home, which raised a good amount of money. I was being auctioned from £1,000 up to £2,500 a dinner. One summer two people battled it out and I went for £2,500 to one gentleman and £2,000 to a lady for whom I have catered at several parties since. She has been a great support to the Get A-Head charity.

I celebrated the millennium with my very first exhibition of over fifty watercolour paintings; this was a dream that I had had for many years. Some of my early works were painted and signed as early as 1994, before I had the cancer. I would finish my work and spend the afternoons with a brush in my hand. I had all sorts of ideas and visions of colours to use. I had amassed quite a large number and put them aside, already mounted by myself. I mentioned my idea of this exhibition to the Get A-Head organizer, Val Spittle, who passed it on to the chairman of Get A-Head, the consultant Mr Watkinson, and the committee, who approved the idea.

From then on it was a non-stop period of work and painting, of success and failure. I am not one who likes to hide the bad paintings, so I tore them up and they went straight into the bin to leave no trace behind. The exhibition was held at the home of one of the committee members, who had a beautifully well-maintained garden in the country. It was a beautiful and sunny day. The guests were arriving and strolling around with drinks in their hands, admiring the paintings in one corner of the garden. I had some volunteers to help me to display them. The paintings were hung on large boards and were beautifully arranged – a mixture of still lifes and landscapes. It was a very proud moment of great achievement that I had waited for all my life. A few yards away on the lawn, I was preparing a buffet for over 200 guests in a marquee with my helpers and other chefs. It was very hard and anxious work but the reward was worth it. So far I have raised a fair amount towards the charity, and it has given me a lot of pleasure, knowing that it will help other patients.

Whilst I was having the radiotherapy a few years back now, a new oncology centre had started being built. Dr John Glaholm had been telling me of the new project to make a more comfortable place for the patients to be treated with radiotherapy or chemotherapy, and how wonderful it would be if some local artists would donate their work to give colour and warmth to the rooms. I nodded my head at the time, promising that I would. In my spare time, I put paint on paper, keeping in mind my promise especially for the new unit. I put aside eight watercolours and I handed them to Dr Glaholm to hang at the centre.

Nearly five years have passed since a radiotherapy technician called my tumour 'the beast'. I have been seen as a hero and an example for conquering the cancer, but I know now that without my family, and the love and reassurance that they gave me, it would not have been possible. The cancer has taught me to love with a deeper love and, for the first time, without any pretence. I don't like to plan my days too far ahead. I am always on the lookout for any sign of the cancer's return, but I feel very much more confident with myself, and feel more loved by those so dear to me. I am glad to still have the energy to create this book, and to enjoy carpentry, gardening and drawing, whilst still running our business. My philosophy on my cancer is: if I could put the clock back, no way would I have wanted such a terrible thing to happen to me as to go through this terrifying experience. I liked my face. I did not have the look of a Rudolph Valentino but I was happy with it. My lips were full and red. My teeth were not the best, but at least I could eat properly and have a nice smile.

Pino, 2002

THIS IS WHAT THE WORLD . . . THINKS OF ME

In ones life one is privileged to meet a few exceptional people who have a core of something special within them separating them from others.

Pino, with the wonderfully supportive love of his wife, Caroline is such a man.

Our family were lucky enough to meet them several years ago and they have cooked sumptuous food for just about every family occasion, be it balmy cricket days, weddings, christenings, funerals and gatherings with friends.

Pino seems to tackle anything that you ask him to do with unfailing, unflappable, expertise and pleasure. Always courteous, always kind. He gathers round him a team of lovely people.

He is an exceptionally generous man and our family feel very glad that we have been fortunate enough to have known him, and look forward to many more years of similar good times together.

This list of his accomplishments is very long and whatever he turns his hand to, he seems to succeed. We wish him well and send him our love and thanks.

Jean Sidwell, Bourton-on-the-Water

I always regretted not learning sufficient Italian to be able to converse with Pino about his cooking and art work as most of his creations sounded much more romantic in Italian than English.

Pino always comes across as being very inquisitive, but it is just his manner of starting a conversation, such as 'Hello Lynne, what are you doing?' or 'Hello Lynne, where are you going?' He is forever the optimist and deserves every success. He always made me feel that my opinion was valued when I helped with his first book.

Lynne Marple, Derbyshire

AGNELLO AL FORNO
ROAST LAMB WITH MINT

This lamb dish is from my area where the lamb is reared in the fields that surround our countryside. It is prepared slightly differently and has a rustic taste. I remember when the older professional chefs would sit in the village square and talk of their cooking days in the far corners of the world.

2kg/4¼lb leg of lamb
Salt
Freshly ground black pepper
3 cloves garlic, roughly chopped
1 large bunch fresh mint, chopped
2–3 tbsp olive oil
Juice of 1 lemon
1 sprig of rosemary
1 stick of celery, finely chopped
1 carrot, finely chopped
1 small onion, finely chopped

Ask your butcher to bone a leg of lamb. Season with salt, add the garlic and half of the chopped mint. Roll it up and tie with kitchen string. Season the outside and place the joint on a rack in a roasting tin, fat side up. Pour over the olive oil, lemon juice and place a sprig of rosemary on top. Surround with the chopped vegetables and place in a preheated oven to roast for 30 minutes.

Turn the heat down, add 300ml/½ pint water and roast for a little over an hour. Be sure to baste the joint every now and then, and make sure that the vegetables don't burn. The meat should be crisp and brown on the outside, but very tender, pink and juicy inside. (Allow another half hour if well done meat is preferred).

Remove the meat to a warm serving platter and keep warm. Strain the cooking juices from the pan into a jug. Skim off as much fat from the juices as you can and return to the pan. Place the roasting tin over direct heat. Add one glass of white wine and reduce the sauce a little. Mix in the rest of the mint. Carve and pour a little of the sauce over each serving.

Serve: 6–8
Preparation: 30 minutes
Cooking: 1 hour 30 minutes
Oven: 200°C/400°F/Gas 6
After half an hour, turn down to 170°C/325°F/Gas 3 and cook for a further hour.

FUNCHI CON PANNA ACIDA
MUSHROOMS WITH SOUR CREAM

This lovely Italian dish is full of flavour and can be served as a starter on its own with crusty fresh bread, or as an accompaniment to a main course dish.

1kg/2lb 4oz button mushrooms
100ml/3fl oz sour cream
100ml/3fl oz double cream
90g/3oz butter
1 small onion, finely chopped
3 tbsp lemon juice
Salt
Freshly ground black pepper

Wipe the mushrooms with a damp cloth and slice them finely. Melt half the butter in a frying pan; add the mushrooms and fry on a high heat, stirring all the time with a wooden spoon until all the water has evaporated.

Add the remaining butter, the chopped onion, lemon juice, salt and pepper. Cook on a moderate heat to soften the onion.

Mix the two creams together and add to the mushrooms. Stir well, adjust seasoning, pour into a buttered shallow ovenproof dish and bake until the top is golden brown.

Serves: 6
Preparation: 15 minutes
Cooking: 30–35 minutes
Oven: 170°C/325°F/Gas 3

TRIGLIA CON POMPELMO E SALSA AL CURRY
FILLET OF RED MULLET WITH A GRAPEFRUIT AND CURRY SAUCE

6 red mullet, filleted, weighing about 170g/6oz each
Salt
Fleshly ground black pepper
Flour for dusting
Olive oil and butter for frying

Garnish and sauce:
2 pink grapefruits, segmented and warmed in water
300ml/10fl oz double cream
200ml/6fl oz vegetable stock, or water
1½ level tbsp mild or a medium-hot curry powder
Salt
Freshly ground black pepper
Few coriander leaves

Order the fish and ask the fishmonger to fillet it, as it isn't easy to remove all the tiny bones.

First segment the grapefruit. Cut off the ends of the fruit with a sharp knife. Cut off the peel in sections by cutting downwards and making sure you remove all the pith. Cut down between the membranes to remove each segment. Set aside in a bowl.

Melt the butter in a frying pan with the olive oil. Season the fish on both sides and dust with flour. Fry gently skin side down for 2–3 minutes, then turn and fry for a little longer. The fish must not be dry – it should take about 5–6 minutes in all. Transfer the fish to a dish and keep warm.

Drain off the fat, add the curry powder and stock, and bring to the boil. Add the cream and reduce a little. Season with a little salt, and strain into a clean pan. Keep warm.

To serve: Warm up the grapefruit segments by pouring hot water over them in the bowl. Spoon the sauce onto warm plates, place the fish on the sauce and garnish with grapefruit segments and a few coriander leaves.

Serves: 6
Preparation: 30 minutes
Cooking: 5–6 minutes

PANNA CON RABARBARO
CRÈME BRÛLÉE WITH RHUBARB

This rich and velvety crème brûlée lets you rediscover the taste of a real dessert.

300g/12oz fresh rhubarb
110g/4oz caster sugar
50g/1½oz unsalted butter
The rind of 1 small orange
568ml/1pint double cream
1 vanilla pod or vanilla essence
6 egg yolks
3 tbsp caster sugar
3 tbsp brown sugar, to caramelise the top

You will need 1.100 litre/2 pint soufflé dish.

Melt the butter in a frying pan . Add the sugar, the rhubarb (washed, string removed and cut into chunks) and the orange rinds. Cook over a low heat with the pan covered for a few minutes until soft. Put the cooked rhubarb into the soufflé dish and leave to cool.

In a large mixing bowl, cream together the egg yolks and sugar until a pale straw colour. Bring the double cream with the vanilla pod or vanilla essence to the boil. Draw off the heat and leave to stand for a few minutes. Lift out and scrape the vanilla pod. Pour the cream onto the eggs and sugar, whisking continuously, then return the mixture to the saucepan over a low heat and stir to bind the custard to a thick consistency with a wooden spoon. Strain immediately into the soufflé dish, leave to cool until well set. Sieve the brown sugar over the cream custard evenly and place under a very hot, preheated grill until lightly caramelised. Wait for the sugar to set for a minute or two to harden. Serve immediately.

Serves: 6
Preparation: 30 minutes

Chef's note: Place the sieve over the soufflé dish ready to strain the crème brûlée. Maintain the low heat and keep stirring at all time, any distraction or overheating could curdle the custard. Don't be afraid to try! Serve on its own or with a fruit salad of sliced bananas and seedless grapes.

EPILOGUE
by Caroline Iacaruso

Now that we are in the year of 2007, it is with joy that I inscribe the following epilogue. It is eleven years ago that Pino had cancer. Maybe Pino will have to write a third book. There is still lots more to tell!

I have read the manuscript and have loved it. I have also edited this book. How much can I take out or put in? It is Pino's book and I feel that, yes, I could have changed certain passages, but then it would loose Pino's touch. I have laughed so many times remembering Pino's stories. Then I read about his cancer; I thought I knew Pino, but all I knew was how we were all hurting for him, and he never showed me his distress. It is good that he has been able to write it down.

In August 2004, Pino, Edilio and I went to Italy and the village of Rosello had many fabulous days organised for the people in the area. One that had been arranged was that Pino put on a watercolour exhibition. The opening day arrived and the village was very much in party mood. The square was filled with people. There was a wonderful band, a dais for the speeches and the dignitaries arrived, the main person being Remo Gaspari, a lawyer and a retired Member of Parliament. Remo Gaspari was presented with the keys of the village by the Mayor of Rosello, Alessio Monaco. Pino's exhibition was held in the Mayor's office on the first floor of the municipal building in the square. It was perfect. Remo Gaspari came up to open the event followed by all the other dignitaries and Pino's work was so well received and we were quite overwhelmed by everything and everybody. Our dear friends, Rita, Franca and Michele, helped us set it all up, and over the following days they helped Pino and myself, and Edilio videoed the whole event.

Edilio and I are very proud of Pino and of what he has achieved, not just for his cooking, his watercolours, our beautiful garden, his chatter and inquisitive manner but the man himself. He is definitely a one-off. I always love to hear my girlfriends say, "Oh, Car, we could not possibly live with Pino; he is always on the go with so many ideas on cooking, art, painting, music . . . and so on." I love it – all this activity – and his reading has become a firm favourite. They just do not know how lucky I am!

In 2004, just before Christmas, Pino was diagnosed with a third cancer on his tongue. Our dear friend, John Watkinson, had told us to bring Pino into the Queen Elizabeth Hospital and he was to be operated on just two days before Christmas. I was horrified as I thought it meant drastic surgery, but they were able to laser the cancer off. Pino had the procedure and within hours of the operation he was eating lunch and we were allowed to take him home the next day. I thought we had a patient on our hands. Edilio and I had visions of us cooking over Christmas. We had Ann, John, Georgina, Annabel, Patrick, Daisy and Milly coming to see us over the Christmas period. Within half an hour of coming home Pino was stuffing the turkey. I need say no more. On Christmas Day itself John, Esmé, Hellie and William were spending Christmas in Wales but John still had time to give us a ring to see how Pino was. What a remarkable man and such a dear friend! Truly they are a gorgeous family.

In 2005, again just before Christmas, Pino had a fourth cancer and this time the operation was more delicate and more serious. The cancer was in the lymph glands and nodes on the left side of his neck. In fact, this made Pino equal on both sides so one could say it has been an improvement, and quickly John Watkinson had the dreaded cancer removed.

Pino's attitude has always been very positive right from the start and it has always been 'The sooner the cancer is out, then the sooner I can get on with my life!'

Several weeks later we were back with John Glaholm, Pino's oncologist, who also is a very dear friend and who was there right at the beginning with John Watkinson. The radiotherapy commenced, but this time with a twist in that John had sourced some drugs that had been created by a Swedish doctor that might well work better on Pino because of the scleroderma. Four weeks went by and then began the general healing. It was a little slower this time, but Pino is taking life a day at a time and looks well.

I am constantly amazed at this man I married. If I say he is quite outstanding among men, I mean it. He is a true gentleman. He has taught me an awful lot. I love to be outspoken; maybe I am a little too loud, and as he says I am rather personal with people I do not know. Yes, I admit that and sometimes to my cost and Pino quietly reminds me that I should keep my own judgement. He is younger than me by nearly five years but he is wiser.

We have a brilliant partnership and we adore each other. Don't get me wrong – even though we have the perfect marriage we also squabble and exhaust ourselves with shouting. Then comes that twinkle in his eyes; I cannot resist, and then we burst out laughing, forgetting what stupid thing had started our dispute.

The most splendid young man in our lives is our son, Edilio. It was such an enormous shock when I found out that I was pregnant. For so many years I had been told that I would never have any more children, and he was a honeymoon baby. Now this year he will be thirty-one, and we have a special relationship with him.

Another happening in my life is my reunion with my eldest son, Anthony. I had lost him for thirty years, and for the past ten years I have felt so privileged to have the opportunity of getting to know him. He has always been in my heart. I never thought he would be allowed to know who I was, but adoption has come a long way since the sixties.

Life is precious and Pino and I have great contentment.

Caroline Iacaruso, Rosello, Harbury, 2007

All shall be well and all shall be well and all manner of thing shall be well
Mother Julian of Norwich (1343–1443)

Avt tace avt loquere meliora silento
Be quiet, unless your speech be better than silence

251

AUTUMN

In the long and empty avenue the leaves are gently falling on the wet and silent
 ground.
Gathering at the feet of ancient trees, the red copper, burnt sienna and brown
 leaves blown by the soft wind –

A young couple in love sitting on a wooden bench holding hands –
Looking at the naked branches and the swirling birds on a grey sky ready for
 their long departure –

The fog rises in the early morning like smoke,
The days grow shorter and cold –
All around is quiet and nature goes to sleep.

Pino Iacaruso, Harbury, 3 April 2006

AUTUNNO

*Nel lungo viale le foglie cadono dolcemente al bagnato suolo radunandosi ai
piedi di un vecchio albero: il rosso rame, il siena bruciato e le foglie marroni
soffiate dal vento soffice.*

*Due giovani innamorati seduti su una panchina di legno si stringevano le mani
guardando dei rami nudi e il volo degli uccelli per il loro lungo viaggio.*

*La nebbia sale lenta al mattino presto come una nuvola.
I giorni si accorciano e diventano freddi.
Tutto intorno è quieto e la natura s'addormenta.*

ACKNOWLEDGEMENTS

No project of this nature could ever be accomplished without the help, support, love and respect of our families, and our friends, which we have made through the years of our married life. They know full well what a tough assignment this has been for me – almost a dream come true. I never thought that so many of my hopes and desires would be a reality.

If there is one person and only one person who made all this a reality, and for all her love, patience, support, and her strength that has kept me going to achieve my dreams, it is Caroline, my Honey.

For many evenings she sat on her own sewing her beautiful tapestries, reading endless books which are her passion, writing letters (and maybe talking a little too much on the phone!) whilst I was typing the manuscript in our small sitting room upstairs. I cannot express my gratitude deeply enough to Caroline. In fact, if – and I mean a big if – I don't think I would have been here now even to type this acknowledgement.

None of this could have happened without her. How lucky I am to have met such a wonderful partner – always looking out for me and after me, making sure that I recovered from my illness and making all my dreams in my life come true. The love I have for her and for our wonderful son, Edilio, is infinite.

Elisabeth, Lady Hamilton for her enthusiasm and love of my first book and writing the forward for this, my second book.

To my dear friends Rita and Donato Candolfo, who live in Ferrara, Italy. For their support as always and correcting in Italian some of my work in this book.

Enisio for letting me using his beautiful poetry.

Thomas Cox a wonderful friend and a computer whiz kid.

And Pat and Mathew Rankin for their wonderful friendship and support.

Pino Iacaruso, Harbury, 2007

RECIPES

STARTERS

SOUPS and SAUCES

SALADS and SIDES

MAIN COURSES

Aubergine with Tomato Sauce and Mozzarella	222
Chicken Fricassée with Peppers and Tomatoes	41
Fillet of Beef with Wild Mushrooms	98
Fillet of Red Mullet with a Grapefruit and Curry Sauce	248
Fillet of Sea Bass with Herbs	224
Lasagne Alla Bolognese	94
Macaroni with Three Cheeses	40
Noisette of Lamb with Coriander Sauce	159
Quail on a Bed of Straw	191
Roast Duck in Orange Sauce	180
Roast Chicken Scarborough Fair –	
with Parsley, Sage, Rosemary and Thyme	228
Roast Lamb with Mint	246
Roast Venison with Chocolate Sauce	148
Salmon in Pastry with Dill Butter	170
Scallops and Asparagus in a Pastry Shell	201
Shepherd's Pie	108
Sole Fillets in White Wine Sauce	60
Spaghetti with Bacon	28
Spaghetti with Pancetta, Tomatoes and Rosemary	74
Steak with Peppercorns	212
Veal Escalopes with Parma Ham	51

PUDDINGS and CAKES

Apricot Pie	42
Baked Apples	52
Chantilly Cream	84
Chocolate Cream Ganache	88
Chocolate Rum Truffles	83
Chocolate Sauce	77
Chocolate Soufflé with Green Chartreuse	160
Chocolate Sponge	87
Chocolate Truffle Gateau	86
Cold Lemon Soufflé with Crystalised Tangerine	134
Crêpes Flambées	202
Crème Brûlée with Rhubarb	249
Crêpes	179
Hazelnut Meringue with Raspberry Sauce	185